Management Strategy

Achieving Sustained Competitive Advantage

Management Strategy

Achieving Sustained Competitive Advantage *Second Edition*

Alfred A. Marcus
Carlson School of Management
University of Minnesota—Minneapolis

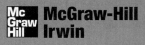

McGraw-Hill
Irwin

The McGraw·Hill Companies

McGraw-Hill
Irwin

MANAGEMENT STRATEGY: ACHIEVING SUSTAINED COMPETITIVE ADVANTAGE
Published by McGraw-Hill/Irwin, a business unit of The McGraw-Hill Companies, Inc., 1221
Avenue of the Americas, New York, NY, 10020.

Some ancillaries, including electronic and print components, may not be available to customers
outside the United States.

This book is printed on acid-free paper.

1 2 3 4 5 6 7 8 9 0 DOC/DOC 1 0 9 8 7 6 5 4 3 2 1 0

ISBN-13: 978-0-07-813712-9
ISBN-10: 0-07-813712-8

Vice president and editor-in-chief: *Brent Gordon*
Publisher: *Paul Ducham*
Director of development: *Ann Torbert*
Managing development editor: *Laura Hurst Spell*
Editorial assistant: *Jane Beck*
Vice president and director of marketing: *Robin J. Zwettler*
Associate marketing manager: *Jaime Halteman*
Vice president of editing, design and production: *Sesha Bolisetty*
Senior project manager: *Harvey Yep*
Lead production supervisor: *Michael R. McCormick*
Design coordinator: *Joanne Mennemeier*
Media project manager: *Suresh Babu, Hurix Systems Pvt. Ltd.*
Cover design: *Joanne Mennemeier*
Cover image: *Chad Baker/Getty Images*
Typeface: *10/12 Times New Roman*
Compositor: *Aptara®, Inc.*
Printer: *R. R. Donnelley*

Library of Congress Cataloging-in-Publication Data

Marcus, Alfred Allen, 1950-
    Management strategy : achieving sustained competitive advantage / Alfred A. Marcus. —2nd ed.
        p. cm.
    Includes index.
    ISBN-13: 978-0-07-813712-9 (alk. paper)
    ISBN-10: 0-07-813712-8 (alk. paper)
    1. Strategic planning. 2. Management. 3. Competition. I. Title.
HD30.28.M3527 2011
658.4'012—dc22

                                                                    2009038447

To my wife, Judy, and to my sons, David Isaac and Ariel Jonathan, philosophically inclined and always questioning everything.

About the Author

Alfred A. Marcus

Alfred A. Marcus is the Edson Spencer Chair of Strategy and Technological Leadership at the University of Minnesota, Carlson School of Management and the Center for Technological Leadership. He has been on the faculty at Minnesota since 1984. His articles have appeared in the *Strategic Management Journal, Academy of Management Journal, Academy of Management Review,* and *Organization Science,* among other places. He is the author or co-author of 14 other books, including *Strategic Foresight,* published by Palgrave Macmillan, and *Big Winners and Big Losers,* published by Wharton School Press. His PhD is from Harvard, and he has undergraduate and graduate degrees from the University of Chicago. Prior to joining Minnesota's faculty, he taught at the University of Pittsburgh Graduate School of Business and was a research scientist at the Battelle Human Affairs Research Centers in Seattle, Washington. He has consulted or worked with many corporations, including 3M, Corning, Excel Energy, Medtronic, General Mills, and IBM. In 1991–1992, he spent his sabbatical at the Sloan School of Management, MIT. He has taught strategy and management courses in Norway, Hungary, the Czech Republic, Romania, and Costa Rica, and was involved in a multinational research project sponsored by the NSF that included companies in the United States, Finland, Israel, and India. Much of his work involves the interface between strategy and changes in the macroenvironment of the firm, including major changes in government and in environmental policies. Since 2005 Professor Marcus has spent a 7-week semester per year at the Technion, teaching courses in its MBA.

Preface

This book is written for those who are interested in strategy. It is a practical book designed to assist those who engage in the art and practice of strategy in organizations large and small in countries throughout the world. Instruction in strategy and reflection upon its key lessons takes place in the world's leading business schools in executive, MBA, and undergraduate programs and in in-house corporate programs designed for managers and executives. Strategy is probably the most basic and at the same time the most advanced discipline in management. It is a discipline whose fundamental principles regularly need to be reconsidered by managers at the most advanced levels and absorbed by undergraduates just starting out in their business career. The basics of business strategy have to be understood by individuals pursuing nonbusiness careers in institutions in the public and not-for-profit sectors who will regularly come into contact with business. The lessons of strategy are likely to have important implications for managers of these organizations as well.

This book is a revised edition of a previously published text. The new book has been thoroughly updated. Material no longer relevant has been discarded and new material introduced. Here are some of the main ways in which this edition of the book differs from the earlier one.

What's New

- This edition places emphasis on employees at all levels with the organization. Employees in lower-level positions are often in possession of important information that needs to be considered in crafting and implementing strategy, but they often lack the tools and the capacity to make good strategic arguments to people higher up in the organization. This book therefore aims to provide everyone in an organization with these tools. By learning the language of strategy, students will have more influence on their organizations and more control of their destiny. All employees in an organization must be cognizant of the basic principles of strategy. All must consider themselves participants in the process of crafting and implementing an organization's strategy.

- This book provides everyone who works in an organization with the tools needed to effectively participate in the process of crafting and implementing an organization's strategy. Students will learn about the types of analysis needed to be an effective contributor in crafting and implementing an organization's strategy and about the variety of moves your organization can make not only to improve its chances of survival but also to achieve sustained competitive advantage. As all employees in an organization are affected by an organization's strategy, it is incumbent on everyone to understand the basic principles.

- This edition takes into account the ongoing global economic crisis and provides insight into how firms must adjust their strategies. Industries are shifting, new ones emerging, and old ones reaching rapid obsolescence and maturity. In an environment that is this uncertain, managers have to hedge their bets about the future. They must be able to protect their firms from the obvious dangers but also detect the opportunities that appear and aggressively take advantage of them. A new discussion found in this edition of the book concerns the hedging strategies managers must use when they are confronted with pervasive uncertainty.

- This edition further develops ideas on how the green economy is emerging, how issues associated with it heavily impinge on companies, and how firms must be proactive in how they adjust. The emergence of a green economy provides many business opportunities, but not all firms have been able to exploit these opportunities. Examples are provided of firms that have successfully adjusted and firms that have not. Lessons are learned from an analysis of the automobile industry and how different firms in this industry have innovated or failed to do so in the face of ups and downs in fuel costs, reduced consumer spending, and imminent warnings of global climate change.

This book remains short and to the point. It is conceptual in nature, although it has numerous examples, and it should be used in conjunction with the many fine cases available in strategic management. An especially good fit for this book is the revised case book *Winning Moves* published by Marsh Press and written by Alfred Marcus.

Many books purport to give instruction in the fundamentals of strategy; however, as the academic discipline of strategy has evolved in arcane and specialized ways, these books often miss the most basic ideas in strategy. The basic purpose of strategy is to make a series of moves designed to achieve sustained competitive advantage. In his classic and landmark 1980s books on strategy, Michael Porter of the Harvard Business School established that sustained competitive advantage is strategy's basic purpose. But even Porter was weak on an actual definition of sustained competitive advantage, and as a consequence the ways he proposed to achieve it were overdetermined and ultimately too complex for most practicing managers to efficiently use. The definition of sustained competitive advantage used in this book is that it consists not of some temporary advantage but of consistent superior performance in comparison to key competitors. Sustained competitive advantage is not about winning one championship but about being a dynasty, that is, performing substantially better than other companies for a long period. Achieving this goal, clearly, is not easy. While Porter coalesced what was known at the time and extended an emerging discipline, he never provided a simple analytical method or series of steps the strategist could employ.

This book provides its readers with a simple but disciplined approach to engaging in the effort to achieve sustained competitive advantage. Its core insight, indeed, can be reduced to a formula, which is introduced in Chapter 1 and fully explicated in Chapter 8 but is worth revealing here. This formula is that sustained competitive advantage rests on an analogy with other endeavors in which strategy is critical, specifically a game like chess, a military campaign, or a sports contest. In each of these endeavors, strategy has an analytical component followed by the well-considered moves that the organization makes based on the analysis that has been done. Then, after making the moves, the organization obtains feedback from them and resets the strategy, making additional moves and obtaining additional performance feedback in an iterative process in which a more complete and better, but never perfect, understanding of the situation evolves.

Simply, what you will need to know to recommend moves that your organization should make is (1) an understanding of the external situation and (2) an understanding of your organization's strengths and weaknesses. In military terms, an organization must be cognizant of the enemy and itself and must be able to match what is known about the enemy (external opportunities and threats) with what is known about itself (internal strengths and weaknesses). An organization's moves build on what the organization has been good at in the past (its mission), while simultaneously establishing an image of where it would like to go in the future (its vision).

After establishing in Chapter 1 that the goal of strategy is to achieve *sustained competitive advantage* (SCA) and that this basic process is behind its achievement, each subsequent chapter takes up in turn the remaining elements of a model or formula for achieving SCA. Specifically, Chapter 2 presents three approaches to doing *external analysis* (EA), including classic industry analysis (Porter's five forces); an assessment of the macroenvironment, which impinges on the five forces; and the application of stakeholder analysis to managing the external environment. Chapter 3 takes up various methods for doing *internal analysis* (IA), including the insights of classic management and contingency approaches; frameworks like the 7 Ss and the value chain; and a method for analyzing strengths and weaknesses that came to prominence in the 1990s, the resource-based view (RBV). RBV will introduce you to ideas about an organization's capabilities and competencies as well as its resources. With these tools in hand for external and internal analysis, you can approach the formidable problem of actually making *moves* (M).

This book treats four types of general moves that your organization should consider. These moves are not discrete and separate choices but can be and often are carried out together or as a sequence of moves depending on the situation. That is, one move may very well hinge on or follow another, as in chess or war where a series of moves have to be made to achieve victory. Chapter 4 is a pivotal chapter inasmuch as it treats both the timing of moves that your organization can make, by going over the elementary principles of game theory, and the actual content of moves at the business level—generic positioning or Porter's ideas about "low cost" and "differentiation" and the space in-between, which Porter maintains is to be avoided, but which this book considers essential territory to occupy and labels "best value." Chapter 4 is about *business strategy* (BS). Chapter 5 is also pivotal in that it treats not competition within an established business, as Chapter 4 does, but rather it introduces you to competition at the corporate level where the main issues are what businesses an organization should participate in and what the scope of its activities should be. Main tools for determining the outcome of these decisions are mergers, acquisitions, and divestitures. Chapter 5 is about *corporate strategy* (CS). Chapter 6 builds on and deepens central concepts of business and corporate level strategy by considering another type of move, that is, globalization, or how to best align a firm's resources, capabilities, and competencies to meet competition in a hotly contested global marketplace. Chapter 6 is about *global strategy* (GS). The final type of general move that the strategist can make is to be entrepreneurial and to innovate. The perils and pitfalls of being entrepreneurial and innovating are the subject of Chapter 7. Chapter 7 is about *innovation strategy* (IS).

In short, the strategic model that is central to this book is the following:

ANALYSIS   **MOVES**

SCA = [EA + IA] + [BS + CS + GS + IS] + Implementation

Besides recapitulating the model, the point of Chapter 8 is to say that the process is an iterative one. It has to be repeated again and again. A firm does not simply once have its employees scan the external and internal environment and make a series of moves, but it has to be constantly engaged in these activities, refining, refocusing, and repositioning itself over time. There is nothing more common in business than a stale strategy whose basic assumptions have not been criticized based on performance feedback and that has not been thoroughly reexamined and reset so that the firm is repositioned and better equipped to withstand ongoing competitive challenges.

The point of Chapter 9, the book's last chapter, is that a well-formulated strategy is useful only to the extent to which it has been effectively implemented. Chapter 9 provides solid and practical advice on how to best implement a strategy. This undertaking is difficult, but it can be done successfully if the advice given in Chapter 9 is systematically pursued. Chapter 9 is new to this edition, as is the emphasis on implementation.

Thus, this book has nine basic chapters that are very tightly and logically linked with a goal in mind, SCA, and a series of steps laid out to help the strategist reach that goal. For those teaching strategy at any level this is an ideal book, as these relatively short but deep chapters can be assigned with one or two cases that can come from any number of sources. As indicated, the use of cases to supplement the chapters is critical, for it is essential that those who wish to gain mastery of the art and craft of strategy practice it. The best source for cases is *Winning Moves*, by Alfred Marcus, published in a second edition in 2009 by Marsh Press.

Each chapter begins with a profile of an executive or academic who has made a significant contribution to strategy (Andy Grove, Michael Porter, Michael Dell, Michael Eisner, Gary Hamel, Bill Gates) or a short vignette of a situation that illustrates the main chapter theme (KFC goes to Japan). Each chapter also exemplifies the main concepts with which it deals in discussing businesses that have been competitors (e.g. Intel vs. AMD, Amazon.com vs. Barnes & Noble, Dell vs. Acer, Best Buy vs. Circuit City, Disney vs. AOL Time Warner, Coke vs. Pepsi, Wal-Mart vs. Spartan Foods.). This book is rich in examples and practical applications.

To sum it up, the rationale for the book is the following:

- Most strategy books have lost sight of the basic purpose of strategy—making a series of moves that are designed to achieve sustained competitive advantage.
- Most books fail to relate moves back to their outcomes, that is, the extent to which these moves actually affect business performance.
- This book is focused on the moves corporations can make and the types of analyses required to make these moves effective.

- It shows managers how to undertake an analysis of the industry environment and an analysis of a company's internal resources before making moves.
- It provides solid advice on how to implement a strategy, once it is formulated.

The main moves that flow from the analysis are positioning of the firm vis-à-vis its competitors (1) in terms of the cost and quality of its products, (2) in terms of the scope of businesses in which it is involved, (3) in terms of its global versus domestic reach, and (4) with respect to the extent to which it will strive to be an innovator as opposed to a follower.

Acknowledgments

So much of what I know about strategy I have learned from my colleagues in the Strategic Management and Organization Department at the Carlson School of Management. They let me serve as department chair from 1994–2000 (I kept urging them to have a coup d'état) and in that capacity I read their papers and came to especially value and appreciate their work. Fundamental to my thinking about strategy are ideas about the external environment and how to analyze it. At Minnesota we always have been strong in this area, and I would like to especially thank my colleagues Bruce Erickson and Ian Maitland. Andy Van de Ven, who writes about innovation, has been very influential in my thinking. Past colleagues such as Margie Peteraf (Dartmouth), Bala Chakravarthy (IMD), and Phil Bomiley (University of California, Irvine) also have influenced me especially with regard to the resource-based view, the issues of competency acquisition and strategic groups, and the behavioral theory of decision making. From Aks Zaheer I have learned about strategic alliances, from Harry Sapienza and Shakra Zahra about entrepreneurial activities, and from a host of colleagues past and present, such as Stefanie Lenway, Tom Murtha, Sri Zaheer, and Myles Shaver, I have gained insights into the processes of globalization.

I would also like to acknowledge these people who are or have been in my department: Anne Cohen, who wrote Chapter 9 on implementation, is a new colleague at the Carlson School. She is an enthusiastic and knowledgeable lecturer in our department and possesses real-world savvy. Her contribution to this book is much appreciated. Dan Forbes is a colleague whose research and teaching I have learned from; John Mauriel was department chair when I first came to Minnesota, and he probably would be surprised to know that the structure of this book owes much to some ideas about strategy he once shared with me; and Ray Willis, who became chair of the department after John, first gave me the chance to teach strategy at the MBA level at Carlson. I thank Ray for his thinking about scenarios and planning given the inherent uncertainty in situations. I have learned about timing from Stu Albert, about negotiations from Pri Shah, and about groups from Mary Zellmer-Bruhn. I have relied on our former and current PhD students, such as Adam Fremeth at Western Ontario; Bill McEvily at the University of Toronto; Sumit Majumdar at University of Texas-Dallas; Isaac Fox, who teaches at Minnesota; Marc Anderson, who is at Iowa State; Tim Hargrave, who is at the University of Washington and Mazhar Islam, who is still toiling away on his dissertation.

In addition to teaching at the Carlson School I have taught strategy in the Management of Technology program at the University of Minnesota's Technology Leadership Institute (TLI). This program is sponsored by the engineering school of the University of Minnesota and is mainly composed of mid-career engineers from local companies. From my students in this program I have learned and continue to learn a great deal. The head of this program, Massoud Amin, is a true gem and a great colleague. Other faculty such as Lockwood Carlson and Dennis Polla are in the same category. The students have to write capstone papers, and they must present them to faculty committees. The capstones involve real-world company problems and I have learned a great deal from how the students have approached these problems and tried to solve them. The staff members in the Management of Technology program are superb and have assisted me a great deal in all the work that I have done there.

Don Geffen, who has worked with me both on research and on consulting projects has been an indefatigable source of ideas and opinions. As an ex–financial analyst and physics professor, he has clearly sharpened my thinking. I also would like to acknowledge Eitan Naveh of the Technion in Israel, who was a postdoctoral student at Minnesota who worked with me for a number of years. Eitan forced me to keep up with the literature on organizational learning, implementation, and other areas related and unrelated to strategy. Terry Foecke, an adjunct faculty member at Minnesota, has been a mentor on management of the physical environment, and there are many colleagues external to Minnesota who have helped me with this topic. In this regard, special mention also should go to Ken Sexton of the University of Texas (previously at Minnesota); Stu Hart of Cornell; Magali Delmas and Cathy Ramus of the Bren School, University of California, Santa Barbara; and the faculty of INCAE in Costa Rica, including Sara Cordero, Renee Castro, and Lawrence Pratt, with whom I have taught a course on managing the physical environment for the past 8 years.

Other sources of my learning about strategy have been the Academy of Management, Business Policy Division, and the Strategic Management Society. Their conferences, journals, and opportunities for the exchange of ideas are superb. And, of course, there is my family, who does not complain (or does not complain a lot) about my constant working.

Finally, I would like to acknowledge the thorough, constructive reviews that were completed for this second edition by an outstanding group of reviewers:

Jill R. Hough, *University of Tulsa*
Paul Miesing, *University at Albany*
James Pappas, *Oklahoma State University–Stillwater*
Trexler Proffitt, *Franklin and Marshall College*
Barbara Ribbens, *Western Illinois University*

Brief Contents

Contents

CHAPTER ONE

Strategy Basics

"A key warning sign [of] a strategic inflection point is when . . . all of a sudden, the company . . . you worry about has shifted. You . . . dealt with one . . . competitor all your life, and all of [a] sudden you do not care about them, you care about . . . somebody else. A mental silver bullet test [is] if you had one bullet, whom would you shoot with it? If you change the direction of the gun, that . . . signals . . . you may be dealing with . . . more than an ordinary shift in the competitive landscape."[1]

Andy Grove, former CEO of Intel Corporation

Chapter Learning Objectives

- Understanding *strategy* as the moves managers make to achieve sustained competitive advantage (SCA).
- Comprehending that SCA is not a few years of good performance but persistent performance over time that is superior to one's competitors.
- Identifying inflection points—extraordinary shifts in the competitive landscape that change the basis for SCA.
- Using analogies from chess, war, and sports to help achieve SCA, including attentiveness to the rules, knowing your enemy and yourself, concentrating forces, relying on teamwork, and keeping score.
- Being conscious of the connection between SCA and comparative advantage.
- Seeing strategy not as detailed planning but as a series of action-response cycles.
- Knowing how to keep score and important measures of SCA.
- Being aware that firms simultaneously are located in the past, striving to achieve their *mission*, or what they have been good at previously, while at the same time they have to move toward a *vision* of what they would like to excel at in the future.

Introduction

A **strategic inflection point** occurs when a company faces major changes in its competitive environment. According to Andy Grove, former CEO of Intel Corporation, these changes may arise from new technologies, different regulatory conditions, or transformations in customer values and preferences. Strategic inflection points require alterations in a company's strategy. Top management may miss the inflections, while managers and lower-level employees in the company's front lines encounter them first. Their job is to alert top management and mobilize support for changes in a company's strategy.

This book is meant for everyone in a company, not just top management. It is meant to sensitize everyone to the need to identify inflection points and adjust a company's strategy. This book provides you with the tools to make effective arguments within your organization that can change its strategy. These tools will enable you to bring inflection points to the attention of management and other employees.[2] Such inflections challenge employees in a company to adjust their organizations' strategies. Based on these adjustments, a company can advance to new heights or plummet to new depths from which it is unable to recover. General Motors' bankruptcy, with its severe pain to employees, suppliers, and regional economies, is a direct consequence of a failure to adjust. In contrast, the investment bank Goldman Sachs has made a remarkably rapid and successful adjustment to the economic recession of the end of the 21st century's first decade.

A company's future depends on the *moves* it makes in response to shifts in the external environment. The reason for mastering the tools of strategic management is to help your organization make these adjustments. Strategic management is explained in this book in terms of its goal: achieving long-term or sustained competitive advantage. This goal is important, for in an environment of radical change all companies are vulnerable. Not all of them will survive. Their survival depends on alert employees well schooled in the art of strategic management, keenly aware of inflections, and analytically equipped to make sound arguments for changes in strategic direction. This book elaborates on the moves you can propose your companies make and on the types of analysis you must do to put your companies in a more advantageous position in relation to their competitors.

Strategy, then, is the moves companies can make to better achieve sustained competitive advantage. These moves are based on an understanding of the opportunities and threats that exist in a firm's external environment and the strengths and weaknesses that exist internally. Strategic moves help a business compete by positioning it with respect to the cost and quality of the goods and services it offers. That is the domain of *business strategy.* An understanding of external and internal environments also helps employees decide in which types of businesses their firm should compete. That is the domain of *corporate strategy.* Business strategy involves questions of product and service positioning, while corporate strategy involves such moves as mergers, acquisitions, divestitures, and alliances.

This chapter is meant to acquaint you with the basics of strategic management. It establishes a framework that will be used in the rest of this book. The framework provides you with a means to become more alert to strategic inflections, to analyze the significance of these inflections for your business, and to make persuasive arguments within your organization about the changes in strategic direction that should be made. The premise of the book is that the task of strategy is not reserved for top management alone. Everyone who works for a firm is affected by the consequences of the firm's decisions, and everyone should have tools to analyze and understand inflections and make recommendations for change.

This chapter compares strategy to three analogous activities—chess, war, and sports. Comparisons with these activities will help you better understand the basics of strategy: how to recognize inflections and better adjust your organization to environmental change.

Sustained Competitive Advantage

The analytical tools that this book provides will assist you in making recommendations within your firm about how to achieve long term competitive advantage. The goal of strategy is **sustained competitive advantage (SCA),** or above-average performance in an industry for at least 10 years or more.[3] Though many firms perform better than their main competitors for a short time, few sustain competitive advantage over a significant period. Very few companies have consistently outperformed their industry for more than 10 years.[4] Dominant winners (and losers) are rare. **Natural parity** is the condition in most industries, and companies that achieve sustained competitive advantage in most industries are **outliers.**[5]

Over a long period, performance converges toward a mean. This condition is not one that your company should accept. There is no excuse for mediocrity, but many top management teams have no better aspiration than to keep up with industry norms. They benchmark what others are doing, rather than trying to be industry leaders. According to one study, only about 5 percent of firms achieve sustained competitive advantage with respect to an indicator of profitability (return on assets), and only about 2 percent do so with respect to an indicator of stock market performance.[6] From 1992 to 2002, just 3 percent of the 1,000 largest U.S. corporations outperformed their industry's average stock market performance and 6 percent underperformed the average. Exhibit 1.1 lists

EXHIBIT 1.1
Sustained Competitive Advantage and Disadvantage, 1992–2002*

Comparisons	Companies	1997–2002 Average Annual Market Return (%)	Sector
Advantage	Amphenol	34.0	Technology
Disadvantage	LSI Logic	3.4	
Advantage	SPX	28.8	Manufacturing/appliance
Disadvantage	Snap-on	1.7	
Advantage	FiServ	31.2	Software
Disadvantage	Parametric	−21.2	
Advantage	Dreyers	22.4	Food
Disadvantage	Campbell Soup	−2.8	
Advantage	Forest Labs	58.5	Drugs/chemicals
Disadvantage	IMC Global	−18.7	
Advantage	Ball	23.9	Manufacturing/industrial
Disadvantage	Goodyear	−11.5	
Advantage	Brown & Brown	48.7	Financial
Disadvantage	Safeco	−1.0	
Advantage	Family Dollar	36.1	Retail
Disadvantage	Gap	9.8	
Advantage	Activision	24.1	Entertainment/toys
Disadvantage	Hasbro	−0.1	

*The criteria used to choose these winning firms were (1) as of January 1, 2002, the companies' 10-year, 5-year, 3-year, and 1-year average market return exceeded that of their industry; (2) their five-year average market return was double or more than double their industry average; and (3) their six-month average return, January 1 to June 1 of 2002, also was greater than that of their industry. Nine opposite cases involving losing firms with the reverse characteristics are shown in the table. Excluded from the analysis, but also showing sustained competitive advantage, were Alliant Tech, Southwest, Donaldson, RGS Energy, and Equitable Resources. See *The Wall Street Journal,* February 25, 2002, pp. B10–B12.

EXHIBIT 1.2
Recession-
Proof and
Recession
Reversed
Competitive
Battles:
2005–2009

	Returns 2005–2009* %	Returns 2005–2007† %	Winner 2005–2009*	Winner 2005–2007†	Sectors
Amphenol	75	100	**WW**	**W**	Technology
LSI Logic	−90	−10	**LL**	**L**	Technology
SPX	−10	40	w	1	Tools
Snap-on	−20	50	1	w	Tools
Fiserv	−15	40	—	1	Software
Parametric	−15	60	—	w	Software
Ball	4	5	w	1	Manufacturing
Goodyear	−6	18	1	w	Manufacturing
Family Dollar	−10	−12	—	**L**	Retail
Gap	−10	250	—	**W**	Retail
Activision	120	140	**WW**	**W**	Games
Hasbro	12	15	**LL**	**L**	Games

*Feb. 25, 2005 to Feb. 25, 2009.
†Feb. 25, 2005 to Jan. 1, 2007.
—a tie
WW = decisive winner long term
W = decisive winner short term
w = short- and long-term weak winner
LL = decisive loser long term
L = decisive loser short term
l = short- and long-term weak loser

examples in each category with their 1997–2002 comparative stock market performance. Surprisingly, these high performers were not regularly cited in the business press as exemplars. They often operated under the radar, and their stories were not told. This book is meant to provide you with the analytical tools to make recommendations in your firm to overcome low achievement levels and become an industry leader.

It is hard to be an industry leader for long periods. Winners and losers in 1992 to 2002 often shifted position between 2005 and 2009. Nestlé acquired big winner Dreyers, the ice cream company; Cargill bought big loser IMC Global, the fertilizer firm, and spun it off as Mosaic; and Liberty Mutual Group acquired big loser Safeco, the insurance company, which became a Liberty Mutual subsidiary. Exhibit 1.2 shows the 2005 to 2009 performance of the other firms found in Exhibit 1.1. Amphenol continued to dominate LSI Logic, and Activision substantially beat Hasbro; however, SPX and Ball were only slight winners over Snap-on and Goodyear. The performance of Fiserv and Parametric and Family Dollar and the Gap was close to equal. Only two years earlier this pattern had been very different, with Snap-on beating SPX, Parametric ahead of Fiserv, Goodyear dominating Ball, and the Gap having a large lead over Family Dollar. The economic meltdown that started in 2007 reversed these trends. Prior performance of firms was not guaranteed in the face of this economic disturbance. This book is meant to give employees within a firm who experience the signs of such change the capacity to alert others and work for alterations in their firms' strategic direction.

The current economic meltdown affecting the world is overturning many competitive relations. The major challenge facing employees at all levels is how to deal with it. Some companies undoubtedly will thrive, but continued success will be harder and harder to achieve. The burden on a company's employees is great.

The inability of companies to maintain competitive advantage for long periods suggests that firms must regularly change their business models. Existing models have to be adjusted to new circumstances. If companies do not adjust rapidly enough, they can fail. All employees within a firm must be empowered with the tools of strategy to assist in the process of bringing about change. What a company has done in the past is no guarantee of its success in the future. Without an effort on the part of all employees to accommodate new realities, companies will suffer. To prevent this from taking place, employees need the tools of strategic management.

Regaining momentum is as much strategic management's domain as establishing advantage in the first place. To become a dynasty, a company must sustain its advantage through tough times. The goal is to be a dynasty and not have just a few good years. Any firm can be lucky enough to do well for a few years, but to continue its winning ways for a long period is extremely difficult. For competitive advantage to persist, mechanisms must be in place not only to achieve competitive advantage in the first place but to protect it once it has been achieved. These mechanisms may involve:

- *Industry's structure* (see Chapter 2). If an industry is very concentrated, if some firms have high market share, and if there are strong barriers to entry, then long-term above-average returns are more likely.

- *Peculiar configurations of resources, capabilities, and competencies.* These make the positions of leading firms especially hard to copy and highly valuable (see Chapter 3). Such firms maintain an advantage because of rare, nonsubstitutable internal strengths, but even these strengths may be challenged.

- Continuous *positioning and repositioning* via the moves companies make (see Chapter 4). The moves involved in positioning and repositioning a company involve more than pricing and product quality choices. Companies change position via *mergers, acquisitions, divestitures, and alliances* (see Chapter 5). They take advantage of opportunities offered by *globalization* (see Chapter 6). They are *entrepreneurial* and strive to innovate (see Chapter 7). They can engage in *judo tactics* to keep their opponents off balance (Chapter 8). Whatever changes they make must be well implemented (Chapter 9).

These are the common methods of achieving sustained competitive advantage that will be explored in this book. Each employee should master the tools of external analysis (Chapter 2) and internal analysis (Chapter 3), as well as understand the moves a company can make to readjust its relationships to its competitors—product and service positioning (Chapter 4), mergers, acquisitions, divestitures, and alliances (Chapter 5), globalization (Chapter 6), and innovation (Chapter 7). Chapter 8 details how this process must be continuous. Chapter 9 discusses effective strategy implementation.

Empirical examination of the performance of Fortune 1000 firms supports the proposition that there are a number of ways companies can win the battle for sustained high performance.

- They can be dominant in an *absolute* sense by being in an industry that is attracting many entrants. They can choose industries with high mean returns where there is little standard deviation in the returns. All firms in such an industry thrive, and thus the industry is an attractive one in which to compete.

The implication of this route to success is to select the right industry. Be in a successful one and ride the tide of the industry's overall success. Take advantage of good economic conditions in the industry to grow revenues and profits.

- But companies also can win in a *relative* sense by being in a consolidating or declining industry. Such an industry has low mean returns and the deviation in these returns is high.

The implication of this route to success is to possess the unique resources or capabilities to win in a dog-eat-dog environment. It is to have the capacity to survive brutal competition.

Choosing a route to sustained competitive advantage, then, depends on a number of factors, which will be further explored in this book. They include an industry's structure (Chapter 2); a firm's peculiar configurations of resources, capabilities, and competencies (Chapter 3); the moves companies make (Chapters 4 to 8); and implementation (Chapter 9).

Winning Moves

In response to changing external circumstances, a firm's employees constantly must endeavor to find new sources of competitive advantage. This requires that the firm make a sequence of short-term maneuvers and long-term changes in direction that add up to a unique position against which competitors cannot make serious inroads. Critical to long-term advantage are positioning the firm so it can protect its products and markets from competitors and thus finding a free space in which to compete.

Analysis

Before exploring the various moves companies can make to achieve sustained competitive advantage (SCA), it is important to understand the types of analyses employees can carry out to increase the chances that the moves their companies make will yield success. Two types of analysis are needed: (1) an analysis of the company's external environment (see Chapter 2), what is referred to as EA in the formula in the preface, and (2) an analysis of its internal environment, that is, its resources, capabilities, and competencies (see Chapter 3), what is called IA in the preface's formula. Estimating a company's external opportunities and threats and matching them with its internal strengths and weaknesses provide a company with the ability to make better moves. How to estimate and match these factors is covered in detail in the next two chapters.

Moves

The moves that flow from such analyses better position a company to prevail in the ongoing competitive challenges it confronts. This book explores moves that position the firm in relation to its competitors with respect to the cost and quality of the products and services the firm provides (see Chapter 4), called BS in the formula in the preface; the scope of its activities (see Chapter 5), referred to as CS; its global, as opposed to domestic, reach (see Chapter 6), which the formula describes as GS; and the extent to which it innovates and searches for new business opportunities as opposed to exploiting existing ones (see Chapter 7), which the formula denotes as IS. Repeated repositioning of a company vis-à-vis its competitors is the lesson emphasized in Chapter 8, while the need to implement a strategy well once it is chosen is the lesson of Chapter 9. The whole process of mulling over how to achieve SCA as a function of EA, IA, moves, and sound implementation must be continuous. The analytical process cannot come to a halt. Distinct stages of formulation and implementation should not be separated out, but rather ongoing adjustment of strategies as carried out should be the norm (see Chapter 9).

The framework for this book is set out in Exhibit 1.3. Chapters 2 to 4 deal mostly with **business strategy,** that is, how to compete in a given industry; while Chapters 5 to 7 focus on **corporate strategy,** what business a firm should be in. Achieving sustained competitive advantage requires external analysis (EA) and internal analysis (IA) and actions that position the firm's products and services with regard to cost and quality (BS); that establish the scope of the firm via mergers, acquisitions, alliances, and divestitures (CS); that put in place an approach to globalization (GS); and that involve entrepreneurship and innovation (IS). Achieving sustained superior economic performance often is accomplished through highly innovative strategies, but these innovations must be regularly renewed and reinvigorated (Chapter 8) and implemented well (Chapter 9).

To make winning moves, employees in the firm must find profitable patterns and business models that meet customer demands. They must do so repeatedly, not just once. Microsoft, for instance, did not rest with the dominance that it achieved in operating systems. It pushed on to office suite software, tried to meet the challenge the Internet presented through browsers, and then moved into the server business. With each of these moves, it confronted a different competitor: Apple in operating systems; Lotus, Novell, and IBM in office suites; Netscape in browsers; and Sun, Hewlett-Packard, and IBM in servers. Each new competitor provided a new challenge to Microsoft.

EXHIBIT 1.3
The Framework for This Book

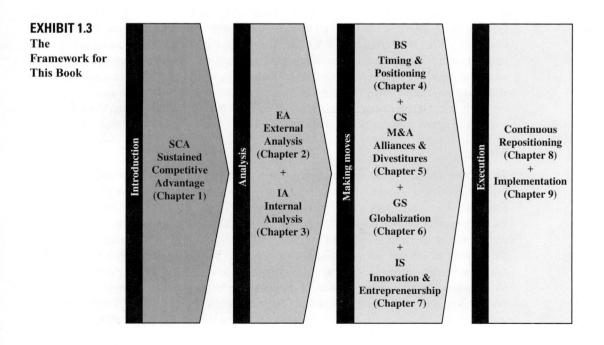

Understanding Management Strategy

The tools of strategic management are best understood through analogies with other areas in life in which competition is fierce, such as chess, war, and sports. Each of these bears important resemblances to strategy.

Chess

Strategy is like chess in that the goal may be seen as checkmate, or thwarting an opponent so that escape is nearly impossible. In driving Kmart to bankruptcy, Walmart came close to this goal, and Best Buy did the same to Circuit City, but in business, the results are rarely so definitive. Rather, the best companies can hope for is sustained dominance, similar to that achieved by Microsoft and Intel in their markets during the 1990s. By disabling their competitors, Microsoft and Intel each captured more than 90 percent of the market in operating systems and microprocessors, respectively.

Operating by the Rules

In both business and chess, dominance has to be achieved according to rules. Following the rules and playing fairly guarantee that the results are a consequence of skill rather than of illegal or unfair practices. In the world of commerce, *skill* means being better able than one's opponents to meet customer needs.

The rules of chess are very well defined and have remained the same for centuries, so few questions arise about the legality or ethics of the moves. In strategy, in contrast, companies operate with a legal framework that is less precise and static, so it is sometimes difficult to ascertain what is permissible. As a result, firms may believe that their job is to test the laws' limits. Managers may have the view that innovative theories propounded by consulting firms and management theorists give them the license to stretch what the law allows. However, when gains are achieved by questionable moves, the extent to which these gains endure depends on how the legal system judges them. The courts may reverse apparent victories. The stories of Enron, Arthur Andersen, WorldCom, Adelphia, and other companies, which came to light after 2000, provide stunning examples and warnings against engaging in illegal activities. They show that society will not tolerate some moves. Blatant cheating, when detected, does not go unpunished.

Therefore, the moves firms make must be aboveboard and in accord with prevailing legal doctrine and ethics. Milton Friedman, who maintained that it was the purpose of managers to maximize shareholder returns, held that doing so must occur within the confines of law and ethics.[7]

However, the law is not always clear regarding some strategic issues. The judgments of legal authorities clarify what the law says and establish precedents for how the game is played. Regulations dealing with competition, for instance, have shifted over time, depending on who the legal authorities were and how they interpreted the law. The Kennedy administration's view of antitrust law was much stricter than today's understanding. The European Union (EU) struck a major blow against Intel in 2009 when it imposed a huge fine on the company for violating the EU's antitrust laws. Microsoft has been treated similarly by the EU, while at the same time U.S. antitrust laws have moderated. Companies must take into account not only the rules in their countries of origins but the rules globally in every nation in which they operate.

According to legal doctrine in the United States in the early 1960s, simply having *very high market share* was proof of possible illegality. Today, high market share does not have this connotation in the United States, but it may in other countries. In the United States there must be proof of actual *anticompetitive behavior.* In the United States, Microsoft was not sued by antitrust authorities because it had more than 90 percent of the market in operating software. The company was sued because it was alleged to have taken specific actions to exclude a competitor, Netscape, from installing a browser on newly manufactured personal computers. The legal challenges Microsoft faced threatened to reverse the gains the company had made in the 1990s. For it to continue as the world's leading software company, Microsoft had to defend itself in the courts. In the face of this challenge, Microsoft almost was broken up into several firms. Intel, too, in the United States has been embroiled in frequent legal controversies with major competitors such as AMD. Intel, for example, tried to use the legal system to block Via Technologies, a Taiwanese company and AMD's primary chipset partner, from making chipsets that would be compatible with Intel's Pentium 4 chips. Via turned around and sued Intel for trying to abridge its rights to operate.

Changing the Rules

Legal suits and countersuits affect the strategic battles in which companies are engaged. Microsoft's opponents, including Sun and Oracle, pressured federal officials to be tough on the software giant. This pressure was a primary reason antitrust authorities acted against Microsoft.

Thus, companies must be aware that the rules of the "game" of strategy tend to shift over time. These shifts occur not only because of variations in the legal and ethical climate but also because of changes in technology and economics. These shifts in the environment in which firms operate are the types of inflection points to which reference was previously given. To some extent, the forces that change the rules of the game are outside the control of a company, but often companies have influence over the rules under which they operate. Some of the changes are hard to entirely direct or block. Once they gain momentum, they can have overwhelming power to change an industry, and a company and its employees have no choice but to adjust.

At the start of the 21st century, executives of Microsoft, Intel, and other leading high-tech companies discovered how strong these forces were, when the bubble burst in their industry, terror struck, global security became an overriding issue, and extremely tough economic conditions set in. Plus, as these events occurred, users were starting to install Linux, a virtually free operating system that could replace Windows. As the 21st century progressed, the world faced the most severe economic collapse it had encountered since the Great Depression.

Changes of this nature are what Andy Grove has called inflection points. Fundamental new forces in the external environment such as these require an alteration in firm strategy. All of the employees in a company must analyze these changes and consider the moves a company can make to better position itself in the face of challenges.

In the face of challenges, employees can promote the idea that a company should shift all or some of its resources to areas where it can better compete. Companies can be *prospectors,* aggressively pursuing new growth opportunities, or *defenders,* clinging to their existing niche and trying to protect their turf. They also can be *analyzers,* both searching for new market opportunities and protecting an existing position. In the worst case, they can be *reactors,* incoherently responding to the changed circumstances.

The success of the moves a company makes ultimately depends on how much flexibility it has to maneuver. Companies always are between two poles—the past and the future. A company's **mission** typically represents what the company has been good at in the past. Its vision, on the other hand, normally is based on its future—what it would like to be good at next.

Envisioning Where to Go Next

Even if the employees in a company have a vision of where they would like the company to go, it may not be possible to achieve this vision quickly. Because of fixed physical or human assets, bureaucracy, or the inflexible worldviews of top managers, the company might not easily make the transition from where it is now to where it would like to be next.

Andy Grove recommends that companies be "agile giants." They need agility to move quickly to new competitive ground, but once they occupy that ground, they must be giants, capable of defending it.[8] In the mid-1980s, Intel's main product was computer memory. When Intel could no longer compete with large and better-capitalized Japanese firms in this business, its employees realized the company had to concentrate on the one thing it did best: It had to focus on an area where it had **comparative advantage.** So Intel shifted to microprocessors based on the reasoning that it was better to be the top player in microprocessors than to be a mediocre player in both microprocessors and memory. Comparative advantage means that a company pursues what it does best. This is the foundation for sustained competitive advantage. Doing what a firm does best, doing what no other firm can do as well in meeting customer needs and expectations, is the key to sustained competitive advantage.

What a company currently is best at is incorporated into its mission, but while pursuing its mission, a firm also must have a vision for where it wants to go next, as conditions do change. Companies such as Intel and Microsoft always are balancing between what they have proven good at in the past and what they would like to be good at in the future. They are trying to develop new options they might use to achieve advantage when their current businesses slacken.

Microsoft, for instance, has been developing a programming language that will allow different Web sites and computer programs to better communicate with each other. It has been attempting to push its operating systems into such non-PC environments as TV set–top boxes, cellular phones, handheld computers, servers, and other areas. In addition, it has been trying to take on Nintendo and Sony in the video game market with its Xbox. All of these efforts are outside its core businesses in operating systems, software suites, and Internet browsers.

Intel, too, is trying to embrace and enter new markets—networks, wireless, and communication—and compete with companies such as Lucent, Motorola, Texas Instruments, and Cisco. It is doing so at the same time that most of its revenues and profits continue to come from its microprocessor business.

Neither Intel nor Microsoft is standing still. One might say they are "throwing spaghetti against the wall to see what might stick." The essence of strategy is to achieve a balance between a firm's past and its future, to adhere to a core mission while trying to realize a new vision for tomorrow. In business, indeed, it is possible to create new games. A company can redefine the game that is in process, play a different game, or walk away from a game and refuse to compete. The employees of a firm have choices in deciding the game or games their company decides to play.

Usually, change is gradual and incremental, but change can be massive and sudden, like Andy Grove's inflection points. Because change cannot be predicted with great certainty, employees must be alert to a variety of different contingencies. They need to develop and propose options that will give their firms the flexibility to move in a number of directions depending on how external conditions evolve.

Weathering Reversals of Fortune

In business, as in chess, one player dominates for a period but then is replaced by another. Dynasties do not last that long. Many companies during the 1990s seemed to have a lock on the top position, only to see reversals of fortune in the early 2000s. Coca-Cola, for instance, lost its dominance over PepsiCo, General Electric over United Technologies, and Nike over Reebok. In each instance, the reversal was caused by moves the companies made:

- Coca-Cola, 80 percent of whose profits came from overseas, stumbled in Europe as a result of product recalls. PepsiCo, in contrast, bought Gatorade from Quaker and introduced numerous new beverage products, including bottled water, earlier than Coca-Cola. At the start of the 21st century, PepsiCo beat both the average stock performance of soft-drink companies and the stock performance of Coca-Cola.
- General Electric's financial division, GE Capital, which had been its star business unit, went downhill in the early 2000s. United Technologies' (UT) stock performance was better because of the defense buildup and the strategic initiatives the company took in areas such as quality and globalization. As a consequence, UT performed at about the same level as companies in its industry, while GE did much worse.
- Nike encountered a public outcry against foreign sweatshops and lost its sponsorship of professional sports leagues and its contracts with well-known athletes. Reebok picked up these sponsorships. Its stock performance was far better than the average footwear company in the early 21st century, whereas Nike's performance was about average.

Dominant companies stumble and companies that are behind move ahead. Thus, management strategy is as much about the ability to make comebacks as it is about achieving dominance in the first place. A prime example is Nike. After stumbling it made a roaring comeback and Reebok collapsed.

Making Moves That Matter

As in chess, the premise of strategy is that the moves a company makes matter. The outcome is determined by the moves, moves that may be negative as well as positive. Enron, for instance, made notoriously wrong moves, however grounded and rationalized in the thinking of the best management consultants of the time. McKinsey & Company advised Enron to be "asset light" and to have "loose tight" internal controls. A reason Enron self-destructed was that it followed this advice. Just as right moves lead to success, the wrong moves can destroy a company.

Of course, Enron self-destructed for many reasons. Fraud, deception, and greed also were involved. Many contests, however, are undecided. The superiority of the players is not apparent, and the games are in a stalemate. Many companies have been neck and neck for a long period, and it is unclear which company will prevail, which will fall, and why. That is why it so important for employees in the firm to observe the external environment from the positions they occupy, to analyze the significance of the changes they see, and to make recommendations for changes in the strategic directions their companies are moving.

War

Another useful analogy in strategy is war. Perhaps this analogy is extreme, but it provides principles of importance. Strategy is like war in that it is based on these two principles: Know your enemy, and know yourself.

Know Your Enemy and Know Yourself

Sun-Tzu's *The Art of War* was published more than 2,500 years ago. In it, he wrote:

> If you know the enemy and know yourself, you need not fear the result of a hundred battles.
> If you know yourself but not the enemy, for every victory gained you will also suffer a defeat.
> If you know neither the enemy nor yourself, you will succumb in every battle.[9]

In strategy, too, employees must examine the external situation in which their company finds itself and understand its strengths and weaknesses. The moves a company makes must be designed to strengthen its competitive position either by changing the external circumstances or by upgrading its internal resources and capabilities.

The principle of "knowing your enemy" was articulated by Winston Churchill, during World War II, who warned against "the treachery of numbers in calculations" that did not "include the great unknown variable of the enemy's reaction."[10]

Napoleon also said, "A general should say to himself many times a day: If the hostile army were to make its appearance in front, on my right, or on my left, what should I do? And if he is embarrassed, his arrangements are bad; there is something wrong, he must rectify his mistake."[11]

Knowing the enemy "goes beyond tabulation of numbers and capabilities; it requires an understanding of culture, values, intentions, customs, organizational doctrines, and operational preferences as well as the personalities of key commanders and staff officers."[12] Knowing an enemy's idiosyncrasies can provide great leverage if properly exploited. Some enemies, for instance,

> act according to reason; others according to emotion. Some wait for events to happen; others make them happen. Some act primarily out of self-interest; others act selflessly. All are creatures of habit; only the habits differ. Some can think clearly through shock; most cannot. All act on the basis of what they believe the situation to be—not necessarily on what the situation is. Most are influenced by what they want to believe.[13]

According to military doctrine, knowing the enemy must be supplemented by insights into one's own characteristics and traits. These insights "aid efforts to unify action, concentrate strengths, and offset vulnerabilities."[14] These two principles, "knowing the enemy" and "knowing yourself," then, are fundamental in both war and strategy.

Not Just Detailed Planning

Like warfare, management strategy also is not just about detailed planning.[15] According to Napoleon, "War consists of nothing but accidents and a commander should never overlook anything that might enable him to exploit these accidents."[16] The Prussian military strategist Carl von Clausewitz wrote in his book *On War,* published in 1832, that detailed planning necessarily fails "due to the inevitable frictions encountered: chance events, imperfections in execution, and the independent will of the opposition."[17] The Prussian general staff "did not expect a plan of operations to survive beyond the first contact with the enemy. It set only the broadest of objectives and emphasized seizing unforeseen opportunities as they arose."[18]

Strategy is not necessarily a lengthy action plan. It is the evolution of a general idea through continually changing circumstances. The results are a consequence of **action-response cycles:** Both sides (one's enemy and oneself) act and both respond[19] (see Exhibit 1.4). The outcomes are not likely to be the intended ones; they materialize from actual encounters with the enemy.

Strategy is as much about this process as it is about design.[20] As design, strategy means planning, rationally choosing alternatives, and implementing the alternatives as close as possible to how they were devised, a model that is unrealistic because it ignores competitors' responses. Competitors react to intended strategies in ways that negate what the firm wishes to do. Then it becomes a matter of adjusting to the actual situation on the ground. The original plans no longer match reality as the situation unfolds, and rigid adherence to the plans is not fruitful.

Realized strategies differ from intended ones. They incorporate the response and counterresponse of other decision makers that affect the result. In many circumstances, the situation changes so much that one would not want to achieve what was originally intended. Strategy as a process introduces flexibility, which strategy as a formal planning exercise eliminates.

Implementing a strategy, then, must be simultaneous with *formulating* one (see Chapter 9). Formulation requires on-the-spot adjustment. In *Strategies for Change,* James Brian Quinn, professor of management at Dartmouth College, argues that strategies should "develop around a few key concepts and thrusts" that provide "cohesion, balance, and focus."[21] The essence is to build a posture that is flexible enough and strong enough for a company to accomplish what it aims to achieve no matter what occurs.

EXHIBIT 1.4
**Strategy
Results**

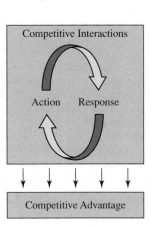

Concentrating Forces

In a letter to one of his generals, Napoleon advised to always keep in mind concentration of strength.[22] Concentrating one's forces is the method to follow in achieving winning strategies over time. In an ever-shifting battlefield, one must apply superior resources where needed to achieve victory. Even a smaller and weaker foe can win if it has mobility to define how encounters take place. If it can mobilize superior means and apply them at critical junctures, the smaller force can win. Thus, speed and flexibility in mobilization and application of resources are as important as possession of these resources.

The corporation's management, therefore, must:

1. Determine what confers superiority.
2. Create a distinctive competence in which the company has comparative advantage.
3. Apply this competence decisively at the proper time and place to increase the chances of winning.

This approach may mean conceding certain positions to concentrate forces where the chances of success are greater. Surprise, speed, and secrecy are needed to move forces to a favorable position. A company also may have to keep capabilities in reserve to be deployed in the face of unexpected contingencies.

Outwitting competitors not only means knowing when, where, and how to fight, but it also means knowing when not to fight and when to retreat. An excellent example is Intel's switch from computer memory to microprocessors as its main product. As mentioned earlier, under Andy Grove's leadership, the company realized it would never be able to compete with Japanese manufacturers in the computer-memory market. It did not have access to enough financial capital to build the huge factories it would need. It could never keep up with the low costs of production that Japanese manufacturers such as NEC, with its attention to detail and incremental process improvement, were capable of attaining.

Although computer memory had been the basis of Intel's business until about 1985, the company no longer had a comparative advantage in this product. It had to concede defeat in this market and fight a different battle. The company switched to microprocessors, where it concentrated forces and achieved superiority. The decision, according to Grove, was whether to be a weak and mediocre producer in both computer memory and microprocessors and risk losing on both fronts or to focus all the company's resources in the one area where it had the chance of being dominant.[23]

Redeploying Assets

In his book *Only the Paranoid Survive,* Grove discusses the importance of being able to recognize key turning points and redeploy assets.[24] Major changes occur in the competitive environment at these inflection points. Conditions change because of shifts in technologies, government regulations, customer values, and other factors.

According to Grove, people at the top of corporations have difficulty recognizing such changes and responding.[25] Just as generals may not get the signals emanating from the battlefield in time to respond effectively, so too top managers may not recognize, or be willing to acknowledge, what is actually occurring. Thus, employees throughout the company must be enlisted for their insights into the signals that are changing conditions on the frontlines and their recommendations for altering the strategic moves a company is making.

Obtaining good signals is not just a matter of having good intelligence; it also involves being receptive to that intelligence. As Grove points out, despite emotional resistance to change, a company must be willing to shed preconceptions and redeploy its assets.[26] This requires seeing where a new opportunity lies and knowing how the corporation's existing base of assets can be reconfigured to meet it. These insights do not belong alone to people at the top of a firm. They are insights had by all employees whose knowledge of conditions the company confronts must be brought to the attention of decision makers. Thus, employees throughout the company need the tools of strategic analysis to make forceful and persuasive arguments about what a company should do.

Hedging Against Uncertainties

How does a company respond to changing circumstances? As times become more uncertain, hedging its moves becomes increasingly important. As Exhibit 1.5 indicates, hedging strategies depend on whether a single best forecast can be made or an outcome can be well described and/or quantitative odds assigned.[27] A brief discussion of these strategies follows.

Gamble on the "Most Probable" Outcome   Companies may act based on what they perceive to be a likely outcome. They make bets with confidence, only to be surprised later if the world does not evolve as they assumed. A prime example of a company that made a large bet based on what it believed to be the most probable future was Iridium's $5 billion investment in its satellite network. When it made this bet it was reasonable to assume that demand would be large, but events did not turn out as Iridium expected. However, making bets of this kind is reasonable in some instances. Investments in new stores by established companies like a McDonald's or a Home Depot are good examples of extending the scope of proven business models and winning by virtue of superior execution without being concerned about the risk of serious upheaval.

Take the Robust Route   Rather than bet on a single future, companies can choose the most robust strategy, or one that is viable regardless of what occurs. This kind of strategy may be referred to as "no regrets." Often-regulated utilities have taken this route. They hedge their bets against a number of possibilities. For instance, the key future question may be about the relative cost of different fuel sources. Utilities create scenarios in which natural gas or wind is the low-cost fuel and invest in *both*.

EXHIBIT 1.5
Levels of Uncertainty and Hedging Strategies

Source: From A. Marcus, *Strategic Foresight* (New York: Palgrave MacMillan, 2009).

Hedging Strategy	Certainty A Single Best Forecast Can Be Made	Risk Quantitative Odds Can Be Confidently Ascribed to Outcomes	Ambiguity Qualitative Outcomes Can Be Described	Unknown
Gamble on the "most probable."	*	*		
Take the robust route.		*	*	
Delay until further clarity emerges.			*	
Commit with fallbacks.			*	
Shape the future.				*

*Stands for preferred hedging strategy.

Delay until Further Clarity Emerges   In the face of uncertainty, a firm may decide to stay the course for now. It delays taking action until the situation becomes clearer. While waiting, the firm makes flexible commitments that minimize downside losses should worst-case situations occur. It can divide its investments into small increments, not fully committing at once but gradually over time in accord with additional clarity it gains and confidence it acquires from moving forward slowly in trial-and-error fashion. The risk is that when the firm decides to fully put its stake in the ground it will be too late. Its competitors already will be there, and it will not be able to dislodge them. Such was the case with both Xerox and Kodak in their slow adjustments to a digital world. Delay, on the other hand, may work in the case of Boeing's decision not to pursue the super-jumbo-jet option.

Commit with Fallbacks   An alternative is to fully commit, but with fallbacks should the plans be unrealistic. This path is not a refusal to commit. It is not avoidance of going full thrust. Instead, the company can justify the risk it is taking because it is convinced that its *initial position* and *capabilities* provide it with an advantage. It thoroughly analyzes the risk on this basis. Major petroleum companies have created fallback positions in renewable energy in the event that fossil fuel supply is severely constrained. BP's "beyond petroleum" initiative is not just a public relations gimmick but a fallback position that preserves the company's flexibility. Committing to fallbacks works best if there is a payoff structure such that investments that fail entail tiny losses, while those that succeed yield very high returns.

Shape the Future   Another alternative is not to be passive in the face of diverse futures, but to try to actively drive and influence what takes place.[28] A firm uses the resources it commands to increase the odds that the most desirable outcome, the one it wants the most, prevails. A shaping strategy revolves around a point of view of where an industry will evolve—where the company wants to see itself in 5 or 10 years. Examples include FedEx's overnight delivery methods, Southwest Airlines' no-frills model for domestic air travel, and the pioneering efforts of Amazon and eBay in Internet commerce. Trying to shape the future makes the most sense when there is discontinuous change and the future is hard to forecast. The returns may be great but so are the risks.

Risk and Uncertainty

The economist Frank Knight distinguished risk from uncertainty based on the capacity to place objective odds on conditions such as flipping a coin or rolling dice.[29] Net present value calculations work best under conditions of risk.[30] These risk conditions are opposed to conditions of uncertainty where the odds are subjectively assigned, and require judgment. According to Knight, competitive advantage and superior economic performance emanate mainly from bets placed under conditions of uncertainty. When the risk is known, the competition is too intense to earn anything but the most mundane returns.

Sports

Another useful analogy for strategy is sports. Management strategy is also in many ways like sports. In sports, the goal is not to win just one championship but to be perpetually successful. It is to create a dynasty, rather than achieving a fluke triumph—a onetime trip to the Super Bowl.

The models to emulate are the perennial powerhouses: in baseball, the New York Yankees, the Boston Red Sox, the Oakland Athletics, and at one time the Atlanta Braves; in professional football, the Pittsburgh Steelers and the New England Patriots; in college basketball, North Carolina and Duke; and in professional basketball, the Los Angeles Lakers and the Boston Celtics.

Getting It Early

How can such long-term success be accomplished? A sports team that is the first to introduce a system can stay ahead of its competitors by refining that system before they make headway against it. San Francisco's National Football League dynasty during the 1980s and 1990s was built on innovations in a West Coast offense that other teams tried unsuccessfully to copy; the other teams were unable to keep up with the refinements and adjustments made by Bill Walsh and his successors.

The same principle can hold in management strategy. A company that is the first to introduce a product or idea—a company that "gets it" early—may be able to build the momentum to win title after title.

When a company gets one thing right, it creates momentum that enables it to get other things right. Exhibit 1.6 depicts the chain of benefits set in motion: Because a company has attracted favorable attention from customers, investors come on board. Because the customers and investors have come on board, highly talented people think the company would be a good place to work, and thus it becomes easier to recruit top-notch individuals. With more highly talented people in place, it is easier to get more customers on board, and the investment community becomes more excited and pours more money into the company. A virtuous cycle is created. In contrast, vicious cycles also are possible: A company's failures can snowball into defeat.

Being first is not always the surest route to success, however, as will be shown in Chapter 4. Often, fast followers, such as Microsoft, prevail over the early leaders. They concentrate superior forces and counterattack. An early leader can never be sure that its lead will stand.

EXHIBIT 1.6
The Reinforcing Nature of "Getting It"

Source: From *Profit Patterns* by Adrian J. Slywotsky. Copyright © 1998 by Adrian J. Slywotsky. Used by permission of Time Books, a division of Random House, Inc.

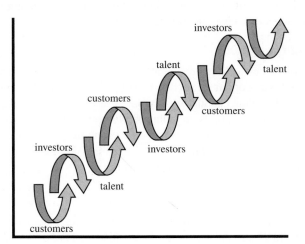

Relying on Teamwork

Management can learn another lesson from sports. Accomplishment comes as much from teamwork as from outstanding stars. Most sports teams have great individual stars, but winning persists because of how teams recruit, socialize, and motivate all their players to work together. Coaches such as the Los Angeles Lakers' Phil Jackson play a significant role. Their understanding of the contributions of superstars like Kobe Bryant and role players like LaMar Odom is as critical as their philosophies of preparing for a game and calling the plays.

A team's management keenly analyzes the situation and makes the right moves that bring together the parts needed for success. Championship teams do not have to excel at everything, but they have to be able to blend the different parts to create a winning combination.

The best teams have a unique character. One will win with an innovative offense and just an adequate defense. Another will dominate because its defense is superior, while its offense barely gets the job done. The St. Louis Rams won a Super Bowl with its offense; the Baltimore Ravens, with its defense. Neither sports teams nor companies have to be good at everything.

Planning and Improvising

Winning involves a mix of planning and improvising (see Chapter 9). A football coach scripts the first 10 to 15 offensive plays of the half, but then changes plans in response to what happens. A pitcher adjusts to the way batters have been reacting to his pitches. Plays that have been run to perfection in practice can break down in actual games. Some options in a possible breakdown are anticipated and practiced; others are made up on the spot, so players must be creative. The creative players are on the field, not in the boardroom. How well such improvising works is often the difference between winning and losing.

Keeping Score: Performance Measurement

Another sports analogy of relevance is keeping score. Companies have economic, legal, and ethical obligations to many **stakeholders** who affect and are affected by what the firm does. To assess how well they are meeting these responsibilities, companies must measure their performance. There are various ways to do so. Companies evaluate strategic plans on the basis of growth in revenues and market share. They assess product lines and individual businesses by calculating gross margins and cash flows. They appraise individual business units in terms of return on assets. Capital investments are analyzed according to net present value, and prospective acquisitions are examined on the basis of their likely contribution to earnings. Several popular approaches to measurement are discussed below.

The Balanced Scorecard

One means of measuring the different elements that may be associated with success is the **balanced scorecard,** a multidimensional approach to corporate performance that incorporates both financial and nonfinancial factors (see Exhibit 1.7).[31] Both hard and soft variables are considered.

As in sports, a company can be less than stellar in some areas and still achieve long-term advantage; conversely, a company can excel in a variety of areas but still lose. Not all the areas where a company or sports team excels weigh equally on the bottom line. For instance,

EXHIBIT 1.7
Balanced Scorecard

Source:Adapted from Robert Grant, *Contemporary Strategic Analysis,* 4th ed. (Oxford, England: Blackwell, 2002). Reprinted with permission of Blackwell Publishing.

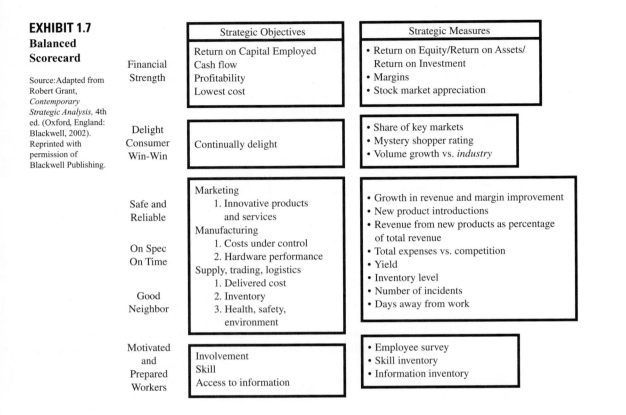

	Strategic Objectives	Strategic Measures
Financial Strength	Return on Capital Employed Cash flow Profitability Lowest cost	• Return on Equity/Return on Assets/ Return on Investment • Margins • Stock market appreciation
Delight Consumer Win-Win	Continually delight	• Share of key markets • Mystery shopper rating • Volume growth vs. *industry*

Safe and Reliable
 	
On Spec On Time
 	
Good Neighbor
	Marketing
	  1. Innovative products
	    and services
	Manufacturing
	  1. Costs under control
	  2. Hardware performance
	Supply, trading, logistics
	  1. Delivered cost
	  2. Inventory
	  3. Health, safety,
	    environment
		• Growth in revenue and margin improvement
		• New product introductions
		• Revenue from new products as percentage of total revenue
		• Total expenses vs. competition
		• Yield
		• Inventory level
		• Number of incidents
		• Days away from work

Motivated and Prepared Workers	Involvement Skill Access to information	• Employee survey • Skill inventory • Information inventory

a company can win awards for having top-notch quality and yet fail in getting new goods to the market early enough to remain competitive. Although it wins in one area, it loses overall. Employees contemplating change in a company's strategy need to decide which performance areas are paramount. Where does the company really have to be great? Organizations should be searching for the winning *blend* of elements. Each organization has a unique internal environment and a different external context, and must make its own match between the two.

Measures of Overall Dominance

Overall dominance is typically measured by two means:

- *Accounting data,* which are based on past performance.
- *Stock market data,* which are supposed to project what a company is likely to do in the future.

Both have their limits. Accounting data, despite the best efforts of the accounting profession and legal authorities to prevent distortion, can be skewed. Firms can manipulate accounting results by recording revenue too soon or too late, recording revenue of questionable quality or of a bogus nature, boosting income with onetime gains, shifting current expenses to later or earlier time periods, and failing to record liabilities or improperly reducing them. Companies such as Cendant, Sunbeam, Waste Management, Lucent,

Dynegy, and Global Crossing, as well as Enron and WorldCom, have been caught engaging in fraud.

Without adequate accounting data, investors can be fooled and stock prices can be based on inaccurate information. Investors do not always have the analytical capability to accurately assess a company's likely future performance. Stock market data depend on investor psychology, and investors are not entirely rational; they become caught up in fads and get swayed by irrational fears as well as enthusiasms.

Economic Value Added

A methodology for assessing a company's overall performance came to prominence in the 1990s: evaluating its **economic value added (EVA).** EVA is defined as net operating profit minus the opportunity cost of capital. It measures how much better or worse a company's earnings are than the amount investors could obtain by putting their money in alternative investments of comparable risk.

Typically, more than 50 percent of the top U.S. companies do not have a positive EVA, which means they did not earn more than their cost of capital. Investors probably would have done better if they put their money in Treasury bonds. Doing better than the rate of return from Treasury bonds is a minimal test of the performance of a company's strategy.

Investor's Business Daily's Rankings

The newspaper *Investor's Business Daily (IBD)* releases a composite score for companies that combines a number of elements:[32]

1. Accounting performance (earnings per share).
2. Market performance (relative price strength in the past 12 months compared to all other firms).
3. Industry performance (a market rating).
4. An amalgam of accounting components (sales plus profit margins plus return on equity).
5. Investor psychology (amount of buying and selling of the company's shares in the last 12 months) and stock price.

The *IBD* ratings rely on accounting (number 1) and stock market performance (number 2) both of which are relevant to strategy. The use of an industry index (number 3) also is relevant in that strategy is based on the premise that industry matters. A large element of the success of a company can be predicted on the basis of its industry (see Chapter 2). The use of sales and profit margins (number 4) also is relevant to strategy; the two main positions a business can occupy are low cost, which necessitates a high level of sales, or differentiation, which rests on high profit margins. Investor psychology plays a role in determining stock market returns (number 5). Thus, overall, the *IBD* ratings provide good surrogates for strategic performance. However, they are based on past performance and say nothing about how well a company will do next.

Industry Boundaries

Since strategic management is premised on performing better than other companies in an industry, one of the trickiest aspects in making evaluations is determining the industry in which a company competes. Over time the industry in which a company competes is likely to shift. The game it is playing is different. For instance, if Microsoft is considered to be in the operating system and software applications industry, then its main competitors throughout much of the 1990s were Apple and Lotus. If Yahoo! is considered to be in the portal industry, then its main competitors in the 1990s were Excite and Infoseek. On this basis, Microsoft and Yahoo! achieved clear dominance over their main competitors at that time.

However, by the start of the next decade, Microsoft and Apple still could be considered competitors, but IBM had bought Lotus, and Yahoo! and Microsoft now were competing, as Microsoft had its own portal. Microsoft was still in the lead, but its dominance in a broader industry category that included software and portals had been reduced.

Industry is a primary category in strategic management, as it establishes the basis upon which competition occurs. Most discussions assume that industries exist and that companies can be categorized based on the industries in which they compete.

Given the importance of the concept of industry in strategic management, an understanding of industries is fundamentally important. But the boundary problem plagues industry definitions, as industry boundaries are in great flux. In a world of rapid technological change, globalization, and hypercompetition, boundaries are not stable. New industries emerge out of old ones and old ones go out of existence. *Strategic groups* are clusters or groups of firms within industries that tend to resemble each other, are likely to respond similarly to external disturbances, recognize a mutual dependence, and can anticipate each other's actions. By conceptualizing the competitive environment in terms of strategic groups, employees can better isolate boundaries where competitive activity is most critical.

Industries and strategic groups are the result of managers' perceptions. Managers have mental models of their firm's identity, its competitors, suppliers, and customers, and beliefs about what it takes to succeed. Firms often have multiple industry and strategic group identifications. Commitments to multiple industries and groups derive from perceptions of uncertain opportunities. Companies have a portfolio of identifications, some to the past and to industries and strategic groups where opportunities have been previously exploited (their company's mission) and some to the future and to industries and strategic groups that show promise as opportunities for future exploitation (their company's vision). Industry and strategic groups have life cycles. They pass through stages of introduction, growth, maturity, and decline. Companies may participate in tangential industries and strategic groups that eventually become important enough to conceptualize them as their central spheres of activity. The boundaries of the games a company is playing are regularly shifting. Companies do not need to gamble wildly on the future of a single industry or strategic group, but can hedge their bets until the uncertain viability of an emerging industry or strategic group can be more fully established.

Summary

Sustained competitive advantage is achieved through a series of strategic moves over time. To make winning moves, a company must be aware of the rules of the game and changes in the rules of the game and have a vision of where to go next. It must anticipate inflection points—major transformations that require adjustments in strategy—and develop contingency moves to meet different external conditions. SCA typically involves competing in more than one area at a time and dealing with likely reversals in fortune.

To win, employees in a firm must know their enemies—those against whom they compete—*and* themselves. They engage in action-response cycles with their competitors, in which focus and flexibility are needed. They have to recognize patterns that emerge during the competition and adjust accordingly. The aim is not to win just once but to create a dynasty. Doing so means instituting systems for both planning and improvisation and relying on performance measurement systems that are as accurate as possible. SCA is not just doing well for a few years but having persistent performance that is superior to competitors.

This chapter has used analogies from chess, war, and sports to help you think about how to achieve SCA. Some of the lessons to be learned are to concentrate forces and rely on teamwork. Companies must be conscious of the connection between SCA and comparative advantage. Employees must know how to keep score. Some of the more important measures of SCA have been presented in the chapter.

A firm is simultaneously located in the past, striving to achieve what it was good at previously (its *mission*), and at the same time moving toward a *vision* of what it would like to excel at next. To consistently receive strong returns, it has to make better moves than its competitors. To do so, its employees have to develop the ability to analyze external opportunities and threats and internal strengths and weaknesses. The frameworks and methodologies you can use to conduct this type of analysis are the subject of the next two chapters.

Endnotes

1. A. Grove, "On Competitiveness," *Academy of Management Executive* 13, no. 1 (1999), p. 16.
2. A. Marcus, *Strategic Foresight* (New York: Palgrave MacMillan, 2009).
3. R. Wiggins and T. Ruefli, "Sustained Competitive Advantage: Temporal Dynamics and the Incidence and Persistence of Superior Economic Performance," *Organization Science* 13, no. 1 (2002), pp. 82–107.
4. G. Hawawini, V. Subramanian, and P. Verdin, "Is Performance Driven by Industry or Firm-Specific Factors?" *Strategic Management Journal* 24, no. 1 (2003), pp. 1–17.
5. T. Powell, "Varieties of Competitive Parity," *Strategic Management Journal* 24, no. 1 (2003), pp. 61–87.
6. Hawawini, Subramanian, and Verdin, "Is Performance Driven by Industry or Firm-Specific Factors?"
7. M. Friedman, "The Social Responsibility of Business Is to Increase Its Profits," in *The Management of Values,* ed. C. McCoy (Boston: Pitman, 1985), pp. 253–60.
8. "Taking Risks at Intel: Andy Grove, CEO, Intel Corp.," video, Hedrick Smith, *The View from the Top: Managing Change in the Global Marketplace,* 1994.
9. Sun-Tzu, *The Art of War* (New York: Barnes & Noble Books, 1994).
10. E. Luttwak, *Strategy: The Logic of War and Peace* (Cambridge, MA: Harvard University Press, 1987), p. 55.
11. J. B. Quinn, *Strategies for Change: Logical Incrementalism* (Burr Ridge, IL: Richard D. Irwin, 1980).
12. J. Toth, handout, Industrial College of the Armed Forces, www.ndu.edu/icaf/, 2001.
13. Ibid.
14. Ibid.
15. H. Mintzberg, B. Ahlstrand, and J. Lampel, *Strategy Safari: A Guided Tour through the Wilds of Strategic Management* (New York: Simon and Schuster, 1998).
16. "The Return of von Clausewitz," *Economist* 362, no. 8263 (September 2002), pp. 18–21.
17. Ibid.

18. Ibid.

19. C. Grimm and K. Smith, *Strategy for Action: Industry Rivalry and Coordination* (Mason, OH: South-Western College Publishers, 1997).

20. Mintzberg, Ahlstrand, and Lampel, *Strategy Safari.*

21. Quinn, *Strategies for Change.*

22. "The Return of von Clausewitz."

23. "Taking Risks at Intel."

24. A. Grove, *Only the Paranoid Survive* (New York: Random House, 1996).

25. Grove, "On Competitiveness."

26. Ibid.

27. See A. Marcus, *Strategic Foresight* (New York: Palgrave MacMillan, 2009); H. Courtney, *20/20 Foresight* (Boston: Harvard Business School Press, 2001); and M. Raynor, *The Strategy Paradox* (New York: Doubleday, 2007). The discussion that follows is indebted to their work.

28. On shaping the future, see G. Hamel and C. Prahalad, *Competing for the Future* (Boston: Harvard Business School Press, 1994).

29. F. Knight, *Risk, Uncertainty, and Profit* (New York: Houghton Mifflin, 1921).

30. A past model may be deficient because of missing variables.

31. R. Kaplan and D. Norton, *The Balanced Scorecard: Translating Strategy into Action* (Boston: Harvard Business School Press, 1996).

32. See www.investors.com.

CHAPTER TWO

External Analysis

"The essence of strategy . . . is . . . competition. Yet it is easy to view competition too narrowly . . . competition is not manifested only in the other players . . . competitive forces exist . . . well beyond the established combatants. Customers, suppliers, potential entrants, and substitute products are all competitors that may be more or less prominent or active depending on the industry. The collective strength of these forces determines the . . . profit potential of an industry. The corporate strategist's goal is to find a position in the industry where his or her company can best defend itself against these forces or can influence them in its favor."[1]

Michael Porter, professor of strategy, Harvard Business School

Chapter Learning Objectives

- Understanding how to analyze the external environment of the firm.
- Being aware that the external environment consists of three elements—the immediate industry environment, the larger macroenvironment, and the environment of groups with a stake in the firm.
- Using these three elements to identify opportunities and threats, and the inflection points, the firm faces.
- Using them to construct scenarios of possible futures and repertoires of responses and other moves that the firm might take in light of divergent contingencies.

Introduction

The chess analogy presented in Chapter 1 is not perfect. In chess, the player has all the information, while information is missing in management strategy and you do not have the time or resources to obtain it all, but like the chess player who looks at the board before making a move, the strategist too scans the external environment to obtain as much information as possible, to analyze it, and to use it to inform decisions. The strategist examines the immediate context in which the firm operates, the **industry environment.** He or she assesses the broader **macroenvironment,** consisting of forces such as politics and law, technology, demography, society, the economic climate, and the state of the physical

EXHIBIT 2.1
Strategic
Thinking:
Linking the
Firm and the
External
Environment

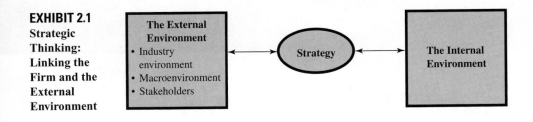

environment. These forces affect the immediate industry environment. The strategist also examines **stakeholder groups,** groups that affect and are affected by the firm's activities, and maps out how the firm will relate to these groups. This chapter provides you with a working knowledge of industry, macroenvironmental, and stakeholder analyses and explains how they can be used to further the strategist's goal of making better moves. These three constitute **external analysis.** Along with internal analysis (Chapter 3), they help the strategist make better moves. Exhibit 2.1 depicts the relationship between external and internal analysis.

Industry Analysis

McKinsey & Company and Bain & Company, major business strategy consultants, include many top companies among their clients. Both McKinsey and Bain include strategy case studies on their Web sites.[2] The case studies pose questions such as:

- Should Buy & Fly, a credit card company, enter Brazil?
- How can Friendly Cookies turn around a sharp decline in profits when cookie prices are rising and its revenue is down by just a few percentage points?

There are no right answers to these questions, just better and worse approaches.

McKinsey and Bain say that although it is a mistake to force-fit every case into a familiar business framework, it is important to be logical and take a well-structured approach.

Industry analysis can help you develop a logical, well-structured approach to problems, but it has to be applied carefully and used thoughtfully. The originator of industry analysis is Michael Porter, professor of strategy at the Harvard Business School and author of a number of important books on strategy.[3]

Porter holds that in developing a strategy you must address two critical questions:[4]

1. *Is the game good?* The strategist should examine the structure and attractiveness of an industry. Some industries are inherently more profitable than others. Knowing which industries they are and why they are more profitable than other industries is important, as the strategist needs to understand how good the "game" is that the company is playing. In the case studies mentioned earlier, it would be important to know how attractive are the credit card industry in Brazil and the cookie industry in the United States. If these industries are not attractive, there is no reason to enter or stay in them. The company can shift resources to other industries.

2. *What is the company's position in the game?* This question focuses on the company's position in the industry. What does it take to succeed in the game the company is playing? Perhaps Buy & Fly or Friendly Cookies can be the best company in an industry whose overall profit levels are low; being the best in such an industry may be better than abandoning it.

Industrial Organization Economics

Porter derives these questions from **industrial organization (IO) economics.** IO economics is a specialty within the field of economics; its original purpose was to help government officials prevent monopolies from arising, but Porter has turned it on its head. His advice to top management is to use the insights of IO economics to create near-monopoly conditions.

The best industry a company can be in is one in which it has virtually no competition. A company should strive to be a "category of one." Being in this position is, in effect, being a near-monopolist. In contrast, multiple competitors mean aggressive price competition, depressing an industry's profitability. If companies are very similar, have the same or similar goals and cost structure, and offer similar products, and growth in the industry is sluggish, then an industry is not attractive. Overcapacity and barriers to exit may characterize the industry. A better industry from the company's viewpoint has more features of a monopoly than it does of perfect competition, including fewer firms, higher entry barriers, and less homogeneous products. If the industry is growing rapidly, this industry is the one to which a firm should belong.

The Five Forces

According to Porter, a number of basic forces have to be examined to determine industry attractiveness. The **five forces** to examine are existing rivals, new entrants, substitutes, customers, and suppliers (see Exhibit 2.2).

Existing Rivals and New Entrants

The first force, *existing rivals*, engage in repeated and regular moves against each other. In addition to examining existing rivals, the strategist must be concerned with *new entrants*.

EXHIBIT 2.2
Porter's Five Forces Affecting Industry Attractiveness

Source: Adapted from M. Porter, "How Competitive Forces Shape Strategy," *Harvard Business Review,* March–April 1979: 86–93.

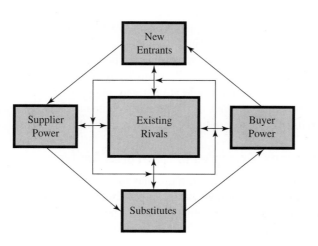

Each industry is open to varying degrees of competition from new entrants, which have the capacity to erode industry profitability and attractiveness. Before entering an industry, a new entrant has to estimate the extent to which the incumbents will retaliate. Barriers to entry, according to Porter, are affected by incumbents' willingness to retaliate. Some incumbents lash out at new entrants with price wars that dissuade potential entrants from moving into the industry. They protect their turf and quickly retaliate in the face of threats from rivals. Other incumbents are more lax.

A new entrant will find it easier to enter a rapidly growing industry than a declining one that is crowded with many competitors. In a slow-growing or declining industry, the incumbents are likely to have excess capacity and thus can cut prices. The likelihood of retaliation against new entrants is great and the chances of retaliation succeeding are high.

Substitutes

Another force affecting industry attractiveness is the power of *substitutes*. A good substitute for the product or service limits prices and lowers industry profitability. Among packaging materials, for instance, plastic, aluminum, metal, and paper often can be substituted for each other. Each constrains the prices that companies making the other products can charge. In the entertainment business, competition among substitutes is fierce: Books, movies, plays, concerts, and sports all compete against each other for the leisure dollar.

Suppliers and Customers

Suppliers and *customers* also affect industry attractiveness. A supplier can move forward in the supply chain. Rather than provide inputs for another company's products, it can make the product itself. Similarly, a customer can move back in the supply chain. Rather than procure goods or services from another company, it can produce them itself. If suppliers and customers have credible options, they are less dependent; they have the power to bargain away the profits a company earns. Companies that depend on just a few suppliers and have nowhere else to go for critical inputs are in a weak position. Suppliers that have many options for selling their goods and services can exact a high price from such companies, thereby eroding profits. Similarly, if customers have many choices, they do not have to buy from a particular company. That company is in a weak position; it may have to lower prices to entice sales, thus diminishing profits.

Being in an advantageous position means having power over suppliers, customers, competitors, new entrants, and substitutes. A company seeks to buy inputs at relatively low prices and convert them to outputs sold at relatively high prices. The differences between its costs and prices are its *margins,* or the profits a company earns. In Porter's framework, a dominant firm in an attractive industry has power over all five forces.

Industry Differences: Examples of Five-Force Analysis

Historically, one of the most attractive industries in which to participate was the pharmaceutical industry, and one of the least attractive was the airline industry. (See Exhibit 2.3 for data on industry profitability from 1985 to 1995.) The differences in these two industries' performances can be explained using Porter's five-force analysis.[5]

EXHIBIT 2.3
Profitability of U.S. Industries, 1985–1995

Source: Federal Trade Commission and Fortune 500, adapted from R. Grant, *Contemporary Strategy Analysis,* 3rd ed. (Oxford, England: Blackwell, 1998).

Industry	Return on Equity
Pharmaceuticals	19.39%
Food and kindred products	13.85
Instruments and related products	11.24
Printing and publishing	10.16
Electrical and electronic equipment	10.00
Rubber and miscellaneous plastics products	9.95
Paper and allied products	8.47
Retail trade corporations	8.37
Aircraft, guided missiles, and parts	8.36
Fabricated metal products	8.15
Petroleum and coal products	7.88
Textile mill products	7.25
Wholesale trade corporations	6.23
Stone, glass, and clay products	5.72
Machinery, excluding electrical	4.29
Nonferrous metals	4.21
Motor vehicles and equipment	2.61
Iron and steel	1.30
Mining corporations	1.24
Airlines	−2.84

Pharmaceuticals—A Five-Star Industry

Porter called pharmaceuticals a five-star industry because, until recently, all five forces were aligned to the industry's benefit.

Historically, companies in the pharmaceutical industry did not try to undermine each other through ruthless price-cutting. Their competitive positions were based on small differences in brand and reputation. Within the industry, there was room for all companies to earn high returns.

Barriers to entry into the pharmaceutical industry were high for the following reasons:

- Pharmaceutical companies had large sales forces of "detail" people, who made regular visits to physicians, informed them about new drugs, and gave them plenty of samples, which the physicians valued. The physicians tended to become familiar with these sales reps and to trust them. It was difficult for an industry newcomer to duplicate the relationships the detail people had developed with doctors.
- The cost of research and development was extremely high. A new entrant could not easily duplicate the trained staff and laboratories of an established company because of the difficulties involved in attracting scientific talent and setting up complex and sophisticated laboratories. A new entrant also would not have experience obtaining government approval for new drugs, a process that could constitute more than 60 percent of drug development costs. Obtaining approval was an arduous process, containing many pitfalls.

Only experienced pharmaceutical companies were likely to have the requisite social and political capital and the know-how to not only develop a drug but also get it approved. With entry barriers such as these, it was little wonder there were few new entrants into the industry.

Because the pharmaceutical companies held patents on their new products, substitutes were scarce or nonexistent.

The buyers—doctors, patients, and health insurance companies—were not particularly price sensitive. According to the physician, the patient had to have the drug in question—there was no choice. If the patient's illness was life threatening or extremely debilitating, the patient was not likely to bargain about price. In addition, because health insurance organizations were increasingly covering the costs of drugs, many patients had little incentive to protest. Consumer bargaining power was weak.

The bargaining power of suppliers also was weak. The ingredients in most drugs were not very expensive; they were commodities and accounted for only a fraction of the cost of finished products. There were many suppliers, so a pharmaceutical company could choose where it would buy ingredients.

But the favorable forces that historically had prevailed in pharmaceuticals began to erode in the 1990s. Three important changes occurred:

1. *The buyer, who previously had been indifferent about price, became increasingly cost conscious.* With the price of pharmaceuticals rising much more rapidly than the inflation rate, insurance companies and government agencies became concerned and demanded cost-containment.

2. *Generic drugs became more widely available as substitutes for brand-name drugs.* Generic drugs provide the same therapeutic properties and benefits as name brands but at lower cost. Government insurance programs, as a consequence of concern about the costs of health care, required that generics be dispensed when available, rather than brand-name drugs.

3. *Advanced research methods lowered the cost of drug development, weakening barriers to entry.* Companies with skills in biotechnology, such as Genentech, were able to enter the industry. They had the potential to revolutionize the drug development process and thereby undermine the structure of the industry and lower its overall profitability.

Airlines—A No-Star Industry

Before its deregulation in the late 1970s, the airline industry had been very attractive. With its prices fixed by the government, consumers had few choices and little power. The airlines competed on nonessentials such as food or the color of their planes. Essentially, no new major airline was created during the period of airline regulation.

But all that changed beginning in the 1980s, prompting Porter to rank the airline industry with no stars, compared with the pharmaceutical industry's five stars.

After deregulation, the government relinquished its right to set rates for airline travel, and it permitted new entrants into the industry. The high returns in the airline industry started to deteriorate as new entrants flooded consumers with previously unavailable options.

Buyer loyalty was low because there was little to differentiate one airline from another. Thus, ticket price became the main factor determining which airline a consumer would use. Information about prices was readily available on the Internet. Customers could easily do comparative shopping and get the best price.

Consumers had substitutes for air travel. Advances in telecommunications enabled business conferences to occur on the Internet. Some travelers could drive, go by rail, or take a bus to their destinations instead of flying.

The main suppliers to the industry had power. The companies that manufactured the engines, assembled the planes, and supplied the fuel were large corporations with clout. The pilots themselves were a highly skilled group that was unionized and that had influence.

By the late 1990s, the airlines had little power over customers and suppliers, their rivalry was intense and sometimes bitter, and they could not prevent entry. Since carriers were going to make scheduled flights regardless of how full the planes were, the costs of adding an incremental passenger were low. Thus, price wars among carriers ensued, and these wars lowered the profit levels of all the carriers. The airlines tried various means to rectify these problems. They consolidated to gain bargaining power over suppliers and prevent new entrants from moving into the industry. Many of the most celebrated new entrants failed and were taken over by other airlines. People's Express, for example, went bankrupt, and its assets were acquired by Continental.

The existing carriers also created hub-and-spoke systems. A hub is a central airport through which flights are routed, and spokes are the routes that planes take out of the hub airport. Most major airlines have multiple hubs. Under a direct-route, or point-to-point, system, airlines fly directly between small markets, which results in unprofitable, half-empty flights. The hub-and-spoke system attempts to make sure that planes are fuller. In addition to filling planes, these systems give the airlines greater power over customers by limiting choices. Some cities are served by only a single airline, leaving customers no choice.

To keep customers from defecting, the airlines established frequent-flyer programs. In addition, they created sophisticated management information systems used for ticketing and routing. Developing these systems involved huge investments that raised the barriers to entry. To keep their costs in line, the airlines tried to renegotiate contracts with the powerful pilot, flight attendant, and mechanics unions. They also purchased newer, more fuel-efficient aircraft. When Boeing acquired McDonnell Douglas, the airlines reduced their reliance on the consolidating U.S. aircraft manufacturing industry by buying more jets from the highly subsidized European manufacturer Airbus. Despite these steps the airlines were unable to make the five forces more favorable for their industry.

Conclusions from the Analyses

Industry attractiveness is transient. Airlines remain one of the poorer-performing U.S. industries, but pharmaceuticals no longer are among the best performers. In fact, in 2006 they were among the worst-performing industries in terms of their annual returns to shareholders (see Exhibit 2.4).

EXHIBIT 2.4
Best and Worst Performing Industries, 2006*

Source: BigCharts.com.

10 Best Performing Industries 2006		10 Worst Performing Industries 2006	
Industry Name	**Percent Change 10 Years**	**Industry Name**	**Percent Change 10 Years**
General mining	860.40%	Automobiles	−40.14%
Consumer electronics	389.37	Airlines	−38.83
Nonferrous metals	289.10	Tires	−35.18
Exploration & production	208.42	Gas distribution	−32.30
Steel	205.84	Automobiles & parts	−25.73
Coal	203.65	Fixed line telecommunications	−21.18
Gambling	173.41	Pharmaceuticals	−19.90
Home construction	149.68	Telecommunications	−18.22
Commercial vehicles & trucks	139.50	Aluminum	−17.48
Oil equipment & services	138.14	Broadcasting & entertainment . . .	−16.84

*The industries are ranked based on their one-year share price performance.

For the airlines and pharmaceutical industries, the severe economic downturn that started in 2007 has meant continued difficult times. The airline industry carries substantial risk because earnings swing rapidly when fuel prices and the macroeconomic outlook change. The continued profitability of the industry is heavily impacted by jet fuel prices and the overall economy's health. The majority of passenger airlines posted sizable losses in recent years, but drops in fuel prices could improve their bottom lines. On the other hand, the deep economic recession lowered leisure flight demand; this cut heavily into airlines' business. In response, most carriers have had to substantially cut seating capacity by reducing the number of flights. Capacity reductions have increased their load factors; however, pricing and occupancy rates remain under pressure. With a weak economy, the airlines have had difficulty raising fares.

A weak economy also has stressed pharmaceutical companies. Their inability to develop drugs fast enough to offset expiring patents has generated new competition from generic drug manufacturers. In an effort to control costs, given looming patent expirations, the industry cut thousands of jobs, with many more job cuts anticipated. Food and Drug Administration (FDA) approval of new drugs, just 18 to 24 per year from 2005 to 2008, was not enough to make up for patent expirations. The FDA, though, has approved dozens of new formulations and new uses for existing drugs. Pharmaceutical companies have been seeking to offset billions of dollars in lost sales due to patent expirations by purchasing competitors and consolidating their business. They also are always searching for new niches to expand their product pipelines. Finally, they are trying to develop generic biotech drugs, called biosimilars, as a new type of revenue source. Generic biotechs are not yet allowed in the United States but are being sold in Europe.

Like the airlines, pharmaceuticals remain a troubled and risky industry. Many factors weigh against the attractiveness of either industry. Though both the pharmaceutical and airline industries were stressed, their performance was about in the middle of the pack among all industries in the 2003–2008 period. Pharmaceuticals continued to outperform the airlines (see Exhibit 2.5). Of the 129 industries listed by Morningstar, pharmaceuticals were in 61st place and airlines were in 81st place.

The Strategist's Role in Industry Analysis

To counter the negative forces an industry confronts, industry analysis should be carried out. The strategist should examine industry structure and have a fundamental understanding of the five forces. Each industry, however, is different. Different forces are significant. The strategist must figure out which are the most important forces and what can be done about them. He or she should give greatest attention to the forces that can be most readily influenced in a way that improves company performance.

Finding the right way to influence these forces is difficult, as the airline and pharmaceutical examples demonstrate. Understanding how an industry is likely to evolve and what the strategist can do to shape its future direction are ongoing challenges with no easy answers. The structures of some industries might be such that the forces cannot be influenced for the better.

The most sensible choice if one's company cannot be the dominant player in its industry is to exit the industry. If exiting is not possible, as is often the case, the strategist must be careful that the moves advocated do not cause industry structure to deteriorate. A favorite

EXHIBIT 2.5
Industry Total Returns (%), 2003–2008*

Source: Adapted with permission from Morningstar, http://news.morningstar.com/stockReturns/CapWtdIndustryReturns.html.

Rank	Industry Name	1-Year Return	3-Year Return	5-Year Return
	Top 8 Performers			
1	Agrochemical	−35.8	18.38	30.12
2	Business/Online services	−32.8	−7.97	20.79
3	Steel/Iron	−68.23	−9.19	13.14
4	Agriculture	−39.2	−5.27	6.96
5	Gold & silver	−31.02	0.5	6.52
6	Land transport	−40.58	−10.72	6.43
7	Tobacco	−32.71	−0.91	6.29
8	Diagnostics	−14	−0.68	4.39
	Industries Ranked 57–65			
57	Medical equipment	−36.21	−11.98	−6.66
58	Environmental control	−69.71	−23.55	−6.82
59	Electric equipment	−48.95	−16.45	−7.05
60	Security services	−57.34	−20.54	−7.36
61	Pharmaceuticals	−25.6	−10	−7.49
62	Business support	−37.65	−20.22	−7.63
63	Insurance (general)	−48.32	−13.86	−7.9
64	Development tools	−45.02	−20.51	−7.91
65	Photography & imaging	−35.92	−14.74	−8.95
	Industries Ranked 77–85			
77	Manufacturing—Misc.	−46.26	−19.57	−10.62
78	Insurance (title)	−21.12	−16.05	−10.87
79	Building materials	−64.48	−31.2	−10.91
80	Transportation—Misc.	−45.16	−22.46	−11.04
81	Airlines	−54.6	−27.3	−11.1
82	Entertainment/Education media	−54.71	−22.17	−11.4
83	Employment	−47.57	−26.22	−11.65
84	Personal services	−37.57	−18.37	−11.82
85	Clothing stores	−50.49	−27.13	−12.31
	Worst 8 Performers			
122	Finance	−56.06	−37.64	−23.97
123	Optical equipment	−59.43	−32.22	−24.22
124	Home building	−56.21	−43.3	−24.68
125	Textiles	−72.41	−37.95	−25.41
126	Contract manufacturers	−66.7	−39.81	−31.36
127	Wireline equipment	−59.06	−41.42	−32.25
128	Radio	−95.98	−69.77	−53.92
129	Oil/Gas products	−57.5	−26.8	−56.1

*5-year rank as of March 1, 2008.

category of moves—price cutting—can be ruinous. The actions a company takes can weaken an industry as well as strengthen it. Whatever moves the strategist proposes must be tested against industry structure. Will the structure improve or deteriorate?

In forecasting the future, the strategist must be aware that the past is not necessarily a good indicator of the future. There might be fundamental new changes in industry structure brought on by changes in macroenvironmental conditions such as the society, politics, and the economy. The factors driving these changes may be very hard to influence. Factors that decrease an industry's profitability may be difficult to alter. Often, the only options are to exit, migrate to a new industry, or create a new industry niche that can be better protected. If an industry cannot be abandoned it must be reshaped. The fundamental rules in the industry will have to be reformed.

Long-Term Industry Attractiveness

Industries that are attractive for long periods have very effective **barriers to entry.**[6] The stronger these barriers are, the more secure the industry will be. Erecting barriers to entry is a way to alter the forces affecting industry profitability. The main entry barriers are:

- *Scale economies.* Economies of scale prevent a new entrant from moving into an industry because it would face severe cost disadvantages: Its per-unit costs would be higher than those of existing competitors. In areas such as manufacturing, research, sales, marketing, or distribution, the new entrant would be behind existing competitors.
- *Product differentiation.* Companies are deterred from entering an industry in which customers have already developed strong brand loyalty. Customers often associate existing companies' products with unique features established over time. These special attributes would be hard for a new entrant to match.
- *Capital requirements.* The capital required to enter an industry raises the level of debt a new company would have to assume. For a new entrant, incurring additional debt is risky, since the break-even point for new entrants is higher than for existing competitors. Given the high level of debt, the new entrant may choose not to compete.
- *Learning- and experience-curve effects.* Existing companies gain an advantage from learning from experience. The accumulated knowledge of existing companies in areas such as production, marketing, and research may give potential entrants second thoughts about whether to move into an industry.
- *Distribution channels.* If existing competitors have a choke hold on distribution channels, new entrants cannot compete. Without access to these channels, new entrants have nowhere to sell their products and services.
- *Government policies.* Some government policies keep new entrants out by establishing requirements they cannot meet. For example, regulations may impose high pollution control costs, require costly measures to ensure worker safety, or mandate complex procedures for providing benefits to employees. A start-up would not have the money or expertise to comply. For example, to protect its stakes in the high-definition television screen business, 3M has used energy labeling standards promulgated by the government to erect barriers to entry.

Although established competitors can keep new entrants out, constraints on entry are becoming increasingly easier to overcome. In industry after industry, boundaries have been scuttled, and the industries revolutionized. Again and again industry definitions have been challenged to the advantage of new entrants that have found ways to enter industries from which they have been previously barred.

Macroenvironmental Analysis

Industry boundaries have been permeable and industries fundamentally transformed because industry structure is not created in a vacuum. The five forces that define industry attractiveness are unstable. They continually evolve. The dynamism arises from forces in the macroenvironment that drive continuous change, create inflections, and alter industry attractiveness. Government, for instance, has a profound impact on industry structure as the pharmaceutical and airline industries show. The global economy too has a huge impact; the recent economic meltdown has removed advantages that the financial services sector once had. Large investment banks no longer exist. The macro factors to which managers must pay special attention include not only government and the economy but also technology, social structure and demography, and energy and the natural environment (see Exhibit 2.6).

Components of the External Environment

The external elements examined below affect an industry's future: (1) government, (2) national and international economies, (3) technology, (4) social structure and demography, and (5) energy and the natural environment (see Exhibit 2.6). Each has an important impact on Porter's five forces. The five forces are dynamic. Disruptive change in industry conditions is the norm.

Government

Government imposes constraints on businesses and generates opportunities. Trends in government budgets and taxes, trade and antitrust legislation, privatization and deregulation, defense spending, and national security affect companies. Also, issues that capture the attention of governments influence business. These include the menace of global terrorism, the relationships between prosperous and poor nations, and the move toward market economies in countries such as Russia and China.

EXHIBIT 2.6
From Industry Analysis to Analysis of the Macroenvironment

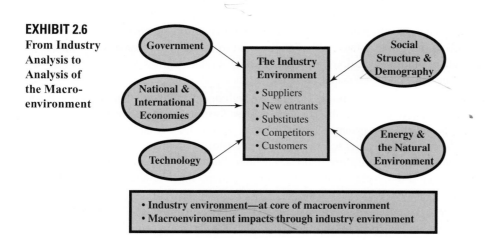

Government Growth   Governments throughout the world have grown, and they have done so for many reasons. The size and scope of governments in different parts of the world vary tremendously. The United States trails most nations in total taxes as a percentage of gross national product (GNP), and the relative size of the U.S. government actually is smaller than that of any developed country except Japan.[7] However, the size of the U.S. government in proportion to GNP was changing as a result of the economic crisis of 2008. Just as the size and scope of the U.S. government expanded during the Great Depression, more than doubling in terms of proportion of GNP and employment between 1929 and World War II, so again the role of government in the U.S. economy was rapidly expanding. The vast stimulus proposed and passed by the Obama administration in 2009 and the ongoing bailout of the banks were profoundly affecting business–government relations.

Many theories have been offered to explain government size and scope. Some theorists have focused on the expansion of public revenues through taxation. A progressive income tax, coupled with inflation and unindexed tax brackets, moves taxpayers into higher marginal brackets and thus leads to increased public revenues and real increases in public expenditures. Other theorists explain the growth of government in terms of the needs that arise from economic development and industrialization. In undeveloped nations, taxes and social security generally account for a lower percentage of GNP than they do in developed countries.

In developed societies, people are more interdependent. As a consequence, government plays a larger role in maintaining public order, administering justice, and regulating business and other activities. Government must account for the unintended harm of private economic activities. It also has to alleviate the burden on the victims and help those who are unable to care for themselves. Government spending, taxation, and monetary policies related to these needs affect the overall economy.

Politics   Party politics, voting, special interests, legislative decision making, and bureaucratic processes play a role in understanding the size and scope of government activities.

- *Party politics.* The extent to which left- or right-wing parties control a government is a strong indicator of the activities it will undertake.
- *Voting.* The degree to which people exercise their right to vote also affects government actions. In the United States, although the right to vote has been broadly extended, the percentage of the population that actually votes is relatively low and is skewed toward higher-income, better-educated, and older adults.
- *Special interests.* Special-interest groups are well organized in the United States. Farmers, retirees, and the gun lobby, for instance, are formidable blocs. Businesses too have many special-interest groups. Special-interest groups have a large stake in particular policies, and find it easier to organize and exert influence over policy than do groups representing large and diffuse publics. The latter have less of a stake in particular policies, so even if the overall impact of policies on their constituencies is greater, they are less likely to voice their concerns.
- *Legislative decision making.* Legislators tend to support bills that favor their own districts. Plus, they support those offered by other legislators as long as bills that benefit

their own districts are supported in return (log-rolling). As a result, many bills are passed that help special interests.

- *Bureaucratic processes.* "Bureaucratic drift" is an example of such processes: Short-sighted yearly decisions lead to cumulative long-term problems.

All of these factors—party politics, voting, special interests, legislative decision making, and bureaucracies—must be analyzed by strategists if they are to understand the movements in government policies that affect their industries.

Government–Business Differences   Governments differ from businesses in fundamental ways (see Exhibit 2.7). Generally, business executives value efficiency, while government officials value equity, accountability, and responsiveness, as well as efficiency.[8]

EXHIBIT 2.7   **How Government Agencies Differ from Businesses**

Government Agencies	Business
Less Market Pressure	**More Market Pressure**
• Fewer incentives for cost reduction and operating efficiency	• More incentives for cost reduction and operating efficiency
• Lower efficiency in allocating institutional resources, less reflection of consumer preferences, and minimal pressure to have supply meet demand	• Higher efficiency in allocating resources, more reflection of consumer preferences, and maximum pressure to have supply meet demand
More External Control and Direction	**Less External Control and Direction**
• Formal specifications and controls from the executive, legislative, and judicial branches of government	• No formal specifications and controls from the executive, legislative, and judicial branches of government
• Need to act based on interpretations of government rules and statutes	• Less need to act based on interpreting government rules and statutes
• High degree of legal and institutional constraints on procedures and spheres of operation	• Fewer legal and institutional constraints on procedures and spheres of operation
• Public opinion and political pressure more likely to influence decisions	• Public opinion and political pressure less likely to influence decisions
Greater Need to Seek Consensus	**Less Need to Seek Consensus**
• Support needed from executive, legislative, and judicial branches to operate	• No explicit support needed from executive, legislative, and judicial branches to operate
• High level of bargaining needed to obtain financial and human resources	• Less bargaining needed to obtain financial and human resources
• More diverse stakeholders with multiple and often conflicting objectives	• More uniform stakeholders with fewer, more singular objectives
• More explicit trade-offs needed between economic and social costs of actions and benefits to the environment and public health	• Less explicit need to make trade-offs between different types of costs—economic, social, environmental, and public health
More Public Accountability and Scrutiny	**Less Public Accountability and Scrutiny**
• Oversight by congressional committees that review use of public resources	• No oversight by congressional committees that review use of public resources
• Freedom of Information (FOI) requests from stakeholders	• No direct Freedom of Information (FOI) requests from stakeholders
• Frequent target of media exposés on government ineffectiveness and inefficiency	• Less frequent target of media exposés on government ineffectiveness and inefficiency

Business executives must operate according to quantifiable and discrete financial targets, and their performance is evaluated using specific indicators such as market share, profits, and return on investment. Government officials often have indefinite goals that are not as easily measured (e.g., improving public health or environmental quality), and their performance is judged according to more subjective criteria (such as the status of public health or the general state of the environment).

In general, risk taking is more valued by business executives than government officials and is more prevalent in businesses than in regulatory agencies. Business managers have increasingly adopted organization structures designed to allow them to respond quickly to rapid changes in the marketplace, while government officials in the United States—reflecting the checks and balances of the Constitution—have complicated, bureaucratic, and overlapping structures that operate at a more measured pace. Government officials must cope with distributional conflicts that arise among diverse interests operating in their jurisdictions, and the institutional rewards typically go to those who can forge compromises in this setting. Business managers, on the other hand, must cope with the needs of their customers and the expectations of shareholders. Although they, too, must forge compromises, typically they are rewarded for taking quick action in the marketplace rather than waiting for the best compromise to emerge.

Blocs of Nations   Another important development is the growing power of blocs of nations, such as the North American Free Trade Agreement (NAFTA) among the United States, Canada, and Mexico, and the European Union (EU). The EU has become a formidable counterpart to the United States as a power center.[9]

The process of European integration was launched in 1950 when France officially proposed the creation of a European federation. Six countries (Belgium, West Germany, France, Italy, Luxembourg, and the Netherlands) joined at that time. Since then, many additional countries have become members including Denmark, Ireland, the United Kingdom, Greece, Spain, Portugal, Austria, Finland, Sweden, and many nations from the ex-Soviet bloc including the Czech Republic and Hungary. The EU's principal objectives are far-reaching. They include establishing a single European citizenship; promoting economic and social progress through a single market, a common currency, job creation, regional development, and environmental protection; and aggressively asserting Europe's role in the world. Five institutions run the EU, with each playing a specific role: the European Parliament, elected by the citizens of the member states; the Council of the Union, composed of the governments of the member states; the European Commission, an executive body; the Court of Justice, which ensures compliance with the law; and the Court of Auditors, which guarantees sound and lawful management of the EU budget.

In an interdependent business world, strategists analyzing the role of government must consider blocs of nations throughout the world, as well as individual nations, as these blocs have influence on their industries.

National and International Economies

The world economy of the 21st century is one of heightened interdependence. After the horrific terrorist attacks of 9/11, consumer spending declined and there was a slowdown in business investment throughout the world. The relatively quick recovery that occurred was built on government actions—loose monetary policies, tax cuts, increased military spending in the United States, and foreign investments, primarily from Asia, in the United States. The U.S. economy was then hit by a decline in the housing market, which spilled over into a worldwide banking and investment crisis. Businesses faltered and companies cut payrolls, taking huge amounts of purchasing power out of the economy.[10] The Federal Reserve cut interest rates to encourage investment and spur economic activity, and Presidents Bush and Obama proposed Keynesian stimuli that Congress passed. The U.S. government intervened in an unprecedented way, and large parts of the economy came under government control.

Similarities to the Great Depression were noted, including a major expansion of consumer credit and home buying that preceded the downturn. Also similar were rising income inequalities. However, most bank deposits were insured, and such programs as Social Security, Medicare, and unemployment compensation put a lid on widespread destitution. A rigid gold standard was not in place, which kept the money supply tight, as was the case in the 1930s, and the governments of the 21st century had not yet resorted to massive trade protectionism as they did during the Great Depression.

As this example shows, governments affect trends in national and global economics. In considering these trends, the analyst should be familiar with such data as growth rates in gross domestic product, changes in inflation, unemployment, government outlays and deficits, and changes in the money supply and interest rates. **Gross domestic product (GDP),** a measure of an economy's total market value, consists of four components—personal consumption, private investment, government spending, and exports. **GDP per capita** indicates how wealthy the individuals in a country are at a given moment in comparison to individuals in other countries. Also important are data on exchange rates and the balance of payments. Because corporations that operate globally are dependent on revenue and profit streams from abroad, changes in exchange rates and the balance of payments can have major effects on their performance.

Current data on most of these measures can be found in many sources. *The Economist,* for instance, updates them in each weekly issue. It also publishes predictions, based on surveys of economic forecasters, of what these measures are likely to be in the future. Examples of this type of information as compiled at the Web site www.economagic.com are presented in Exhibit 2.8.

Technology

The world needs technological innovation for economic growth to be sustainable. The economist Joseph Schumpeter argued that new technologies replace old ones in waves ("creative destruction") as certain sectors (e.g., textiles, steel, railroads, automotive, chemicals, pharmaceuticals, telecommunications, computers, biotechnology) dominate the global economy at particular intervals.[11] Technological change, according to Schumpeter, is like a "series of explosions," with innovations concentrated in specific sectors, or leading-edge industries, that provide growth's momentum. These leading sectors propel the economy forward.

EXHIBIT 2.8
Economic Interdependence and the Meltdown: U.S. Economic Performance 1948–2008

Source: Reprinted with permission from Economagic.com.

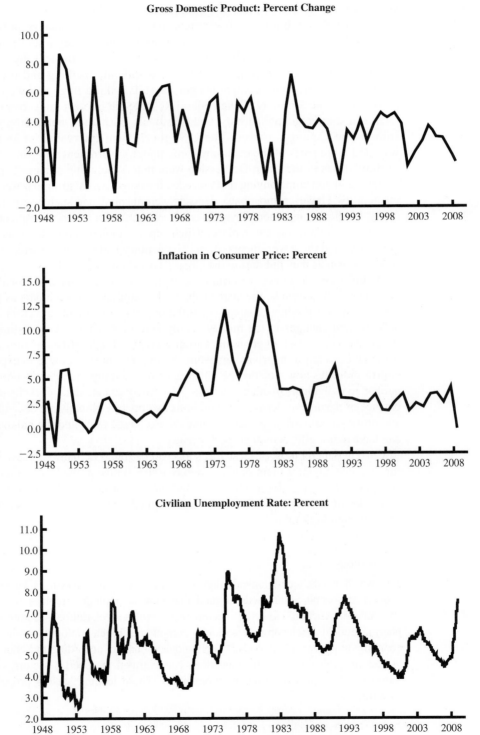

Gross Domestic Product: Percent Change

Inflation in Consumer Price: Percent

Civilian Unemployment Rate: Percent

EXHIBIT 2.9
Promising
Technological
Developments

- *Genetic Engineering.* The genetic code of living organisms has been mapped in preparation for the ongoing restructuring and remodeling of genes to enhance or eliminate various traits in humans and other life forms. The map may provide scientists with the ability to predict and correct genetic diseases. It may allow them to create drugs to better fight diseases such as cancer. It should give them the ability to create crops that are pest-resistant and drought-proof, and have other useful properties.
- *Advanced Computing.* Evolving chip technologies are opening up the promise of even faster and more powerful computers. Information from audio, video, and film is being digitized so that it can be retrieved more quickly and used more effectively. The use of memory systems such as optical disks, film, and bar-code readers also is being expanded. Parallel processing permits many computers to be used simultaneously. It greatly enhances computer power and performance and thereby increases the complexity of the scientific and technical tasks that can be handled. Computer use is continuing to expand to areas where human intelligence has been applied. Computers are increasing their ability to carry out such activities as learning, adapting, recognizing, and self-correction.
- *Telecommunications.* Fiber optics, which carry many signals at once (such as television, telephone, radio, and computer), are greatly improving and expanding communications. Microwaves send wireless digital information to satellite dishes. Advanced satellites can be used for pinpoint surveillance and mapping.
- *Biomedical Engineering.* Microwave scalpels equipped with lasers (light amplified by the stimulated emission of radiation) are replacing metal scalpels used in surgery. Through bioelectricity, damaged or malfunctioning nerves, muscles, and glands can be stimulated to promote their repair and restore their healthy functioning. This technique can be used in humans with severed bones or defective hearts or lungs. It speeds the healing rates of wounds.
- *Material Sciences.* Many new materials are becoming more widely available. Lighter, stronger, more resistant to heat, and able to conduct electricity, new polymers can be used in many products from garbage bags to tanks, ball bearings, batteries, and running shoes. New materials can be constructed molecule by molecule and atom by atom using supercomputers in their design. Tailor-made enzymes for industrial use are being developed. High-tech ceramics resistant to corrosion, wear, and high temperatures are being used in autos and elsewhere to create cleaner-running and more efficient engines. Lightweight and noncorrosive fiber-reinforced composites that are stronger than steel are being used in buildings, bridges, and aircraft.
- *Energy.* Many new energy technologies exist such as fuel cells, which use hydrogen as opposed to fossil fuels like oil. Solar energy cells already are being used in pocket calculators and remote power applications. Superconductors carry electricity with less loss of energy. They make possible cheaper and more advanced magnetic imaging machines for hospitals. They can also be used in TV antennas and faster computer circuits.

Particularly promising technological developments are occurring in such fields as genetic engineering, advanced computing, telecommunications, biomedical engineering, the material sciences, and energy. Exhibit 2.9 discusses advances in these fields.

Even for promising technologies, large obstacles stand in the way of their wide-scale adoption and use. A promising technology is an invention, which is not the same as an innovation. **Invention** is the creation of an item or process, usually in a laboratory. It is a test of the principle involved, an act of technical creativity in which a concept that may be suitable for patenting is described. **Innovation** is the process of putting an invention into widespread use. It is the effort to commercially exploit the invention's introduction to ensure its broad application. However promising new technologies may be, many fail to be adopted in a wide-scale way.

Better management does not necessarily reduce the failure rate.[12] Most managers have powerful reasons to keep risk to a minimum. In deliberating about whether to undertake a particular project, the strategist has to consider the project's technical *and* commercial feasibility. In doing so, he or she must estimate:

- Probable development, production, and marketing costs.
- The approximate timing of these costs.
- Probable future income streams.
- The time these income streams are likely to occur.

All of these calculations are fraught with difficulty (see Chapter 7).

Social Structure and Demography

In deciding if a business venture is likely to succeed, a strategist must pay attention to the potential market. Key factors to consider about the potential market are social structure and demography, such factors as a population's age, education, extent of ethnic diversity, and median household income.

For instance, the U.S. population is getting older. In 1970, the median age was 28. By 2050, it will be 38.[13] The population also is better educated. In 1940, only 25 percent of the population had a high school diploma and 5 percent had a bachelor's degree or more, but by the year 2000, 84 percent had a high school diploma and 26 percent had a bachelor's degree or more.[14]

Immigration to the United States is increasing. The six states projected to have the largest net increases in immigrants by 2025 are California, New York, Florida, New Jersey, Illinois, and Texas.[15] Largely because of the rise in the number of two-income families, median household income has grown. In 1970, it was about $34,000 in 2001 dollars, but by 2001, it was more than $42,000.[16]

Other important factors are the size of the population, consumption patterns, leisure and work habits, extent of new household formation, and geographic distribution of the population. In determining industry attractiveness, the strategist needs to understand demographics and how they shift the relative power of buyers, suppliers, and competitors.

For more than 200 years, Thomas Robert Malthus, whose views centered on the dangers of overpopulation, inspired most thinking about population growth. However, today population growth is neither exponential nor arithmetic, but the opposite; it is slowing to historically low levels and in some cases shrinking. This is a part of a larger pattern of demographic transition (see Exhibit 2.10) where population has moved from high fertility and mortality in traditional societies to low fertility and mortality in advanced societies.

This shift has occurred over a long period and in an unbalanced way. As economies grow and health conditions improve, mortality rates decline but only substantially later do fertility rates follow. Demographic transition occurs in stages, with a pretransition stage (stage 1) characterized by a high birthrate, high infant and maternal mortality rates, and very short life spans. Population growth in this phase is stagnant. An early transition stage (stage 2) starts when infant mortality starts to fall off because of advances in GDP. With GDP growth, developments such as increased variety in the food supply, better housing, improved sanitation, and progress in preventative and curative medicine occur. As a consequence, the death rate falls and populations surge, creating bulges. The key driver in stage 2 is the delay between declines in fertility and mortality.

Demographic transition theory suggests that population growth is not unlimited. Stage 3 in Exhibit 2.10 has a declining birthrate; population grows, but mainly because

EXHIBIT 2.10
Demographic
Transition
Theory

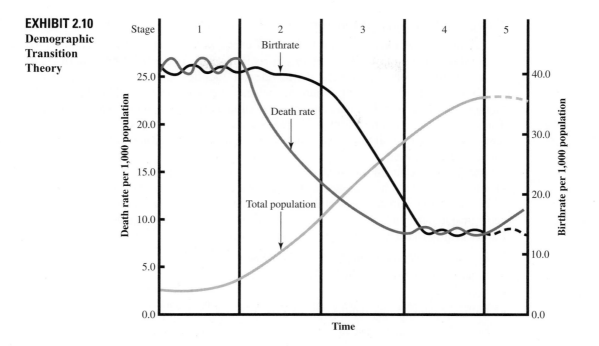

the death rate continues to fall. The average age of the population starts to increase. Late transition (stage 4) is characterized by a birthrate at or below the replacement level, substantially lower than at the start of the transition. This stage is marked by continuous advances in medicine and life-extending activities, which prolong life and lead to large increases in the number of elderly, a phenomenon now common in many advanced industrial countries. In stage 5, the birthrate is stable, but the death rate grows mainly because of aging.

As well as changes in the number of people globally, their attitudes and values shift. Social values reflect how people feel about leisure. Political values influence voting preferences and feelings about public issues. Cultural values indicate the extent to which people are tolerant of different lifestyles. Religious values affect lifestyle decisions people make.

According to the sociologist Daniel Bell, people's values originate in three realms—economic, political, and sociocultural.[17] In economics, society is moving from producing goods to offering services. Knowledge is in the foreground and is a central source of change. Politics is open to different groups demanding recognition, equal rights, and equal status. The *sociocultural* realm recognizes and emphasizes the individual's right to self-expression. A primary source of tension is disjunction among these realms. In the economy, meritocratic values govern. These principles are not completely compatible with principles of equality and open access, which govern politics. Values such as self-fulfillment and self-enhancement, which influence culture and society, may be in conflict with economic and political values. The strategist has to be alert to these tensions. The social field is not a homogenous entity.

Energy and the Natural Environment

The strategist also must consider the role of energy and the natural environment. All corporations rely on critical energy resources.[18] In 1973, 1979, and 1990, the rulers of Persian Gulf nations interrupted worldwide oil supplies, causing oil prices to rise dramatically. Alternative energy sources, such as wind, solar power, and bio-based fuels, that will make the world less dependent on fossil fuels still are in the development stage. The use of existing nonrenewable resources such as coal and oil can create serious problems—atmospheric pollution, hazardous wastes, and carbon dioxide buildup, which can cause global warming.

The Business Council for Sustainable Development (BCSD) coined the concept of **eco-efficiency** in 1992.[19] It is defined as the delivery of competitively priced goods and services that satisfy human needs and enhance quality of life while progressively reducing ecological impacts and resource intensity throughout the life cycle to a level in line with the Earth's estimated carrying capacity.[20] To achieve eco-efficiency, a firm must:

- Reduce the material intensity of goods and services.
- Reduce the energy intensity of goods and services.
- Reduce toxic dispersion.
- Enhance material recyclability.
- Maximize sustainable use of renewable resources.
- Increase material durability.
- Increase the service intensity of goods and services.

Managers need to understand that the natural world is the source of critical resources corporations require to operate efficiently and profitably. To minimize adverse environmental consequences, they can cut back on environmentally unsafe operations, carry out R&D on environmentally safe activities, develop and expand environmental cleanup services, compensate for environmentally risky endeavors, collaborate with environmentalists, take advantage of innovative government compliance programs, and encourage technological advances that reduce pollution from products and manufacturing processes.

Just as managerial strategies have a major effect on the environment, energy and environmental problems have a profound effect on the strategies managers adopt. In the long run, smooth transitions from the use of one set of resources to another should occur if markets function without undue government interference and if technological changes occur in response to market signals. In the short run, however, resource scarcity and price hikes can occur, causing severe adjustment difficulties for businesses and the likelihood of government intervention.

People in business must keep abreast of the drivers of energy and environmental change. The main drivers to consider are demand and supply, war, global politics, and climate modifications that may be induced by greenhouse gases. The oil reserves of the Organization of Petroleum Exporting Countries (OPEC) remain significant, but the actual amounts these countries have are far from certain. This is because the nations in the cartel have an incentive to overreport supply: They are given the right to bring oil to the market on the basis of how much production potential they claim to have.

Though Saudi Arabia is assumed to have more reserves than any country in the world, questions have been raised about its oil fields' viability. Matt Simmons in his book *Twilight in the Desert* argues that the Ghawar field, the Saudis' largest with more than 50 percent of the nation's oil, already is more than 50 percent exhausted, and as additional depletion occurs the cost of extraction will move significantly upward.[21]

Typically, when an oil field reaches a 50 percent exhaustion level, relatively inexpensive primary recovery shifts to much more expensive secondary and tertiary recovery. The Department of Energy's long-term estimates of oil prices at about $60 a barrel assume that Saudi Arabia can produce 18 million to 22 million barrels per day by 2020 to 2025. Observers such as Simmons maintain that it is questionable whether the Saudis can produce more than 10 million to 15 million barrels per day.[22] Of potential significance is the fact that major oil companies spent $8 billion on exploration in 2003 but discovered only $4 billion of commercially useful oil.

Each year production declines by more than 4 million to 5 million barrels per day. To replace what is lost and to provide for added growth, the world requires 6 million to 8 million barrels per day of new oil production.

Energy supply surely will also be affected by climate change. Most scientists agree that something approaching a 5-degree warming brought on by an increasing concentration of global greenhouse gases (GHGs) will change the climate system. How an increase in carbon dioxide and other greenhouse gases actually affect the planet remains complicated because carbon dioxide and other greenhouse gases do not act in isolation. The feedbacks among the different elements in the climate system are quite complex.

If scientists are uncertain about precise temperature changes, they know even less about specific timing. Scientists also have trouble modeling the extent to which people will be able to adapt to climate change.

Efforts to prevent climate change so far have not been successful. In December 1997, representatives from 160 countries met in Kyoto, Japan, to deliberate about a treaty that would limit the world's greenhouse gas emissions. The Kyoto Protocol was signed by nearly every nation in the world except the United States, but it was not ratified until 2005. By 2008, it was clear that Kyoto's goals were not being achieved. Many countries, including Canada, Spain, and others, had exceeded their Kyoto commitments.

To remedy this problem, a technological revolution is needed, since no known technology can deliver enough carbon-free energy required to stabilize greenhouse gases in the atmosphere.

Systems and Scenarios

The macroenvironment is very complex. The strategist must keep in mind that elements in the macroenvironment are part of a system that has multiple linkages.[23]

Changes in one factor (energy prices, terror, etc.) induce changes in another, which in turn bring about changes in a third, and so on. These changes are connected.[24] Complex systems can be in equilibrium for long periods, but countervailing forces exist and systems therefore can migrate quickly in surprising directions. The financial meltdown of the end of the first decade of the 21st century is an example of a system's very rapid disintegration. A strategist should ask these questions:

- Which element in the macroenvironment is most unstable?
- Which emerging trends are important?
- What choices are available to influence these trends?

The strategist should try to describe the scope, direction, speed, and intensity of changes he or she observes.

A **scenario** is a story or plot that describes how a particular end point might be reached. It reveals various "what-if" possibilities for which the strategist seeks to discover the implications.[25] For instance, Shell has scenarios that are prominently displayed on its Web page. They point to the type of world the company *hopes* will come into existence and to the dangers in the kinds of worlds that actually may appear. Shell's 2005 scenarios were:

- *Open Doors*—a pragmatic world with a strong emphasis on efficiency. It is a secure world of mutual recognition, voluntary best-practice, close links between business and civil society, and cross-border integration.
- *Low Trust Globalization*—a legalistic world of guaranteed state security. It is a risky world, absent market solutions and subject to intrusive checks and controls from overlapping jurisdictions.
- *Flags*—a dogmatic world where social cohesion and security trump efficiency. It is an even riskier world where dogmatism, zero-sum games, and basic conflicts over values stifle continuing globalization.

A **cross-impact matrix** is a useful device for creating scenarios. It shows how trends intersect with the scenarios. In Exhibit 2.11, four scenarios are developed around possible regime change in Saudi Arabia. In the first scenario, the United States–Saudi relationship remains fairly stable. In the second scenario, radicalization increases in Saudi Arabia. The third scenario considers what might happen if the government were taken over by religious extremists. Potential changes in oil supply and demand, the world economy, technology, social forces, and the environment are considered, with the final rows being reserved for estimates about world oil prices in different time periods.

The purpose is not to predict the future, but to consider possible futures and influence, prepare, and rehearse for what might happen. The firm's strategists should develop possible moves the firm could make to cope with the scenarios (see Chapter 1 on hedging strategies).

Uncertainty

Scenarios are speculative. They point to different types of uncertainty that exist.[26]

- **State uncertainty** refers to incomplete knowledge about the components in the strategist's model (in this instance, oil supply and demand, the world economy, technology, social forces, and the environment) and how they relate to each other. There also is uncertainty about how macro elements affect the five forces in the industry model. What is their impact on the structure of an industry? Does the industry become more or less attractive?
- **Effect uncertainty** refers to impacts on particular firms. Even if the strategist has information about the macroenvironment and the industry, he or she still may not be certain what the effects will be on a particular company.
- **Response uncertainty** refers to lack of knowledge of response options. There may be insufficient imagination and creativity in crafting responses as well as an inability to predict the likely consequences of the response choices.[27]

EXHIBIT 2.11   **A Cross-Impact Analysis of Regime Change in Saudi Arabia**

	Saudi Status Quo	Saudi Arabia Radicalized	Saudi Arabia with Iranian-Style Revolution	Saudi Arabia Modernization
U.S. politics	U.S.-Saudi relations basically the same	U.S.-Saudi relations rupture	U.S.-Saudi relations totally break down; 2 nations become implacable enemies	U.S.-Saudi renewed friendship
Oil supply and demand	World demand increases due to developing countries	Demand up, supply decreases; no new sources discovered	Demand rises sharply; no new sources discovered, and worldwide embargo on supplies to Western nations	Adequate supply to meet demand
World economy	Does not substantially go down	Recession	Massive slump in world economy accompanied by high levels of inflation; return of 1970s-like stagflation	Flourishes
Technology	No big breakthroughs	Drivers appear for possible substitutes	Intense pressures to develop substitutes to fossil fuels; some become commercially ready	Alternative energy technologies in widespread use
Social forces	Gradual but contained Middle East radicalization	Further radicalization in many countries	Entire Middle East inflamed; anti-western sentiment grows in non-Islamic countries	Increased global harmony and celebration of diversity as positive force
Environment	Degrades gradually	Negative effects of global warming start to appear	Severe climate change impacts felt in many places in world, especially poorer countries	Environment improves because new technologies in widespread use
2013 price per barrel crude oil	$85	$100	$175	$75
2018	$95	$115	$190	$65
2023	$115	$140	$235	$100

Uncertainty generally is assumed to be negative, and the strategist usually is expected to take steps to reduce or absorb its impact on the organization. In some cases, however, it may make sense to try to *increase* uncertainty because it opens the possibility for change. The potential losses and reduced power that accompany uncertainty can generate anxiety, with the need to eliminate the anxiety stimulating creative thinking and overcoming a drift toward inertia. Creative management of uncertainty is an important task of the strategist.

An Enacted Environment: The Industry and Its Boundaries[28]

Ultimately, the strategist constructs a model or cognitive map to describe the relations between the macroenvironment and industry structure. It should be based on evidence, the analyst's judgment, and critique of peers. It will have qualitative and subjective elements as well as quantitative and objective ones. The strategist isolates conditions for further scrutiny, uses prior understandings to make sense of these conditions, and decides what should be subject to additional analysis. The strategist should be looking for inflections. Industries and their boundaries are changing (see Chapter 1) and the macroenvironment is the source of much of this upheaval.

The collapse of industry boundaries is a phenomenon to be reckoned with in such industries as commercial banking where the lines have blurred between banks, brokerages, insurance companies, finance companies, and credit card issuers. Another example of the blurring of industry boundaries has been the convergence of computers, telecommunications, media, and entertainment.

Typically, industry boundaries blur because of a combination of changes in government policies, economic conditions, technological possibilities, and social factors. The macro-environment impinges on the five forces and changes their features. An example worth considering is Amazon.com. In what industry does it belong? Is it a bookseller, an online retailer, a general-purpose retailer, or an "Internet shopping center"? Who are its competitors? Barnes & Noble, eBay, Walmart, or all of these companies? No other firm seems to straddle industry boundaries quite like Amazon. This may place it in a unique position to achieve competitive advantage. However, it also may mean it is particularly vulnerable to attack from competitors in many quarters.

Companies increasingly migrate from industry to industry, failing to abide for long periods in a position defined by conventional definitions.

Organizations tend to be socially constructed systems of shared meaning.[29] They create models of their environment. The environment is not an objective "fact," but an imaginative creation that comes into being via an interpretive process in which managers play a role.

Cooperation or Competition?

Increasingly, partnerships, alliances, joint ventures, networks, and other forms of cooperation are proving to be highly advantageous. The best stance to take toward the competition involves being a *collaborator* as well as antagonist.

The **value net,** a modified approach to the five forces, reflects this concept. The idea of the value net is that suppliers, customers, and companies, rather than struggling against each other in a zero-sum game, come together to create new value (see Exhibit 2.12).

Strategy, then, deals with cooperation as well as competition. Brandenburger and Nalebuff refer to this approach where companies work together to create value as **co-opetition.**[30] They quote the financier Bernard Baruch: "You don't have to blow out the other fellow's light to let your own shine."

EXHIBIT 2.12
Value Net—An Alternative to Five Forces?

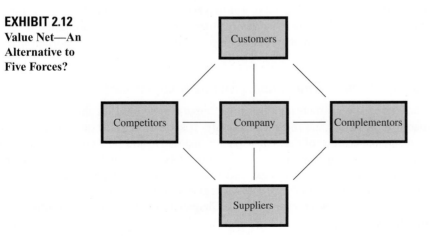

Stakeholder Analysis

Stakeholder analysis is a good way of examining competitive and cooperative relationships.[31] A *stakeholder* is any group that affects and is affected by the firm. Stakeholders bring life to the abstractions in industry and macroenvironmental analysis. They include not only the five forces but also governments, scientific and technical organizations, local communities, the media, the general public, and other representatives from society. There are also internal stakeholder groups, such as shareholders, board members, managers, and employees. The weakening of traditional management hierarchies and increasing reliance on outsiders, to whom functions previously performed within the firm are contracted, argue for treating internal stakeholders in a manner similar to external stakeholders. Each corporation is likely to have a slightly different "map" of its most relevant stakeholders. Exhibit 2.13 shows a sample.

Stakeholder Theory

According to **stakeholder theory,** a firm that obtains high-level contributions from its internal and external stakeholders will be successful. Attaining this level of contribution requires giving stakeholders appropriate incentives. To each stakeholder the firm provides a different type of incentive, and from each stakeholder the firm obtains a different type of contribution. Customers, for instance, get high-quality goods and services; in return, the firm gets customers' money and loyalty. Employees get salaries and wages in exchange for their work. Scientists and engineers get the chance to pursue interesting projects and make discoveries in exchange for helping the firm develop new products and processes.

Agency Theory

Unlike stakeholder theory, which maintains that a firm has duties and obligations to all stakeholders, **agency theory** holds that the internal stakeholders—board members, managers, scientists and engineers, and employees—have to work on behalf of the shareholders.[32]

EXHIBIT 2.13
Stakeholder Map

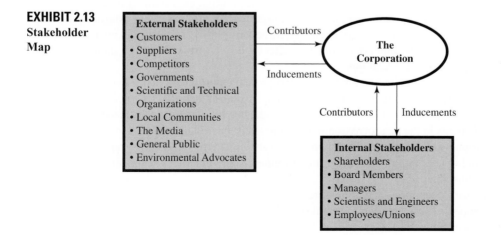

Agency theory argues that the primary stakeholder group is the owners or shareholders, who are the residual claimants. They are taking on the biggest risk: In the event of bankruptcy, they are the last to be paid back. Agency theorists maintain that the purpose of managing relations with other stakeholders is to maximize returns to shareholders. Since doing so is subject to law and ethics, a firm has legal and ethical, as well as economic, obligations to each of its stakeholders, but the obligation to shareholders comes first.

Stakeholder theorists tend to dispute the claim that the primary stakeholder is and has to be the shareholders. They hold that a firm's management actually can choose a group to be its primary stakeholder. Many firms, in fact, do choose customers over shareholders. The interests of other stakeholders are satisfied to the extent needed to induce them to continue to make contributions to the firm, but the firm's primary obligation is to its customers. For example, Johnson & Johnson's mission statement begins with customers and then mentions suppliers, employees, communities, and the environment before stockholders.

A firm also may say it aims to balance the interests of stakeholders. It can work for the greatest good for the greatest number, or it can work for consensus and social harmony.[33] Japanese firms tend to have a more balanced view of their responsibilities and the groups they serve than do U.S. firms. U.S. firms continue to declare that their primary obligation is to shareholders, while Japanese firms mention employees and society before shareholders.

The concern of agency theorists is that giving managers such latitude can lead to abuse: Managers can say they are serving interests other than shareholders when, in fact, they are operating the corporation for their own benefit, enriching themselves at the expense of stakeholders. The separation of ownership from control, which puts day-to-day management of the firm in the hands of relatively few executives, makes such abuses possible.[34] Despite the role that boards are supposed to play on behalf of shareholders in controlling corporate management, these abuses have been common. The top managements in companies such as Enron, WorldCom, and Tyco have stolen from their companies at the expense of its shareholders.[35]

Summary

The three main tools presented for analyzing the external environment in this chapter are related, supplement each other, and can be used together for assessing external opportunities and threats. These tools are (1) a five-force, or industry, analysis; (2) an assessment of the macroenvironmental conditions that affect the five forces; and (3) a methodology for mapping stakeholder relations.

The starting point in any analysis of the external environment is the five forces: competition among (1) existing rivals, (2) new entrants, (3) substitutes, (4) customers, and (5) suppliers. Five forces, however, are dynamic and are affected by elements in the macroenvironment. The elements in the macroenvironment discussed in this chapter have been (1) government, (2) national and international economies, (3) social structure and demography, (4) technology, and (5) energy and the natural environment. The macroenvironment makes the five forces unstable.

Industry definitions and boundaries shift. New industries are created. Old industries lose their appeal. These are the important swings, some predictable and some not, in the attractiveness of industries.

Analysis of the five forces and the macroenvironment can yield insight into inflection points a company confronts. It also can lead to recommendations of moves the firm can make. The pharmaceutical and airline industries provided examples of moves firms can make to alter industry conditions, but there are limitations to these moves in fundamentally changing industry prospects.

Scenarios point to possible outcomes that may come into being because of the effects of the macroenvironment on industry conditions. They give the firm indications of possible futures the firm might confront. With this understanding, the strategist can build repertoires of moves the firm can take to meet different challenges. Given that the future is uncertain, the firm can rehearse its responses to different possibilities.

A very useful way of conceptualizing the firm's interactions with the forces in its environment is in the form of stakeholder relations. To each stakeholder group, the firm provides inducements and from each it obtains contributions. The strategist can prioritize a firm's stakeholder relations and economize on the use of the scarce inducements. The stakeholder model is helpful in bridging the firm–environment interface. However, an understanding of the external environment is just the first step in developing options and considering the moves that a firm can make. The internal environment also must be understood and analyzed. The purpose of the next chapter, therefore, is to present the tools for internal analysis.

Endnotes

1. M. Porter, "How Competitive Forces Shape Strategy," *Harvard Business School Press,* March–April 1979, p. 137.

2. The McKinsey case studies can be accessed at www.mckinsey.com/careers/, and the Bain case studies can be accessed at www.bain.com/bainweb/Join_Bain/case_interviews.asp.

3. M. Porter, *Competitive Strategy: Techniques for Analyzing Industries and Competitors* (New York: Free Press, 1980); M. Porter, *Competitive Advantage: Creating and Sustaining Superior Performance* (New York: Free Press, 1985); and M. Porter, *The Competitive Advantage of Nations: With a New Introduction* (New York: Simon and Schuster, 1998).

4. "Michael Porter on Competitive Strategy," Harvard Business School video, 1988.

5. Ibid.

6. M. Porter, "How Competitive Forces Shape Strategy."

7. A. Marcus, *Strategic Foresight* (New York: Palgrave MacMillan, 2009); and A. Marcus, *Business and Society* (Burr Ridge, IL: Richard D. Irwin, 1993).

8. A. Marcus, D. Geffen, and K. Sexton, *Reinventing Environmental Regulation* (Washington, DC: Resources for the Future Press, 2002).

9. See the European Union's Web site at http://europa.eu.int/index_en.htm.

10. The government pays nearly 50 percent of all health care expenditures through programs such as Medicare and Medicaid, and more than 50 percent of all U.S. bankruptcies are due in part to medical expenses.

11. J. Schumpeter, *Capitalism, Socialism and Democracy* (New York: Harper, 1975) [orig. pub. 1942], pp. 82–85.

12. Economists distinguish between a condition where the odds of success are known with certainty (e.g., flipping a coin), which they call risk, and a condition where the odds of success are not known with certainty, which they call uncertainty. See F. Knight, *Risk, Uncertainty, and Profit* (Boston: Houghton Mifflin, 1921).

13. U.S. Census Bureau, 1999.

14. U.S. Census Bureau, Population Division, 2000.

15. Ibid.

16. U.S. Census Bureau, Current Population Survey, 2002.

17. D. Bell, *The Cultural Contradictions of Capitalism* (New York: Basic Books, 1976).

18. A. Marcus, *Controversial Issues in Energy Policy* (Newbury Park, CA: Sage, 1992).

19. S. Schmidheiny, *Changing Course* (Cambridge, MA: MIT Press, 1992).

20. See the Business Council for Sustainable Development Web site at www.iisd.ca/consume/unep.html.

21. M. Simmons, *Twilight in the Desert* (New York: Wiley and Sons, 2006).

22. Ibid.

23. V. Narayanan and L. Fahey, "Macroenvironmental Analysis," in *The Portable MBA in Strategy,* ed. L. Fahey and R. Randall (New York: Wiley and Sons, 2001).

24. D. Loveridge, *Foresight* (New York: Routledge, 2009). Loveridge has attempted to integrate systems theory and foresight.

25. P. Schwartz, *The Art of the Long View*, 2nd ed. (New York: Currency Doubleday, 1996).

26. F. Milliken, "Three Types of Perceived Uncertainty about the Environment," *Academy of Management Review* 7, no. 2 (1982), p. 134.

27. Ibid.

28. K. Weick, "Enactment Processes in Organizations," in *New Directions in Organizational Behavior,* ed. B. Staw and G. Salancik (Chicago: St. Clair Press, 1977).

29. L. Smircich and C. Stubbart, "Strategic Management in an Enacted World," *Academy of Management Review* 4 (1985), pp. 724–36.

30. A. Brandenberger and B. Nalebuff, *Co-opetition* (New York: Currency Doubleday, 1996).

31. R. Freeman, *Strategic Management: A Stakeholder Approach* (Boston: Pitman, 1984).

32. M. Jensen and W. Meckling, "Theory of the Firm, Managerial Behavior, Agency Costs, and Ownership Structure," *Journal of Economics* 3 (1976), pp. 225–39.

33. Freeman, *Strategic Management.*

34. A. Berle and G. Means, *The Modern Corporation and Private Property* (New York: Harcourt, Brace, and World, 1932).

35. J. Cassidy, "The Greed Cycle," *The New Yorker,* September 23, 2002, pp. 64–80.

Internal Analysis

"Core competencies are the collective learning in organizations, especially how to coordinate diverse production skills and integrate multiple streams of technologies. . . . Core competence is communication, involvement, and a deep commitment to working across organizational boundaries. . . . Few companies are likely to build world leadership in more than five or six fundamental competencies. A company that compiles a list of 20 to 30 capabilities has probably not produced a list of core competencies. Still, it is probably a good discipline to generate a list of this sort and to see aggregate capabilities as building blocks."[1]

C. K. Prahalad and Gary Hamel, "The Core Competence of the Corporation"

Chapter Learning Objectives

- Reviewing the basics of management theory.
- Providing a number of approaches for analyzing a firm's internal strengths and weaknesses including the seven S's, the value chain, and the resource-based view (RBV).
- Distinguishing between resources, capabilities, and competencies.
- Explaining how RBV may be used to achieve sustained competitive advantage (SCA).

Introduction

Clearly, an imperative for all organizations is to build a company's internal strengths and eliminate its weaknesses. In response to the deep recession in the world economy that commenced in the latter years of the first decade of the 21st century, staff at McKinsey's Global Institute projected four views of the future.[2]

Regenerated Global Momentum

The optimistic view was that the government's stimulus and monetary policies have their desired result and will prevent the recession from being lasting or deep. Confidence rebounds and the world economy resumes its growth.

Battered But Resilient

In a less optimistic scenario, the world economy takes longer to rebound. The downward spiral is long and severe. Economic prosperity returns, but only very slowly.

Stalled Globalization

Another possibility is that different nations or regions suffer for different intervals. Some snap back more quickly than others.

The Long Freeze

However, it also is possible that the global economy will not rebound for a generation or more. The decline will be intense and long-lasting.

With uncertainties of this magnitude, what should strategists do? They must bolster their organizations' internal strengths and eliminate their organizations' internal weaknesses. **Internal analysis (IA)** is the process of examining an organization's strengths and weaknesses. IA focuses on the question of how organizations can enhance their resources, capabilities, and competencies. What can they do to ensure that they will do well in tough times? The purpose of this chapter is to provide you with the skills to carry out internal analysis. From this chapter you will learn what can be done to boost a firm's internal strengths and eradicate its weaknesses.

As Exhibit 3.1 shows, both internal (IA) and external (EA) analyses are necessary to craft a firm's strategy. As in chess, after scanning the external environment, the strategist examines how his or her pieces are aligned. Operating according to the military maxim "Know your enemy but also know yourself," the strategist must understand the firm's capabilities. Starting with *management theory* there are many ways to dissect and diagnose a firm's capabilities. Porter introduced a method for internal analysis called *value chain analysis*.[3] This chapter discusses both *management theory* and *value chain analysis*. It also discusses Prahalad and Hamel's idea of a *core competency*.[4] A core competency has three main attributes: It (1) provides access to new markets, (2) gives customers benefits,

EXHIBIT 3.1
Strategy Requires External Analysis and Internal Analysis

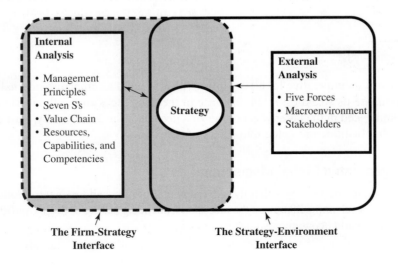

The Firm-Strategy Interface

The Strategy-Environment Interface

and (3) is difficult for competitors to imitate. Unlike physical assets, which deteriorate over time, a core competency is the engine for new business growth and development, clearly essential in tough economic times. A core competency entails learning, coordinating, integrating, and operating outside the organization's boundaries. It has constituted the basis for the success of an organization such as Dell, which drew on the strengths of other organizations to complement its own, creating close ties with suppliers and customers.[5] The *resource-based view* (RBV) of the firm, partially derived from ideas of Prahalad and Hamel, is examined in this chapter. An alternative to the industrial organization (IO) economics approach to strategy that was the focus of the last chapter, it emphasizes internal strengths rather than industry conditions as the main factors driving sustained competitive advantage (SCA).

Management Theory

The classic ideas of **management theory** are hierarchical. Managers are the agents of the owners; Owners in publicly traded corporations are stockholders. Managers are not supposed to pursue their own interests at shareholders' expense.[6] A company needs a very strong top leadership team headed by a talented, experienced, and accomplished chief executive officer (CEO) who can deliver high returns to shareholders. Quantifiable, financial results motivate the top management team, which is held accountable by the board of directors, who represent shareholder interests.

To achieve these quantifiable goals the top management team should articulate the company's mission (what it has been good at in the past). They also must have a vision of where the company should be going. They have to establish core values and a structure for carrying out the company's strategy. Strategy comes from the top down in response to shareholder needs. The board of directors monitors, controls, and advises the top management team. It approves its strategy and aligns strategy with the interests of shareholders. A sufficient number of independent outsiders should be on the board to bring fresh ideas and perspectives and to ensure accountability. This approach to organizational strengths also closely corresponds to Frederick Taylor's scientific method of dividing the work based on the specific tasks involved and investigating systematically the best way to carry out each task.[7] Top management assigns to everyone in the organization a specific role and function that best serves shareholder interests.

According to classic management theory, the organization, therefore, must have:

- A well-defined hierarchy.
- A division of labor to allow high degrees of specialization.
- A very specific and well-defined set of assignments of authority and responsibility.
- Unity of command and direction so that there is subordination of individual interests to the good of shareholders.

The organization's internal strengths and weaknesses are best understood by concentrating on the top management team and its interaction with the board and employees.

Because of its suppression of bottom-up initiatives and individual creativity, the classic approach has limitations. In its rigidity it is a caricature of bureaucracy run wild. Not all organizations are likely to thrive under this model and thus advertising agencies, consultancies, and movie studios typically do not organize themselves in this fashion. More democratic, task and team oriented, each project on which they work is somewhat different. Organizations of this nature provide ample opportunity for employee participation. They need employees to feel free of arbitrary constraint so they can express their originality.

Firms that operate in fast-moving environments understand that there is no one best way dictated from the top, to get the job done. The work that they do requires resourcefulness and responsiveness to unpredictable demands, which a rigid hierarchy will stifle. The way to evaluate an organization's strengths and weaknesses is to look at the extent to which the organization is flexible and capable of rapid adjustment. Does it innovate quickly?

The Human Relations Approach

Because of the drawbacks of the classic approach, it has been supplemented by a variety of other approaches that may be used to assess an organization's strengths and weaknesses. The **human relations approach to management theory** is considered by proponents to be more employee-friendly.[8] It stresses motivation and values. It asserts that:

- Informal coordination in groups should replace centralized controls.
- Communications between employees and managers should be two-way.
- Compensation should be based on performance, not on following orders.
- Management should foster an environment that is conducive to employees' development and learning.

Under this approach, employees may be given an ownership stake through employee stock ownership plans (ESOPs).

This model is not just confined to small firms. Indeed, a company that has tried to install it is Walmart. While Walmart stifles attempts at unionization, it also tries to avoid antagonism between employees and management by means of a servant leadership model where employees are provided with the tools they need to succeed and they are given substantial leeway to carry out their tasks. Though Walmart expects employees to work hard for low wages, it incents them for doing so by making employees partial owners. Employees share in the profits when the company's stock price goes up. Many long-time Walmart employees have become very rich. The capacity of an organization to mobilize the talent and energy of its employees is as much an indicator of its strengths and weaknesses as the capabilities of its top management team.

Contingency Theory

Contingency theory holds that depending on the external environment a company faces there are two models it can follow: *mechanistic* or *organic*.[9] The *mechanistic* model relies on hierarchy, functional specialization, and a formal and impersonal structure. Employee rewards are primarily economic, in the form of wages; employees rarely have ownership rights. The *organic* form, in contrast, is less rigid and hierarchical than the mechanistic. It relies more on decentralization, participation, and a democratic personal structure. Employee motivation is less dependent on economic rewards; it arises from employees' sense of belonging and their identification with the organization's mission and values. The task of analyzing an organization's strengths and weaknesses comes down to understanding which of these forms is most appropriate, given external demands.

Contingency theorists argue that the mechanistic model works better in stable organization environments, while the organic model works better in turbulent environments. The theory's basic proposition is that corporate performance is a consequence of a *fit* between the external environment and the organization's internal characteristics. The analyst of an organization's strengths and weaknesses has to determine if the appropriate level of fit has been achieved. However, whether the appropriate level has been achieved is hard to determine. The precise meaning of *fit* is unclear, and the process of clearly identifying and measuring external and internal environments is problematic.

In regard to the external environment, a number of questions arise: Is the best way to assess it in terms of industry variables (the five forces), macroeconomic factors (government, economics, technology, social structure, the natural environment), and/or stakeholder relations (see Chapter 2)? In what ways do these interact to define an organization's external environment? Similarly, what is the best way to assess an organization's internal environment? Such an analysis could be based on many factors. For instance, an organization's strengths and weaknesses can be described in terms of:

- *Leadership.* The leadership style in an organization includes the types of motivation systems used, patterns of communication in the organization, and interpersonal interactions and relations.
- *Decision making.* This includes not only the way decisions are made, but also the goals that are pursued and the control systems that are in place to ensure that these goals are met.
- *Performance mechanisms.* These are the mechanisms used for performance assessment, training, and socialization.
- *Division of labor.* How is labor divided? Is it divided on the basis of products, markets (industrial, commercial, government), functions (production, sales, marketing, finance, administration, R&D), technologies, or geographic locations? Indeed, many firms have a **hybrid structure,** with some divisions devoted to functions, some to clients, and some to geographic areas. Other organizations have a **matrix structure:** employees have dual reporting arrangements on the basis of functional expertise, customers served, and/or geographic area. Which of these involve a better fit and constitute a strength rather than a weakness?
- *Integrating mechanisms.* They determine how the organization brings together people, products, and processes, rather than separating them into different roles and functions. These mechanisms are important. In each organization, they tend to vary and might include informal contacts among employees, the use of task forces, and/or permanent and temporary coordinating teams. How do the integrating mechanisms contribute or fail to contribute to an organization's strengths and weaknesses?
- *Culture.* An organization's *culture* also can be a key strength. Cultures vary from strong to weak, depending on a variety of attributes: attitudes toward customers and competitors, levels of individual autonomy and management support, achievement orientation, compensation equity, moral and ethical integrity, professionalism, and tolerance for risk and conflict. Some corporate cultures are obsessed with product quality; others consider product innovation or market growth more important than product quality. Which culture is a best fit with external conditions?

Contingency analysis is hindered by the presence of multiple contingencies.[10] Under what circumstances are a mix of organizational components appropriate in different environments? When are different combinations a strength rather than a weakness? The best way to organize is hard to determine. Meanwhile, "Dilbert" cartoons that represent people's growing frustration with dysfunctional organizations proliferate. Many organizations have overworked and stressed-out personnel and hostile, counterproductive work climates. There may be a lack of coordination among key divisions, excessive decision making at the top, and inexplicable duplication among functions. Organizational weaknesses often overwhelm strengths. It is unclear how organizations should respond to maintain morale when there is economic uncertainty. When resources are shrinking, job mobility is slim, and layoffs are common, what should organizations do?

The Seven-S Framework

The popular business book of the 1980s, Peters and Waterman's *In Search of Excellence,* was built around a simple concept for analyzing an organization's strengths and weaknesses. The seven S's is a framework for analyzing internal strengths and weaknesses that came from McKinsey & Company, where Peters and Waterman had worked as consultants.[11] Peters and Waterman brought together elements of the mechanistic and organic model. According to their theory of organizational strengths and weaknesses, there are seven attributes **(seven S's)** or basic levers that management can manipulate to steer large and complex organizations to excellence. Exhibit 3.2 describes their interrelationship.

1. **Strategy**—the extent to which an organization has a logical sense of the actions it must take to gain sustainable competitive advantage over the competition, improve its position in relation to customers, and allocate resources to high-return activities.
2. **Structure**—the extent to which an organization has a coherent form for dividing labor, allocating responsibilities, coordinating tasks, and ensuring accountability.
3. **Systems**—the extent to which an organization has explicit descriptions in place to show how processes work and tasks are accomplished in critical areas such as capital budgeting, manufacturing, customer and supplier relations, accounting and performance measurement, and carrying out mergers and acquisitions.
4. **Style**—the degree to which there is tangible evidence that the time, attention, and behavior of management and employees actually are devoted to, and aligned with, the organization's real strategic needs (not just lip service but real action).
5. **Staffing**—the degree to which management and employee expertise and experience match the jobs that have to be carried out, the extent to which the personalities in place are capable of working together, and the degree to which there is sufficient diversity among staff to allow opposing and dissenting voices to be heard.
6. **Skills**—the extent to which an organization as a whole, as opposed to its employees, has the capabilities not only to compete in existing businesses but also to develop new businesses and generate corporate growth.

EXHIBIT 3.2
The Seven S's

Source: From *In Search of Excellence: Lessons From America's Best Run Companies* by Thomas J. Peters and Robert H. Waterman, Jr. Copyright ©1982 by Thomas J. Peters and Robert H. Waterman, Jr. Reprinted by permission of HarperCollins Publishers Inc.

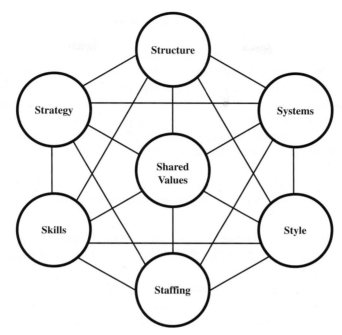

7. **Shared values**—the extent to which there is unity of purpose behind a common vision and culture that is taking the organization to where it should be going.

Peters and Waterman faulted U.S. managers for tending to focus almost exclusively on the mechanistic elements of organizations—strategy, structure, and systems—while missing the importance of the organic side—style, staffing, skills, and shared values.

The qualities of excellence that arose from the blending of these elements were:

1. A bias for action.
2. Closeness to the customer.
3. Autonomy and entrepreneurship.
4. Productivity through people.
5. Hands-on and value-driven operations.
6. A willingness to stick to the knitting.
7. A simple form and lean staff.
8. Simultaneous loose-tight properties.

The seven-S was a very unreliable indicator of future performance. Many of the "excellent" companies Peters and Waterman analyzed became poor performers including Digital Equipment, Westinghouse, Xerox, Kodak, Wang Laboratories, Polaroid, Delta Air Lines, and Kmart.

Value Chain Analysis

Porter's contribution to analyzing a firm's internal strengths and weaknesses was the **value chain.** By *value,* he meant revenue minus costs of production. This standard is built on the *margin* a firm achieves by carrying out the critical activities, primary and support, which together form the *value chain* (see Exhibit 3.3). Each activity must be evaluated for its margin, that is, its costs in comparison to the income it generates. Porter argued that each firm in an industry should compare the margins of its primary and support activities to those of its major competitors to detect signs of internal strength or weakness.

According to Porter, understanding internal strengths and weaknesses means having a thorough understanding of how primary and support activities are linked. The primary activities are:

1. *Inbound logistics*—receiving, storing, and internally transporting product inputs. Warehousing, inventory control, vehicle scheduling, and returns to suppliers fit in this category.

2. *Operations*—transforming product inputs into product outputs. Such tasks as machining, packaging, equipment maintenance, and testing fit in this category.

3. *Outbound logistics*—distributing goods to customers. Tasks such as warehousing, order processing, and scheduling fit in this category.

4. *Marketing and sales*—making the product known to buyers and persuading them to buy. This category includes advertising, product promotion, sales force management, channel selection and relations, and pricing.

5. *Service*—providing customers with service to keep up or improve the value of the product. Such tasks as installation, training, repair, and supplying of parts are in this category.

EXHIBIT 3.3
The Value Chain

Source: Adapted with the permission of The Free Press, a Division of Simon & Schuster Adult Publishing Group, from *Competitive Advantage: Creating and Sustaining Superior Performance* by Michael E. Porter. Copyright © 1985, 1998 by Michael E. Porter. All rights reserved.

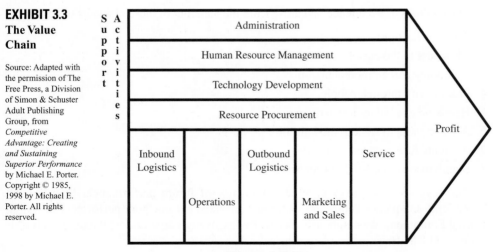

Primary Activities

The support activities are:

1. *Resource procurement*—buying inputs such as machinery, buildings, office and lab equipment, raw materials, supplies, and other items that are used in all value-creating activities including support activities. These purchases are made according to rules for dealing with vendors and require information systems for record keeping.

2. *Technology development*—developing the know-how to carry out the firm's many activities and tasks from running equipment to writing documents, from making products to transporting goods, from designing products to enhancing their reliability, and so on. Technology development may depend on a variety of scientific disciplines and subspecialties such as microelectronics, precision mechanics, fine optics, and bioengineering.

3. *Human resource management*—recruiting, hiring, training, developing, and compensating the firm's personnel. These practices have an important effect on employee socialization and their motivation and skills.

4. *Administration*—finance, accounting, legal affairs, public affairs, planning, and strategy. Some of these activities may be carried out at the business-unit level, and some may be carried out at the corporate level.

Each primary and support activity can be subdivided into further tasks and linked in different ways. Primary and support activities carried out in different ways with different linkages have different effects on cost and performance. Some tasks can be done internally; others can be contracted to outside vendors. An important implication of this type of thinking is that the firm does not have to do everything itself; its internal strengths can be acquired from external sources.

Value Chain Linkages

From Porter's ideas about how to analyze a firm's internal strengths and weaknesses came important insights about how value chains of firms are linked. The value chain of one firm is not isolated from the value chain of other firms. As Exhibit 3.4 shows, supplier value chains are linked to a firm's value chain. The value chain of a firm in turn is linked to the value chains of distribution channels and final purchasers. Internal strengths and weaknesses extend outside a firm's boundaries.

EXHIBIT 3.4
Value Chain Linkages

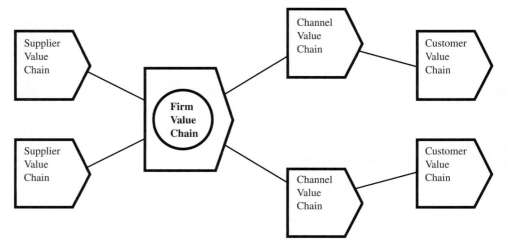

EXHIBIT 3.5
Dell Model

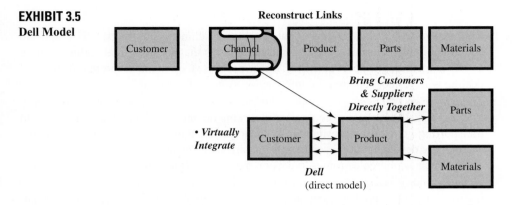

Reconstruct Links

Customer   Channel   Product   Parts   Materials

Bring Customers
& Suppliers
Directly Together

Parts

• *Virtually*
Integrate   Customer ⟷ Product

Materials

Dell
(direct model)

Porter's analysis highlights the interconnectedness of firms' value chains. In isolation firms do not bring value to customers. Coalitions of firms functioning together bring value to customers. The firm's outside ties bolster its internal strengths. These links create sustained competitive advantage. Firms need to assess not only their own internal strengths and weaknesses but also those of the companies in their value chain.

Benefits of Value Chain Linkages: An Example

Dell is an example of a company that built its business model around value chain analysis. Dell did not do everything well. It outsourced component supply and some parts of after-sale service, eliminated all alternative distribution channels, and concentrated on having a direct relationship with the customer, which is what it did best.[12] Intimately linking its value chain with the value chains of its suppliers and its customers allowed it to grow rapidly and become a successful company (see Exhibit 3.5). Dell could not accomplish as much as it did without these linkages.

This model is very different than the industrial organization model of Porter found in the last chapter. While Porter advocates having power *over* suppliers, customers, and competitors, Dell partners *with* its suppliers, customers, and competitors. Dell's basic business model is not to maximize value to itself at the expense of suppliers and customers; rather, it is to maximize value to all firms in its value chain. The rewards for participants in the value chain are not fixed; they are expandable. The pie grows and everyone benefits. Dell's internal strength or key competency that competitors have not been able to match is closeness to customers and the speed with which it executes orders. It is able to accelerate the accomplishment of its business purposes through rapid inventory turnovers and extremely tight management of receivables and payables. By these means, it overcame much larger rivals, including IBM.

The Resource-Based View

Dell never had more physical, financial, and human *resources* than its rivals—IBM, Compaq, and Hewlett-Packard. Nor did it have more patents or a stronger brand name and reputation. It achieved success with superior *capabilities* for coordinating the activities of its supply chain. It has a strong core competence in value chain management.

Dell is an example of how the **resource-based view (RBV)** explains competitive advantage. RBV is a *view* rather than a theory of internal strengths and weaknesses. In explaining why some firms consistently outperform others, it offers an "evocative description" rather than a series of logically deduced and tightly related falsifiable propositions.[13] It has been developed to the point where it challenges IO economics—the theory proposed by Porter in the previous chapter—as the dominant paradigm in strategic management. Dell wins by how it configures its resources, capabilities, and competencies.

RBV versus IO Economics

As discussed in Chapter 2, IO economics holds that an organization achieves superior performance by seeking monopoly or near-monopoly power. The firm strives to be in the right segment or niche in an industry and to neutralize pressure from competitors. It counters the behavior of rivals through the erection of barriers to entry via scale and scope economies, experience- and learning-curve effects, product differentiation, and capital requirements. According to this approach, industry structure and market power determine competitive advantage. While most studies indicate that these factors determine as much as 15 to 20 percent of the competitive advantage a firm can achieve, it is generally conceded that they are not the only sources of such advantage.[14]

RBV sees the organization as a combination of resources, capabilities, and competencies and attempts to understand the influence of these factors on performance. A high percentage of the explanation for competitive advantage comes from how a firm's resources, capabilities, and competencies are arrayed.

RBV starts with the assumption that organizations differ. While they may face similar competitive conditions, they realize different returns. Performance differences within industry groups and segments are as significant as performance differences between them.

Rather than seeking monopoly power, organizations set out to achieve returns on their resources that are above their real costs. As in classic economics, the aim is to economize. Some organizations can draw on fewer resources to support the same level of business, while others support a larger volume of business with an existing resource base. The different results they achieve are best explained in terms of the way they manage their resources, capabilities, and competencies. An assessment of a firm's internal strengths and weaknesses rests on understanding how it does this.

Exhibit 3.6 summarizes the key differences between the IO and RBV models. Because of their differences, IO and RBV present varied approaches to achieving superior performance. While IO economics starts with external analysis and then analyzes the main

EXHIBIT 3.6
Basic
Differences
between IO
and RBV

Industrial Organization Model (IO)	Resource-Based View (RBV)
Sustained advantage is determined by factors . . .	
Outside firm	*Inside* firm
Focus on . . . Industry structure and attractiveness	Identifying, developing, and obtaining these factors

IO Model	Resource-Based View
Emphasis on . . .	
External Factors (Porter's Five Forces)	Internal Factors (Resources, Capabilities, Competencies)
Which affect . . .	
All firms in the industry equally; all have the same prospects.	Each firm in the industry differently; each has different prospects.
Which explains why . . .	
All firms in the same industry perform roughly the same.	Some firms in the same industry perform at a higher level than others.
So select the . . .	
Right industry to achieve superior performance.	Right firm to achieve superior performance.

internal means to support a strong external position, RBV starts with internal analysis and calculates what is the best external position to occupy given the firm's array of internal strengths and weaknesses (see Exhibit 3.7). In other words, IO fits the firm to external threats and opportunities, whereas RBV molds the external environment around what the firm does best.

According to RBV, if no external niche exists for what the firm does best, then the firm can create a new niche that is more to its liking. The firm can be a first or early mover and occupy a new competitive space where it will face little or no serious competition. For instance, before Dell's arrival, the direct marketing model was not believed to be a viable model for long-term success in the personal computer business. Thus, Dell's largest competitors—IBM, Compaq, and HP—did not move in this direction. They ceded first-mover advantage to Dell and then entered this market after Dell already was well entrenched.

In stressing the centrality of internal analysis, RBV helps to explain the blurring of industry boundaries and the creation of new industry categories. Innovation in the way firms structure their resources, capabilities, and competencies in comparison to other firms in the value chain has been the source of industry transformation.

Resources, Capabilities, and Competencies

RBV terminology is complex. The distinction between resources, capabilities, and competencies has been described as "subtle at best."[15] Though subtle, this distinction is fundamental to understanding the organization as a combination of these elements. Each of these elements plays a role in understanding an organization's strengths and weaknesses.

Resources are the organization's basic financial, physical, and human capital. **Capabilities** allow the organization to exploit these resources. They include, for instance, an aptitude for action and the ability to carry out desired plans. The organization has many capabilities but only a few competencies. **Competencies** allow managers to link key resources and capabilities and to combine, transform, and channel them to satisfy customer needs. Together, the organization's resources and capabilities make up a distinctive competence or inadequacy, a strength or a weakness.

Resources

Resources consist of *financial capital* (money from entrepreneurs, equity holders, bonds, banks, and retained earnings) and *physical capital* (plant, equipment, land, natural resources, raw materials, computer hardware and software, manufacturing robots, automated warehouses, semifinished goods, by-products, waste, unsold stocks of finished goods, and other tangible property).

The qualities that best characterize resources are (1) they are usually protected by legal rights and (2) they can be possessed and owned, transferred and traded, and bought and sold. Resources also can include intangible items such as contracts, leases, licenses, trade secrets, trademarks, brand names, and intellectual property. Labor—unskilled and skilled, clerical, administrative, financial, legal, technical, and managerial—to the extent that it is covered by contractual relations and is used as an input in production is also a resource. Exhibit 3.8 lists a number of key organizational resources.

The resource-based view sees the organization as a collection of these primary productive resources, the disposal of which is determined by administrative decision. Resources are bundles of possible services or contributions to the production of goods with value to customers. The organization is distinguished by how it converts its resources into services.

Exactly the same group of resources, when used in different ways and combinations for different purposes, can yield different services.

From this perspective, an organization's final products represent only one of several ways it can use its resources. Resources can be combined in new, different, and better ways; they may be reconstituted to yield something greater than the returns they achieve in their current specialization in particular products.

Performance results not from the mere possession of resources but from their combination in novel and improved ways, for example, by assigning workers to areas where they achieve higher productivity or allocating financial capital to uses that produce a greater yield.

Using the organization's inherited resources, managers can create an image of the possibilities the organization faces and the obstacles it must overcome. This image, along with the managers' views of the organization's competitive position, affects managerial decisions on ways to combine resources into products and plan for future expansion. These managerial decisions are a key component of the organization's strengths and weaknesses.

EXHIBIT 3.8
Key
Organizational
Resources

Tangible	Intangible
Financial and physical capital	Brand names and trademarks
Land	Reputation
Buildings	Patents and licenses
Plant	Technical or marketing know-how
Equipment	Trade secrets and intellectual property
Natural resources and raw materials	
Semifinished and unsold goods	

From Resources to Capabilities

Resources and capabilities are inherently intertwined. Under optimal conditions, they not only complement each other but also increase the value of both. Consider their interplay in the following ways.

1. Measurement. Resources are fixed inputs that allow the organization to perform its tasks. If tangible, they are found in financial statements; they appear on an organization's balance sheet and are valued in its books. However, because of the specialized experience—the capability—the organization has developed for combining, recombining, and using its resources, they may be worth more or less than their accounting value.

2. Market exchange. Because the real value of resources is hard to assess, they may not be bought or sold easily. In addition to bookkeeping feasibility, lack of well-defined property rights presents an obstacle to transactions. Except for patents, which are based on legally enforceable property rights, intangible resources, such as a reputation for toughness or quality, cannot be easily traded. They are dependent on particular organizational practices and business processes that make it difficult to remove them from their context. Similarly, capabilities such as the loyalty of dealers and trust of customers, which have been nurtured through a history of honest dealing, cannot be easily transferred.

3. Difficult to imitate. There are many unique aspects of organizations—the results of specialized experience in combining and using resources—whose complexity makes them difficult to imitate:

   - Product lines, including prices, advertising, packaging, and styling.
   - Marketing and financial methods.
   - Recruitment practices.
   - Relationships with suppliers and customers.

   Another element that is difficult to imitate is the flow of goods and services in the value chain—how production is broken down into operations and linked to form a product.

4. Causally ambiguous. The connection between resources and capabilities is causally ambiguous or not easy to spell out. For outsiders, these complex relations are not easy to comprehend. Because rivals cannot easily understand them, these connections are hard to copy. They afford protection from competitive rivalry.

5. Barriers to entry. Resources do not provide barriers that deter competition when they are standard endowments, such as land, labor, and capital, which can be purchased in the market at known prices. Hard-to-purchase and difficult-to-price resources that are related to capabilities create barriers. Superior returns—those higher than needed for survival and greater than expected in perfectly competitive markets—can best be obtained from *rare, hard-to-imitate, valuable, and nonsubstitutable* resources combined with capabilities that are hard for competitors to imitate.

6. Competitive position. Sustaining superior returns depends on maintaining a strong competitive position that has been achieved through time. The capabilities needed to do so cannot be purchased in markets. They are *path dependent;* that is, they are the cumulative outcomes of historical decisions. Their *flow* can be adjusted in the present, but their *stock* requires long-term development.[16]

EXHIBIT 3.9
Key
Organizational
Capabilities

Company Skills	Routines
Coordination and allocation of resources	Managerial talent
Putting resources to productive use	How managers make decisions
Organization structure and control systems	How internal processes are handled
Cultural norms and values	How employees interact and cooperate
Technological skills	
Production knowledge	
Experience with government	
Customer loyalty	

For a competitor, attempting to imitate the long-term leader in an industry might be time-consuming and costly with little chance of success. The leader's unique combination of resources and capabilities provides it with a head start, leaving competitors with the difficult task of trying to catch up quickly (e.g., by running crash advertising or R&D programs, which usually are less effective than one carried out over a longer period).

In addition, even if the needed resources can be acquired, the competitors still face the major problem of identifying the precise sequence in which the leader's capabilities have developed. As the above points illustrate, a company can have unique and valuable resources, but unless it has the capabilities to fuse them, it will be unable to create and sustain a distinctive competence (see Exhibits 3.9 and 3.10). The focus in analyzing a company's internal strengths and weaknesses should not be on resources per se, but on how resources are combined into unique capabilities and competencies.

Capabilities

Capabilities exist to exploit a firm's resources. They are less measurable, tradable, and imitable than resources, and thus they have more value in deterring competition and sustaining a competitive position. An organization can have many capabilities, such as technological skills, managerial talent, production knowledge, experience with government contracts, and customer loyalty—all of which are largely people-based. Important

EXHIBIT 3.10
Interaction of
Resources and
Capabilities

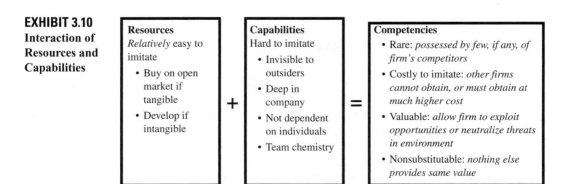

capabilities such as interactions between specialists and the capacity to solve recurrent conflicts have a human foundation. They are embedded in human networks within the organization and with other organizations. They involve functional relationships among organizational members, as well as outside commitments from customers, suppliers, and financial bodies to support the organization. Such relationships may arise from a financial, physical, or technological base, but go well beyond in terms of their importance to the organization.

There are many people-related capabilities that organizations may have: leading, planning, and obtaining feedback; engaging in dialogue; and motivating, compensating, appraising, communicating, and rewarding employees. Time-consuming and difficult to develop, these capabilities are hard to replicate because they cannot be bought off the shelf with money alone. They derive from the organization's inner workings.

For instance, an important example of a capability is an organization's **culture** (see the earlier discussion in this chapter).[17] Culture consists of key managerial values, beliefs, and assumptions about how the organization should conduct its business; treat its employees, customers, suppliers, and others; and foster innovativeness and flexibility. From the perspective of RBV, culture is a source of advantage if it yields lower cost or unique products or services that competitors cannot easily copy. It adds *value* when it contributes to higher sales, lower production costs, and higher margins. When *rare,* a culture enables the organization to be something others cannot be or to do things that cannot be done, or done as well, by other organizations. For example, a strong culture can result in a fixation with customer service and satisfaction and a closeness to the customer that yields timely market information and intense brand loyalty.

A culture is *imperfectly imitable* if other organizations cannot easily duplicate what the culture has to offer. For this to be the case, the culture cannot be easy to characterize. It should be idiosyncratic in some ways, a reflection of the organization's founding, development, unique personalities, and experiences. If path-dependent and historically bound in this way, a culture can contribute to long-term advantage.

In sum, the qualities that best capture capabilities are likely to adhere to people. They include the training, talents, experience, judgment, intelligence, relationships, and insights of workers and managers, their openness to new technologies, and an organization's culture—all elements that cannot be owned, transferred, traded, bought, or sold in the same way that physical property can. An organization's capabilities, as indicators of its strengths and weaknesses, are hard to characterize and assess.

How Capabilities and Resources Relate

According to RBV, an organization's accumulated knowledge, skills, experience, and understanding can be united in different ways to yield different results. In this way they are a source of both competitive power and adaptability. Less visible but no less important than physical, monetary, or other resources, capabilities are comparable to *recipes* while resources are *ingredients; software* while resources are *hardware;* and *artistic sense and technique* while resources are *brushes, canvases, and paint.* Together, resources and capabilities yield superior competencies in areas that bring value to customers such as efficiency, quality, innovation, and responsiveness (see Exhibit 3.11). The ultimate strength of an organization is revealed in competencies that are linked to customer value.

EXHIBIT 3.11
Creation of Distinctive Competencies

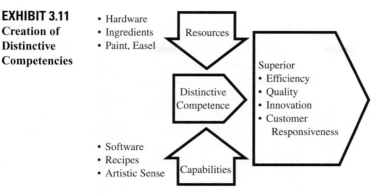

- Hardware
- Ingredients
- Paint, Easel

Resources

Distinctive Competence

Superior
- Efficiency
- Quality
- Innovation
- Customer Responsiveness

- Software
- Recipes
- Artistic Sense

Capabilities

The number of capabilities that produce competencies that deliver customer value is potentially large, and identifying relevant ones and understanding how they relate is complex. Relations among these elements may be called an *organization's capital,* which includes its administrative framework, the reporting system, explicit and implicit planning methods, mechanisms for control and coordination, reputation, informal relations among groups, and alliances between the organization and entities outside it. Organizational capital also includes values, vision, communication, employee empowerment, teamwork, and acceptance and legitimization by key stakeholders. And it includes the way problems are framed, how an organization learns from experience, how it aligns itself and achieves a fit with its environment, and what it declares to be its mission and purpose. A full evaluation of organizational capital as a source of organizational strength and weakness is a painstaking endeavor.

Some capabilities, such as team building and quality management, may be more basic than others if they can combine into higher-order capabilities, such as customer loyalty. If certain groups of capabilities can fit together as a unit and yield higher-order effects, they can be viewed as being of greater significance. For example, first-level capabilities may be conceived of as the basic managerial functions of planning, organizing, directing, supervising, controlling, coordinating, integrating, building trust, reducing conflict, developing teamwork, and creating systems and structures. Higher-level capabilities may be learning about and implementing change, making continuous improvements, and achieving periodic breakthroughs. A still higher level would consist of vision—imagining some future state and allocating resources to achieve it.

To participate in certain industries, a company may need many capabilities; 50 or more "threshold skills" may be needed. To differentiate among capabilities and determine which are essential and which are not as important, an organization needs to identify its key internal strengths, the ones must do internally and it cannot afford to outsource.

Examples of Company Capabilities

Company capabilities are only valuable to the extent that they build competencies in meeting customer needs in unique ways that other firms cannot match. Capabilities must contribute to customer value if they are the sources of enduring organizational strengths. They must:

- Maintain ongoing, effective programs that reduce costs and raise quality; and/or
- Create special cultures that get employees involved.

Some examples follow.[18]

a. Systems such as Advanced Computer-Aided Design and Manufacturing, Statistical Process Control, and Just-in-time Inventory   These systems lower costs and raise quality. For example, at Amphenol, a designer, manufacturer, and marketer of electrical, electronic, and fiber-optic connectors and interconnect systems, as well as cables, there are ongoing programs to rationalize production facilities, reduce expenses, and maximize return on capital. The improvements involve advanced computer-aided design and manufacturing systems, statistical process controls, and just-in-time inventory programs. The firm has been successful at increasing product quality, shortening product delivery schedules, and reducing overhead. It offsets increases in the cost of raw materials, labor, and services by productivity improvements and cost savings. It also imposes aggressive cost controls on its manufacturing and distribution functions.

b. Value Improvement Processes Designed to Increase Economic Value Added   Another example is SPX, a provider of flow technology products, test and measurement products, and industrial products and services. It reduces costs and raises quality by subjecting its businesses to a value improvement process (VIP). The company's goal is to achieve economic value added (EVA) defined as net operating profit after-taxes minus a charge for the cost of the capital. All of its businesses go through this process, which leads to numerous changes. For instance, the company has revamped the business model for specialty tools. The streamlining has resulted in outsourcing production, reducing manufacturing facilities, and discontinuing low value products. Employees work in "high performance teams" that are rewarded for the contributions to long-term profitability, growth, and continuous improvement.

c. Formal Project Review Processes   Still another example is Activision, a creator of online, PC, console, and handheld games. It has created a formal control for the selection, development, and production of games that includes in-depth reviews of each project at important stages by high-ranking operating managers. This system keeps costs down and raises quality. The payoff is in operating margins. Midcourse corrections are common. Each step in the process is coordinated to consider the views of customers.

d. Direct Store Delivery and an Opportunity to Make a Difference   Dreyer's, a manufacturer and distributor of premium ice cream, has had both programs that reduce cost and raise quality and a special culture which has elevated employee involvement. Dreyer's has a direct-store-delivery (DSD) system with very sophisticated information and logistics. It has designed delivery routes to increase the territory distributors service and cut unnecessary stops. The process has realized millions of dollars in savings. Independent distributors that ship Dreyer's products must adhere to strict company guidelines. For example, trucks must have monitors that sound an alarm if the temperature of a cargo falls below a desired level.

Dreyer's culture is centered on employee participation. In 1988, it instituted an "I Can Make a Difference" philosophy that celebrates the individual, trust, and ownership. Nine "Grooves" further define the philosophy:

1. People issues are the primary responsibility of managers and supervisors, not a personnel department (Dreyer's doesn't have a typical HR department).

2. Deciding whom to put on the Dreyer's team is very important (hiring smart).
3. People don't need to be motivated; they need to be liberated, meaning they need to be given a chance to do their job their way.
4. People involvement means just that—allowing people to get involved in Dreyer's business in a broader way than just their specific job or function.
5. Everyone is expected to own some aspect of his or her job.
6. When someone demonstrates ownership, recognize that individual with hoopla.
7. Hire highly motivated, experienced people, and train in order to impart knowledge and skills needed for their jobs.
8. Everyone needs and deserves honest feedback from his or her manager on a regular basis.
9. We need to recognize the people who make a difference in the business.

Creating a Special Culture to Get Employees Involved

a. Selective Hiring to Breed Loyalty   Other companies also have very special cultures. To build its culture, Ball, a packaging supplier to the beverage and food industries, is selective in the hiring process and invests large amounts of money in training. When it launches a plant, it may interview 3,000 people for 80 positions. Loyal employees stay with the company for long periods. Ball runs a nonunion shop to keep worker–management antagonism at a minimum. Its workers are encouraged to be entrepreneurial in spirit to make operations more efficient.

b. An Independent and Aggressive Employee Culture   Brown and Brown, a diversified insurance agency and wholesale brokerage, also has a special culture. That culture gives employees a large measure of independence, while at the same trying to inculcate in them an aggressive "hunt if you want to eat" way of doing things. The company's sales force has to be knowledgeable and energetic and possess strong analytical skills. A high percentage of its managers are certified public accountants (CPAs) and come from major accounting firms. Sales employees have extensive experience in sales, long-time relationships with clients, and tend to be well known in their local communities.

From Capabilities to Competencies

Resources and capabilities together produce complex aggregate-level competencies that are the *highest-level* means the organization has for acquiring, maintaining, renewing, and coordinating diverse resources and capabilities, ensuring their durability, and preventing them from becoming obsolete. The many different capabilities the organization possesses are the building blocks for its competencies; competencies, in turn, integrate and consolidate component capabilities (see Exhibit 3.12). Thus, behind every realized competence there is a blend of many capabilities.

For example, a competency such as low-cost competing (see Chapter 4) is not based only on efficient production; it depends on many complementary elements including skilled people, low-cost supply sources, and efficient delivery and ordering systems. All of these must be brought together and related in complex ways.

Similarly, competing based on a flow of product enhancements and new products depends not just on product conception, design, and development but also on timely

EXHIBIT 3.12
From Capabilities to Competencies

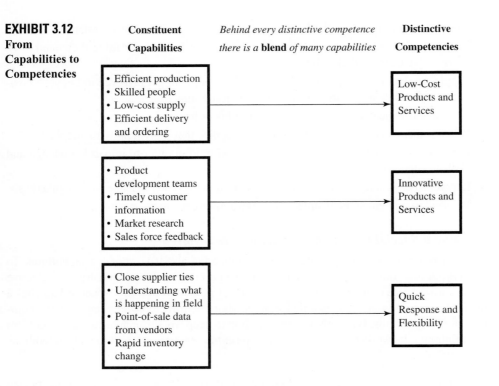

Constituent Capabilities	*Behind every distinctive competence there is a* **blend** *of many capabilities*	Distinctive Competencies

- Efficient production
- Skilled people
- Low-cost supply
- Efficient delivery and ordering

→ Low-Cost Products and Services

- Product development teams
- Timely customer information
- Market research
- Sales force feedback

→ Innovative Products and Services

- Close supplier ties
- Understanding what is happening in field
- Point-of-sale data from vendors
- Rapid inventory change

→ Quick Response and Flexibility

information about how customers use products, their level of satisfaction, and their future requirements. These in turn depend on formal market research, sales force training, feedback, and interaction among engineers, designers, and customers. Additionally, it may be necessary to have computer software that facilitates flexible manufacturing and testing and to have managerial philosophies that espouse patience in building margins and market share.

Competencies

Competencies consist of a management logic and belief about how to *harmonize* the organization's many diverse resources and capabilities. They are the patterns the organization uses to deploy its skills and assets in ways that give value to customers. While their specific aspects vary from company to company, competencies typically are broad in scope. Because they involve such a complex harmonization of separate parts, competencies are difficult to imitate. Indeed, the more complex the integration among discrete elements, the more difficult it is for competitors to comprehend and copy what the organization does and thus the easier it is for the organization to sustain a competitive position.

Unlike physical assets, which wear out and deteriorate over time, competencies may improve. Relatively mobile, they are likely to have important *protean qualities;* they can provide access to a wide variety of markets beyond those the organization is currently serving. For example, 3M built on the capabilities it had in substrates, coatings, and adhesives to expand into a diverse array of products such as sticky tape, removable notes, magnetic tape, photographic film, and pressure-sensitive tapes. Canon applied the capabilities it had in optics, imaging, and microprocessor controls to expand into copiers, laser printers, cameras, and image scanning. Competencies represent the coalescing of capabilities in old *and* new ways. They give the organization the ability to take advantage of new opportunities and to repulse threats. Because they can be used for more than a single product or service, they enable the organization to invent new markets, to quickly enter emerging ones, and to make shifts in product lines and services.[19]

Creating a Distinctive Competence

A **distinctive competence** is the unique accumulation of capabilities and rigidities that an organization has acquired over time. In assessing an organization's strengths and weaknesses, it is important to identify an organization's distinctive competence that gives the organization its special character. It develops such a competence by accepting commitments in the course of adapting to internal and external pressures. Once institutionalized, the adaptations affect the ability the organization has to frame and execute desired policies, but they apply more broadly. A distinctive competence is not only a tool but also a source of employee gratification, institutional integrity, value, and reason for being.

Five elements coalesce to create a distinctive competence.

1. *The knowledge and techniques needed to create useful products and services.* The creation and distribution of goods and services depend on value chain expertise—expertise in the flow of inputs, their conversion to outputs, the distribution of the outputs, and the disposal of waste. The organization is proficient in some combination of R&D, design, manufacturing, physical distribution, retail sales, postsale service, and handling and minimizing waste.

2. *Acquiring and generating resources beyond the supply the organization directly owns and controls.* The organization acquires additional resources through value chain linkages. Working beyond its boundaries and establishing collaborative arrangements with external entities help it expand available resources. It must establish strong relationships—not just financial and economic but also psychological and emotional—with external groups (see the discussion of stakeholders in Chapter 2).

3. *Dealing with novel problems.* Capabilities are embedded in routines. However, excessive reliance on routines poses the problem of inflexibility: An organization can remain committed to familiar tasks even when the evidence strongly argues against it. Search procedures to deal with novel problems are themselves based on existing routines.[20]

4. *Looking toward the future.* An organization is a flow of ad hoc adjustments to external conditions, compromises, and best judgments. The present is a moving front, a transitory position. An organization must look toward the future. How should it redeploy assets to achieve new objectives?

5. *Positioning and repositioning.* Managerial skills are needed to advantageously position and reposition the organization. For this to be accomplished, knowledge of competitive relations, the psychology of interfirm rivalries, and evolving social, legal, technical, economic, and political factors is essential. To position and reposition itself, an organization must be able to adjust to changing conditions. (Positioning is discussed in Chapter 4.)

The Process of Acquisition

To adjust to the challenges it faces, the organization must decide which combinations of resources, capabilities, and competencies should be assembled, and in which sequence. The process of acquiring resources, capabilities, and competencies is affected by uncertainty. It "cannot be optimally derived from normative theory."[21] Uncertainties exist about possible future states and competitive interactions in those states. Complexity is inherent as developing an appropriate mix of resources, capabilities, and competencies. It involves not only identifying and coordinating the needed elements but also planning their future deployment. Organizations must continuously reappraise their resources, capabilities, and competencies, discarding those they no longer need and acquiring those they do need. Two steps to acquisition exist:

1. Looking outside the organization for talent and technology and establishing partnerships and alliances.
2. Finding ways to synthesize, harmonize, and integrate what is learned within the organization.

The goal is not simply to accumulate disparate resources, capabilities, and competencies but to join them in a tapestry that creates a greater whole.[22] The role of every employee is to identify, acquire, build, and deploy such resources, capabilities, and competencies. Clearly, some organizations are better at this process than others. To the extent that they are better, they are stronger and more likely to achieve sustained competitive advantage.

Summary

A number of different approaches are available to analyze a firm's strengths and weaknesses. Internal analysis may be done by relying on classic management theories, or with the seven-S framework, a value chain analysis, or an assessment of an organization's resources, capabilities, and competencies.

The seven-S framework applied well to the excellent companies of the early 1980s but did not stand up to the test of time. Value chain analysis is useful especially when extended outside organizational boundaries. It reveals how organizations are dependent on each other in complex webs.

The resource-based view (RBV) currently is in vogue as a method of analyzing an organization's internal strengths and weaknesses. RBV is not a resource-based theory at all. It might best be described as anti-resource-based theory, as it espouses that capabilities and competencies, not resources, provide the essential element for achieving sustained competitive advantage. RBV is very good at explaining how resources alone as a source of competitive advantage can be quickly dissipated. Still, definitional issues abound in the actual application of RBV. Some of the basic constructs are vague and hard to apply. RBV is often criticized for being tautological in nature and nonrigorous in its basic concepts.[23]

A foolproof method for analyzing an organization's internal strengths and weaknesses does not exist. The strategist must pick and choose among these theories and approaches and use judgment in how to apply the approaches to specific cases. In the end, the strategist must recognize that both internal and external analyses are needed. The matching of the two is necessary for the creation of sustained competitive advantage.

Endnotes

1. C. Prahalad and G. Hamel, "The Core Competence of the Corporation," *Harvard Business Review,* May–June 1990, pp. 79–91.

2. L. Bryan and D. Farrel, "Leading Through Uncertainty," *McKinsey Quarterly,* December 2008, pp. 1–13.

3. M. Porter, *Competitive Advantage* (New York: Free Press, 1985).

4. Prahalad and Hamel, "The Core Competence of the Corporation."

5. "The Power of Virtual Integration: An Interview with Dell Computer's Michael Dell," *Harvard Business Review,* March–April 1998, pp. 73–84.

6. F. Hayek, "The Corporation in a Democratic Society: In Whose Interests Ought It and Will It Be Run," in *Business Strategy,* ed. H. Ansoff (New York: Penguin, 1977), pp. 225–39.

7. F. Taylor, *The Principles of Scientific Management* (New York: Harper, 1911).

8. F. Roethlisberger and W. Dickson, *Management and the Worker* (Cambridge, MA: Harvard University Press, 1939); and F. Herzberg, *Work and the Nature of Man* (New York: Crowell, 1966).

9. J. Woodward, *Industrial Organization* (London: Oxford University Press, 1965).

10. S. Ellis, T. Almor, and O. Shenkar, *"Structural Contingency Revisited: Toward a Dynamic System Model," Emergence* 4, no. 4 (2002), pp. 51–84.

11. T. Peters and R. Waterman, *In Search of Excellence* (New York: Warner Books, 1982).

12. A. Slywotzky and D. Morrison, *The Profit Zone* (New York: Three Rivers Press, 2001).

13. RBV has had nearly 40 years of development, starting with Edith Penrose's 1955 classic, *The Theory of the Growth of the Firm,* and culminating in a flurry of attention in the past 15 years: E. Penrose, *The Theory of the Growth of the Firm* (Oxford, England: Basil Blackwell, 1959); R. Amit and P. Schoemaker, "Strategic Assets and Organizational Rent," *Strategic Management Journal* 14 (1993), pp. 333–46; J. Barney, "Strategic Factor Markets: Expectations, Luck, and Business Strategy," *Management Science* 32, no. 10 (1986), pp. 1231–41; J. Barney, "Organization Culture: Can It Be a Source of Sustained Competitive Advantage?" *Academy of Management Review* 11, no. 3 (1986), pp. 656–65; J. Barney, *Gaining and Sustaining Competitive Advantage* (Reading, MA: Addison-Wesley, 1997); A. Brumagin, "A Hierarchy of Corporate Resources," *Advances in Strategic Management* 10 (1994), pp. 81–112; I. Dierickx and K. Cool, "Asset Stock Accumulation and Sustainability of Competitive Advantage," *Management Science* 35, no. 12 (1989), pp. 1504–13; G. McGrath, R. MacMillan, and S. Venkatraman, "Defining and Developing Competence," *Strategic Management Journal* 16 (1995), pp. 251–75; R. Hall, "A Framework Linking Intangible Resources and Capabilities to Sustainable Competitive Advantage," *Strategic Management Journal* 14 (1993), pp. 607–18; A. Lado, A. Boyd, and P. Wright, "A Competency-Based Model of Sustainable Competitive Advantage: Toward a Conceptual Integration," *Journal of Management* 18, no. 1 (1992) , pp. 77–91; R. Nelson and S. Winter, *An Evolutionary Theory of Economic Change* (Cambridge, MA: Harvard University Press, 1982); R. Reed and R. DeFillippi, "Causal Ambiguity, Barriers to Imitation, and Sustainable Competitive Advantage," *Academy of Management Review* 5, no. 1 (1990), pp. 88–102; B. Wernerfelt, "Resource-Based View of the Firm," *Strategic Management Journal* 5 (1989), pp. 171–80; D. Miller and J. Shamsie, "The Resource-Based View of the Firm in Two Environments," *Academy of Management Journal* 39, no. 3 (1997), pp. 519–43.

14. Lado, Boyd, and Wright, "Competency-Based Model."

15. Barney, *Gaining and Sustaining Competitive Advantage,* p. 144.

16. Dierickx and Cool, "Asset Stock Accumulation."
17. Barney, "Organization Culture: Can It Be a Source of Sustained Competitive Advantage?"
18. A. Marcus, *Big Winners and Big Losers* (Upper Saddle River, NJ: Wharton School Press, 2006).
19. Prahalad and Hamel, "The Core Competence of the Corporation."
20. Nelson and Winter, *An Evolutionary Theory of Economic Change*.
21. Amit and Schoemaker, "Strategic Assets and Organizational Rent."
22. Prahalad and Hamel, "The Core Competence of the Corporation."
23. R. Priem and J. Butler, "Is the Resource Based View a Useful Perspective for Strategic Management Research?" *Academy of Management Review* 26, no. 1 (2001), pp. 22–40.

PART TWO

Making Moves

CHAPTER FOUR

Timing and Positioning

"Strategy requires a theory that pays attention to the sequential moves and countermoves of competitors over long periods of time. As competition has heated up, this dynamic interaction among competitors has become the key to competitive success. Success depends not on how the firm positions itself at a certain point in time, but on how it acts over long periods of time."[1]

Richard D'Aveni, author

Chapter Learning Objectives

- Understanding strategy as a series of moves and countermoves.
- Being aware of the importance of timing in making these moves.
- Gaining an elementary comprehension of game theory and its contribution to strategy.
- Being aware of four generic positions: (*i*) low cost to a narrow group; (*ii*) premium product to a narrow group; (*iii*) low cost to a broad group; and (*iv*) premium product to a broad group.
- Understanding the increasing importance of a best-value position, which combines low cost and differentiation.
- Recognizing examples of company repositioning.
- Explaining strategic groups and the variety of ways a product or service can be segmented.

Introduction

If a "game," the purpose of strategy is to achieve sustained competitive advantage. This book has suggested three ways to achieve sustained competitive advantage. In the first model (Chapter 1), superior concentration of forces is the way to achieve it. As in war, a winning company does not have to possess more resources than its foes; rather, it must be able to *concentrate more firepower* at the scene of the battle. Thus, flexibility, rapidity of movement, and choosing the location of battle can overcome superior might. According to the second model (Chapter 2), which also has military connotations, the way to achieve sustained competitive advantage is to create *an impregnable fortress* that an organization's foes cannot penetrate. Once movement into a new position is made, that position must be defended. This model (Chapter 3) focuses on the best way to create a stronghold that competitors cannot enter: Acquire unique resources, capabilities, and competencies that cannot be easily copied, and combine and recombine them in ways that are rare, valuable, costly to imitate, and nonsubstitutable. Developing unmatchable internal strengths is a way to keep competitors from entering. If they cannot play the game, they cannot win. In this way, the advantage gained is protected.

These models, however, pay insufficient attention to the dynamic element in strategy— the moves and countermoves companies make to achieve and sustain competitive advantages. Therefore, in Part 2, we examine these moves in detail. Chapter 4 focuses on two issues—the timing of the moves and positioning of a company within an industry. Chapter 5 looks at the scope of a company and at mergers, acquisitions, and divestitures. Chapter 6 discusses globalization, and Chapter 7 covers innovation. External analysis (EA) covered in Chapter 2 and internal analysis (IA) covered in Chapter 3 are followed by moves involving business strategy (BS), corporate strategy (CS), global strategy (GS), and innovation strategy (IS).

The premise of these chapters is that strategy is a series of moves and countermoves in these realms. D'Aveni argues, "The value, risks, and effectiveness of every move must be seen in relation to the actions of competitors."[2] When a firm makes a move, it must anticipate the countermoves of its competitors. What will the competitors do next?[3]

The game analogy suggested in Chapter 1 is fleshed out here. The strategist must consider what to do next based on the probable moves that competitors will make. Opponents will try to replicate the position a firm wishes to occupy. They will try to copy the unique accretion of resources, capabilities, and competencies the firm has collected. The countermoves of opponents must be taken into account. Since strategy is a series of moves and countermoves in a game, the strategist must know game theory's elementary principles. This chapter explains these principles in terms of timing and then discusses the concept of positioning. It introduces Porter's concept of generic strategies and various critiques, modifications, and extensions of this concept.

Timing

After examining the external environment and assessing the firm's internal strengths and weaknesses, the strategist is ready to make his or her moves. Does timing matter? In making its moves, does it make a difference if an organization is an early or late mover?[4] First movers take risks in anticipation of high returns. If their new ventures and undertakings work as expected, they gain a head start on the competition, but in doing so they incur high development costs. Through reverse engineering, second movers can copy what first movers do and avoid costly and expensive errors that the first movers make (see Exhibit 4.1). If second movers move aggressively, they can overtake the first movers. First movers can lose their initial advantage if they fail to effectively respond to the second movers' challenges.

EXHIBIT 4.1
Timing
Matters

Advantages for	
Early Movers	**Late Starters**
• Head start on competitors	• Reverse engineering
• Large percent of valuable early adopters	• Less risk
• Customer loyalty	• Lower development costs
	• Fewer mistakes

EXHIBIT 4.2
**Innovators
versus
Followers**

Source: Adapted from
R. Grant, *Contempo-
rary Strategy Analysis,*
4th ed., 2002.
Reprinted with per-
mission of Blackwell
Publishing.

Product	Innovator	Follower	Winner
35mm camera	Leica	Canon	Follower
Commercial jets	de Havilland	Boeing/Airbus	Followers
Ballpoint pen	Reynolds	BIC	Follower
Light beer	Rheingold	Miller	Follower
CAT scanner	EMI	GE	Follower
Float glass	Pilkington	Corning	Innovator
Instant photos	Polaroid	Kodak	Innovator
Fiber optics	Corning	Many	Innovator
Disposable diapers	Procter & Gamble	Kimberly-Clark	Unclear
VCRs	Sony	Matsushita	Follower
Diet cola	RC Cola	Coca-Cola	Follower
Calculator	Bowmar	Texas Instruments	Follower
Video games	Atari	Nintendo	Follower
Copiers	Xerox	Canon	Unclear
Computer operating system	Apple	Microsoft	Follower
Internet browser	Netscape	Microsoft	Follower

For first movers, sustaining initial benefits is very difficult. There have been many in-stances in which second movers overtook them. For example, Canon overtook Leica in the commercial exploitation of the 35 mm camera; General Electric and Johnson & Johnson overtook EMI in the commercial exploitation of (CAT) scanners; and Dell and Hewlett-Packard overtook Apple in the commercial exploitation of personal computers. However, in some cases first movers have triumphed, and in other cases the outcome has swung back and forth (see Exhibit 4.2).

Being the first company to make a move, whether introducing a new product or a new business practice, creates a hard-to-challenge advantage. However, being a first mover is risky, and aggressive second movers often succeed where first movers fail. Consider Best Buy. In 1991, Best Buy's sales were $.66 billion, substantially behind Circuit City's sales of $2.36 billion. But in 1996, Best Buy overtook Circuit City, with sales of $7.21 billion com-pared to Circuit City's $7.02 billion.[5]

Best Buy surpassed Circuit City by rapidly making strategic moves that Circuit City did not match:

1. Best Buy made its stores exciting, fun places to shop.
2. Best Buy removed its high-pressure, commissioned sales force and replaced it with a more laid-back, salaried sales force. Circuit City stuck with commissioned sales.
3. Best Buy's policy of everyday low pricing meant it offered good values at different price points. It did not mean that everything in its stores was sold at a rock-bottom price; Best Buy carried so-called myth items (exciting, high-energy, leading-edge) as well as com-modity ones. Over time, Best Buy increased its emphasis on the myth items so that it would continue to appeal to techno-savvy shoppers, who by their very presence gave Best Buy stores a certain allure.
4. Best Buy attacked its competitor at its core—after-sale service. Circuit City had achieved 75 percent of its operating profit from the sale of extended warranties, so Best Buy offered competing "performance service plans" at 30 percent less than Circuit City's prices.

EXHIBIT 4.3
Competitive Landscape

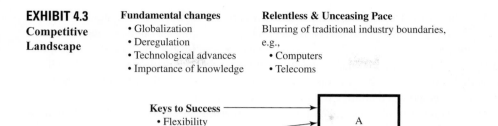

Fundamental changes
• Globalization
• Deregulation
• Technological advances
• Importance of knowledge

Relentless & Unceasing Pace
Blurring of traditional industry boundaries, e.g.,
• Computers
• Telecoms

Keys to Success
• Flexibility
• Innovation
• Speed

A "Dynamic Capability"

As a second mover, Best Buy was very aggressive. By taking these steps, Best Buy differentiated itself from Circuit City. More nimble and strategically adroit than Circuit City, it devised a series of innovative moves that stymied its larger rival. When Circuit City failed to respond effectively, Best Buy surpassed it. When the 2008 economic meltdown struck, Circuit City went bankrupt. Best Buy checkmated its opponent. Circuit City went out of existence. In mass-merchandise retailing, this has been the sorry story of many companies.

The Value of Rapid Adjustment

The ability to rapidly adjust to changing circumstances may be a firm's most enduring competency. Clearly Circuit City was lacking this competency (see Chapter 9). For most firms, the competitive landscape alters rapidly because of the moves made by its competitors and transformations in factors such as the global economy, government regulation, technology, and knowledge.

The relentless pace of change blurs traditional industry boundaries (see Exhibit 4.3). For example:

• The computer, telecommunications, and entertainment industries have been merging such that companies like Microsoft, Comcast, AT&T, and Time Warner compete against each other in each of these domains.

• Commercial and investment banking, brokerage, and insurance industries have amalgamated, turning giant firms such as Citgroup and Goldman Sachs into competitors operating in similar realms. Global financial-services conglomerates such as the following now exist which compete in commercial and investment banking:

• ABN Amro
• Bank of America
• BNP Paribas
• Barclays
• Citigroup
• Credit Suisse
• Daiwa Securities
• Deutsche Bank
• Goldman Sachs
• HSBC
• JPMorgan Chase
• Morgan Stanley
• Nomura Securities Co., Ltd.
• Royal Bank of Scotland Group
• Royal Bank of Canada
• Société Générale
• UBS
• Wells Fargo

After the Great Depression, the U.S. Congress required that banks engage in only one type of banking activity. Commercial banks provided checking accounts, savings accounts, and money market accounts. They accepted time deposits. Investment banks raised capital, traded in securities, and managed corporate mergers and acquisitions. Under the Glass-Steagall Act of 1933, such combinations had been illegal. The Gramm-Leach-Bliley Act of 1999, however, changed all this. It allowed banks to do both.

As the competition between commercial and investment banks picked up, they competed actively for real estate loans. They acquired mortgages by purchasing them from mortgage bankers or dealers. Many of the mortgages issued were to subprime borrowers with little ability to repay. Investment banks provided money at loss leader interest rates so as to securitize the loans, causing the loans to be a popular financing option.

However, when U.S. house prices began to decline in 2006–07, mortgage delinquencies soared. Many securities backed with subprime mortgages lost their value. Securitized loans exacerbated the subprime mortgage crisis. The upshot was a huge capital crisis in the banking world. Throughout the world, credit tightened.

This crisis, triggered by a dramatic rise in mortgage delinquencies and foreclosures, had its roots in weak financial regulation. As part of the response, almost all of the major investment banks became commercial banks. On September 22, 2008, the last two major investment banking firms on Wall Street, Goldman Sachs and Morgan Stanley, became commercial banks so they could receive Troubled Asset Relief Program (TARP) money. TARP gave the federal government the right to purchase up to $700 billion of troubled assets and equity from banks such as Citigroup and Morgan Stanley.

External shocks, such as the collapse of the housing market, transform industries. The key attributes for ongoing business success in the face of these shocks are flexibility, innovation, and speed. Quick moves are needed to remake outmoded business models. All firms strive to be first in introducing new business models, but not all will achieve this goal. Moreover, firms that develop the new business models may not be able to implement them effectively (see Chapter 9).

Management theorists Eisenhardt and Martin maintain that the ability of firms to experiment and achieve "new resource configurations" more rapidly than their competitors is a "dynamic capability."[6] Their ability "to renew, augment, adapt, and reinvent" themselves is a rare and valuable factor that enables them to sustain competitive advantage.[7] Only time will tell which companies within the weakened global banking industry will be able to display such a capability. As of 2009, Goldman Sachs was the winner.

Obstacles to Quick Action

If companies do not take steps to preserve their competitive advantage, their success is transient. Of the top 25 U.S. corporations in 1900, only 2 remain today. In a typical year, more than 150,000 business bankruptcies occur, most of them involving firms that fail to react adequately to change. Of the many reasons for firms' lack of response, inertia and prior strategic commitments stand out.

The *Icarus paradox* highlights the effects of failing to adapt.[8] Icarus, a figure in Greek mythology, was being held hostage on a besieged island. To help him escape, his father made him wings of wax and feathers. Because flying saved his life, Icarus loved to fly. He soared higher and higher until he came too close to the sun, which melted the wax in the wings and Icarus plunged to his death.

Similarly, many companies become so committed to the business models that brought them success that they continue to use them despite new conditions that make the models obsolete. Their absorption in what they once did well keeps them from learning and adapting and leads to their undoing.

A good example is Xerox, which chose not to make the changes that could have ensured future prosperity. Today, consumers do not associate Xerox with the personal computer revolution; the names that come to mind are Apple, Microsoft, Intel, and Dell. Yet Xerox's research division in Palo Alto, California, pioneered almost all the elements that ultimately went into PCs, from the mouse to the printer. Steve Jobs picked up ideas from Xerox researchers, but years after its involvement in this revolution, Xerox was still in the copying business, and even in this business, which it should have dominated, its rivals were overtaking it.

Though Xerox's managers had the potential to be first in the personal computer market, they made a conscious choice to stay out of it, reasoning that PCs were not the firm's line of business. Their timing was notoriously bad. Douglas Smith and Robert Alexander document the company's choice to forgo PCs in a wonderful look at Xerox called *Fumbling the Future.*[9] By examining company records and interviewing executives, the authors show how bureaucratic infighting killed the PC business at Xerox. Factions in the firm that favored being first in the PC market lost out to factions that favored sticking to Xerox's existing lines of business. Xerox's inability to react is a classic example of how a company can miss a once-in-a-lifetime opportunity.

As this case illustrates, the timing of moves is highly important. But determining the optimal timing for moves is a dilemma that depends on competitors' timing as well as one's own. This game is not carried out in isolation. Multiple parties react to each other's moves. A way of conceptualizing this dilemma is to use game theory, the pluses and minuses of which will be explored next.

Game Theory

There are two types of games—*simultaneous* ones like online fantasy football and *sequential* ones like chess.[10] In a simultaneous game, two or more players act at the same time; in a sequential game, one player goes first and the other player gets to observe the results before making his or her move.

In both types of games, a decision *not to go forward* is just as important as a decision to go forward. The choice, in business terms, is whether to stick with an old product, practice, or business model like Xerox sticking with the copier or to start rolling out a new one like Xerox developing the PC while continuing with the old. Such choices are **timing dilemmas.**

Simultaneous Game

In a simultaneous game with two players (here, two firms), each has the choice of producing only its old product or going with the old one plus a new product. The payoffs vary depending on what the other party does. In Exhibit 4.4, if both parties stick with the old product, their payoff is $100 each; if they both innovate and go with old and new products, their payoff is $0 each. When two parties make the same move at the same time, each one cancels the gains the other could have achieved. The two parties, in essence, neutralize each other.

EXHIBIT 4.4
Simultaneous
Game: Payoff
Matrix

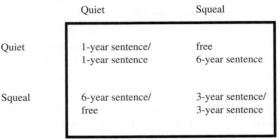

		My Company	
		Old Product	Old and New Product
My Rival	Old Product	$100/ $100	$250/ $−30
	Old and New Product	$−30/ $250	$0/ $0

EXHIBIT 4.5
Prisoner's
Dilemma:
Payoff Matrix

		Prisoner 1	
		Quiet	Squeal
Prisoner 2	Quiet	1-year sentence/ 1-year sentence	free 6-year sentence
	Squeal	6-year sentence/ free	3-year sentence/ 3-year sentence

So far, the choice seems clear. It is safer to stay with the old product than to innovate and add a new one when the other party might do the same. However, what if one party innovates, producing both the old and the new products, and the other does not? Then the payoff is $250 to the innovating party, while the party that holds to the status quo loses $30. Now the choice is between possibly winning $250 or possibly losing $30. Assuming that each side is just as likely to innovate as it is to stay the course, the odds favor innovation: Staying with the old product yields payoffs of $100 and –$30, for an average gain of $35, while innovating yields payoffs of $250 or $0, for an average gain of $125. Both parties, being rational, will choose to innovate, and in doing so, each will cancel out the other's gain. Where both could have achieved $100 if they had been satisfied with staying the course, now both get nothing from innovating.

In game theory, this kind of situation is called the **prisoner's dilemma** (see Exhibit 4.5). In a prisoner's dilemma, both accused parties get a one-year sentence if each refuses to squeal on the other. If one testifies against the other, he or she goes free and the other accused party faces a sentence of six years. If both parties testify against each other, both go to prison for three years. In the prisoner's dilemma, as long as the parties are unable to communicate with each other, it is rational for both of them to squeal. When the suspected criminals rat on their partners in crime, society benefits but the two parties playing the prisoner's dilemma game suffer. Their jail sentences go up, which is in neither party's best interest.

In the example of the new-product dilemma, society also benefits because the innovation is pursued and the new product comes to market, but neither of the innovating parties gains. Companies such as Xerox or Circuit City might have understood the downside of innovating. Their deliberations lead them to a bias against change. Why should a company innovate if a game-like scenario indicates that neither it nor its rival is likely to be better off?

In the real world, however, the payoffs are not known in advance; they can be only roughly approximated. The analyst must calculate the probability of gain or loss times the magnitude of that gain or loss, but both calculations are estimates and, if they are off by even a small amount, can compound the errors. To make these calculations, the analyst might use a confidence interval. For example, there is an 80 percent chance that the payoffs are as specified and a 60 percent chance that the parties will act rationally. But not all rivals are likely to be rational. It might even serve their purposes to surprise one another by being intentionally irrational.

In making estimates about the payoffs and what the two sides will do, the analyst has to consider motivation and level of awareness. A good question, for instance, is why wasn't Circuit City more aggressive in responding to Best Buy's moves? The analyst would also have to investigate organizational politics because they are likely to play a role, as they did in the Xerox case. A **sensitivity analysis** based on different assumptions about motivation, levels of awareness, and organizational politics might be needed to establish odds for a number of outcomes.[11] Without precise numbers for the probable gains and losses and the various moves a competitor might make, the range of results might be so great as to be uninterpretable. These uncertainties plague managers trying to make timing decisions. The longer they work on resolving the uncertainties, the more time they lose.

Sequential Game

As mentioned earlier, in a sequential game, the parties alternate their moves in a series rather than moving simultaneously. With each round, the parties understand the game and the tendencies of their opponents better. Since the parties know that they will be dealing with each other repeatedly and recognize that mutual self-destruction is foolhardy, the likelihood of their cooperating should increase. With cooperation, the prisoner's dilemma can be solved to each of the parties' benefit. Both realize that they walk away with a shorter prison sentence if neither squeals. Simulations with the prisoner's dilemma have shown that when one party introduces cooperative behavior, the other is likely to respond in a tit-for-tat fashion, but these simulations have not been supported by experiments which show that in repeated games cooperators learn from defectors to act against their common interests.

The sequential game concept is a useful model for repeated interactions because its iterative cycles introduce realism. However, as with the simultaneous game model, the payoffs and the odds of what each side will do must be estimated, and their estimation is hampered by uncertainty. Indeed, with an iterative process, there are more calculations and thus greater chances of error.

To illustrate, let's return to our original example: First, one company decides whether to innovate or not. The payoffs of its decision have to be calculated on the basis of what its rival is likely to do next. As shown in Exhibit 4.6, there are four payoffs, or outcomes (O), to be calculated—O1, O2, O3, and O4. So far, the sequential game is similar to a

EXHIBIT 4.6
Sequential
Game Decision
Tree

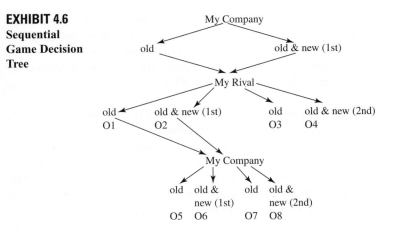

simultaneous game. However, the sequential game enables us to model what will occur after the initial payoff, as the assumption is that the game will continue with additional rounds. Suppose that in the first round a company decides that it is going to stick with its old product, and its rival then decides it will not innovate. The company has to decide whether to innovate or not in the next round, so it must calculate the second-round payoffs on the basis of the first-round results. These outcomes are represented by O5 and O6 in Exhibit 4.6. Now suppose that in the first round the company decides it is going to stick with its old product and its rival then decides to innovate. The company must decide its round-two move and calculate the payoffs on the basis of this result. These additional outcomes are represented by O7 and O8.

More rounds will occur, and more outcomes will have to be estimated and compared. The sequential game model helps prepare the analyst for the repeated character of competitive interactions by forcing the analyst to think several steps ahead, rather than one step at a time. The timing of a move is not a one-only decision for either party. As the rounds continue, important decisions will need to be made at each interval. In a sequential game, the payoffs and the odds of what a player might do must be recomputed often. These repeated calculations compound the possibility of error.

Expanding the Assumptions

The examples discussed above show some of the problems that occur in conceptualizing strategy as a game. One is that rivals have only two options—to innovate or not to innovate. Obviously, the real world provides more possibilities than this schematic choice. There are other options than a company abandoning its old product, or hedging its bets with some proportion of new and old products. The choices depend on the creativity of the strategist. Decision making is not limited to either-or, yes-or-no thinking. It encompasses more than totally supporting or opposing innovation (see Chapter 1 for a discussion of the kinds of choices that might be available). Moreover, with each iteration in the game, the company becomes *more or less* committed to innovating or to sticking with what it had been doing previously. This tendency to commit limits its subsequent choices.

Another assumption is that only two parties are competing. Most real-world situations involve competition between more than two parties. For instance, in a game between cereal makers General Mills and Kellogg, the two sides can go two rounds, first matching each other by offering the right to buy a box of cereal and get one free and then matching each other by removing this promotion. Neither really gains from this game. The moves of one party are neutralized by the moves of the other. The game ends in stalemate. However, there are two other cereal makers in this game. If Post or Ralcorp continue offering the promotion after General Mills and Kellogg have stopped offering it, they may be able to gain market share. As weaker players in the industry, they may prefer market share over profitability. Their actions, as well as those of General Mills and Kellogg, affect the outcome. Games that have more than two players are more common than games involving only two players, but they are harder to model. Sophisticated game theorists understand this problem and have explored complicated games that have many players over many iterations. Readers of this book can consult such works on game theory as Morton Davis's *Game Theory: A Non-Technical Introduction* (Dover Publications, 1997).

Learning from Game Theory

Game theory presents a number of enduring lessons. It emphasizes the importance of considering timing. The strategist must:

- Identify the competitors in a game.
- Try to understand their options.
- Try to compute the payoffs from the combinations of decisions they can make.
- Try to understand the sequence of their moves.[12]

The timing and ordering of strategic moves significantly affect the results. Using these methods, the analyst is able to make better, but not optimal, strategic choices.

Every strategic move has a timing dimension—the firm can act first or wait. In the real world, timing decisions rarely are formally modeled. They are made using *verbal logic.* They rely on arguments about past successes and failures which mislead companies. Wang Laboratories, for instance, was a pioneer in creating word processing software and office equipment to replace the typewriter, but it was unable to maintain the momentum and lost out when PCs became common. In contrast, pharmaceutical giant Hoffmann-LaRoche repeatedly reinvented itself, moving from vitamins at its origins to sulfa drugs in the 1930s and later into the tranquilizers Librium and Valium. A company must repeatedly try to be a leader.[13] Being a first mover only once is not enough.

The arguments for leadership include:

- The lags in time it will take a follower to catch up, during which time the leader can earn substantial profits.
- The ability during these lags to erect learning and scale barriers to entry.
- The ability to establish a reputation and to erect switching costs that make it hard for customers to abandon the firm.
- The preemption of scarce assets and resources, such as raw materials and distribution channels, which a follower cannot obtain.

However, followers are not without adequate defenses, such as:

- If they can avoid high development costs and learn from the leader's mistakes, they can best the first mover.
- They have options such as adding "bells and whistles" to a stripped-down product or service. They can outflank a first mover by creating products that are smaller or larger, more convenient, or lower-priced.
- They can reconceptualize products in ways that may not be open to the leader, which might find it hard to do anything other than what it has so far perfected. Followers may be able to leapfrog the first mover's accomplishments.

Not all first movers dominate, and few dominate forever. Intel has made a name for itself by being a leader in computer memory and microprocessors, whereas Microsoft has not followed this course but, rather, has been an aggressive follower that invaded and conquered markets pioneered by other firms (operating systems and browsers). As D'Aveni points out, a leader can "retain the initiative throughout each interaction, the follower can seize the initiative and retain it or can move back and forth."[14]

The lesson, to paraphrase Abraham Lincoln, is to focus on one's competitors and the moves they might make more than on oneself.[15] The key is not to view the situation exclusively from your own perspective but to be cognizant of competitors. Slip into their "shoes," and understand how they view the situation. Effectiveness is determined not by one's moves alone but by how one anticipates and addresses the moves and countermoves of competitors.

Be aware that a company can repeatedly win games, but still be a loser. When Monsanto's patent on NutraSweet, the artificial sweetener pioneered by Searle, a division of Monsanto, expired in 1987, Holland Sweetener attacked (see Exhibit 4.7).[16] In Europe, it introduced a cheap generic substitute. Monsanto had to lower the price of a pound of NutraSweet from $100 to $26. In Europe, Holland Sweetener brought a successful antidumping suit against Monsanto. It also made an aggressive bid for Monsanto's Coca-Cola and PepsiCo contracts, forcing Monsanto to give the cola companies combined savings of more than $200 million on their contracts for artificial sweeteners. But Monsanto's actions forced Holland Sweetener out of the U.S. market and drove the Dutch company to near bankruptcy. Monsanto protected its NutraSweet franchise; the competitive moves and countermoves were harmful to both companies.

Game theory's lesson is that one company's success is critically dependent on what other companies do. Best Buy's success has depended on what Circuit City did; Circuit City's failure depended on what Best Buy did. Charles Schwab's success has relied on what

EXHIBIT 4.7
NutraSweet: A Losing Game

Monsanto	Holland Sweetener
• NutraSweet patent expires in 1987	• Introduces generic substitute in Europe
• Lowers price from $100 a pound to $26	• Brings successful antidumping suit; makes aggressive bid for Coca-Cola and PepsiCo contracts
• Forced to give Coca-Cola and PepsiCo combined savings of $200 million	• Exits U.S. market near bankruptcy

Morgan Stanley has done; Morgan Stanley's success has depended on what Charles Schwab is doing. Coca-Cola's success depends on what PepsiCo does; PepsiCo's success depends on what Coca-Cola does.

The actions a firm takes elicits responses from its competitors that in turn elicit responses from the firm. Even when the firm decides to do nothing, it is making a choice. The decision not to make a move can be as important as the decision to do so.

Positioning

Positioning is central.[17] Where does a company want to go? According to Porter, moves position a company in four generic spaces based on two unique sources of competitive advantage—offering a similar product at a low cost or offering a unique product at a premium price (see Exhibit 4.8). The scope or breadth of the company's market (see Exhibit 4.9) also distinguishes between the positions a company can occupy. A market can be broad and include a wide range of products, customers, or geographies, or it can be narrow and apply to a focused group. Generic moves are the route to power, a means to control an industry's five forces.

Thus, a company can occupy four separate positions:

- Offering similar products at low cost to a narrow group of customers.
- Offering unique products at a premium price to a narrow group of customers.

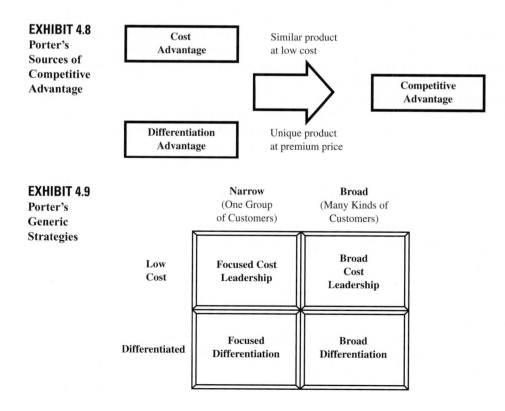

EXHIBIT 4.8
Porter's Sources of Competitive Advantage

EXHIBIT 4.9
Porter's Generic Strategies

EXHIBIT 4.10
Positioning in Retail

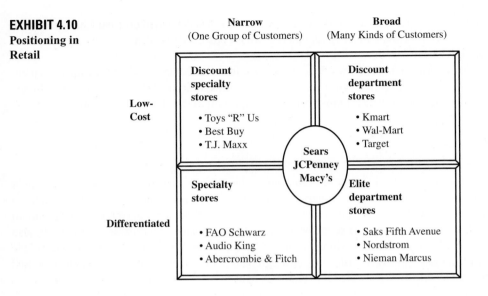

	Narrow (One Group of Customers)	Broad (Many Kinds of Customers)
Low-Cost	**Discount specialty stores** • Toys "R" Us • Best Buy • T.J. Maxx	**Discount department stores** • Kmart • Wal-Mart • Target
Differentiated	**Specialty stores** • FAO Schwarz • Audio King • Abercrombie & Fitch	**Elite department stores** • Saks Fifth Avenue • Nordstrom • Nieman Marcus

(Center: Sears, JCPenney, Macy's)

- Offering similar products at low cost to a broad group of customers.
- Offering unique products at a premium price to a broad group of customers.

Companies have positioning choices. A company can be a broad or narrow cost leader or a broad or a narrow differentiator, but Porter warns against being stuck in the middle, which he considers to be the worst position, a claim considered in more detail later in the chapter. As can be seen in Exhibit 4.10, which categorizes retail stores in this way, Sears, JCPenney, and Macy's occupy the middle ground, offering both low-cost and differentiated products to broad and narrow groups of customers. Exhibit 4.10 does not incorporate all the possibilities—the retail industry is too large and diverse, with many competitors jockeying for position and seizing the empty spaces. Stores such as Kohl's, Mervyns, Sam's Club, Costco, and Family Dollar would push the exhibit's limits.

Some companies own stores in a number of categories: Target once had its namesake stores as well as stores in the Marshall Field's and Mervyns formats. The Gap occupies the narrow low-cost position with its Old Navy stores and the narrow differentiated position with its Banana Republic stores, as well as the position between with its Gap stores. Many companies, including Abercrombie & Fitch, Eddie Bauer, and J. Crew, occupy the same narrow differentiated position as Banana Republic.

Almost every industry can be conceived in this way, from groceries and restaurants to heavy machinery and insurance. Both the low-cost and the differentiated positions are built on unique value chain configurations and linkages that competitors cannot imitate. But both require continuous improvement and the search for new edges to maintain a leadership position.

The **low-cost position** is based on high-volume sales of low-margin items. Low-cost products are usually no-frills items, but this does not mean they can be inferior. They must be of acceptable quality and have features that meet consumers' needs. Superior advantage in a low-cost position comes from creating a significant and sustainable cost gap relative to competitors and managing critical cost drivers well. This cost gap translates into superior margins when the company commands prices at or near industry averages. A cost leader, however, cannot let prices fall so low that they neutralize a cost advantage.

The **differentiated position** is based on low-volume sales of high-margin items. Customers are willing to pay a premium price for a differentiated product or service because the item satisfies some specialized need or craving that cannot otherwise be satisfied. Uniqueness can be achieved through many means—design or brand image, technological features, customer service, and specialized dealer networks, creative advertising, product innovations, a high level of quality, and/or relations with suppliers. The key to following a successful differentiation strategy is to offer customers something for which they are willing to pay substantially more than the costs incurred by the firm in creating it.

The financial services industry provides an example of these contrasting models (see Exhibit 4.11). Online brokers occupy the extreme-low-cost position. Their margins are very low, but they try to compensate for this with a business model that calls for a very high number of transactions. Many firms have occupied or tried to occupy this niche—TD Waterhouse, E-Trade, Siebert and Company, Ameritrade, and Datek. The niche, however, was a very precarious one to sustain when the brokerage industry suffered from the stock market's collapse and stagnancy.

The traditional full-service model was highly differentiated. It rested on personalized, premium-quality, full-service advice. Commissioned brokers were handsomely compensated for providing this service. Again, many firms once competed in this niche, including Merrill Lynch, Morgan Stanley, and Goldman Sachs. By providing very specialized investment products, they were competing for the business of high-net-worth individuals.

Charles Schwab tried to break with the highly differentiated model of the full-service investment firms by being a discount broker. It eliminated advice, reduced commissions, and

EXHIBIT 4.11
Business Models in Financial Services

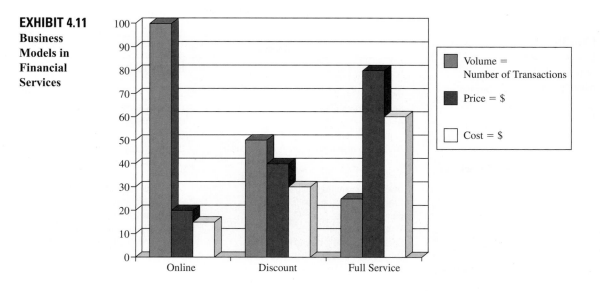

offered transactions only from a salaried sales force. Although it invested in branch offices and technology, its overhead was far lower than that of the full-service brokers, so it could afford to be a low-cost operator.

However, the online brokers, whose cost structure is even lower than Schwab's, out-flanked Schwab, forcing it into the middle. Finding itself between the extreme online discounters and the old-time, full-service brokers, Schwab tried to turn its position into an advantage by calling it a "category of one." It is now a powerful online force but it also has tried to compete with the full-service brokers for the accounts of high-net-worth individuals. It invests in affiliated professional account managers to whom it refers "preferred clients."

Keep in mind that the entire industry has been under duress and has been fighting over a shrinking pie as the global economic meltdown has set in. All of these business models have been in trouble. A firm with an entirely new model and the dynamic capability to revolutionize the industry might be able to pull ahead and emerge as the industry leader. There is opportunity in this disarray.

Are Low Cost and Differentiation Incompatible?

Porter has held that the middle position is untenable. If a middle position is the weakest. Schwab will not be able to sustain its middle position.

Porter maintains that it is essential for managers of a company to understand which type of advantage they are trying to achieve—low cost *or* differentiation—because the internal resources and capabilities needed to support one are not compatible with the internal resources and capabilities needed to support the other (see Exhibit 4.12). In retailing, for example, Sears, JCPenney, and Macy's have been stuck in the middle and have had trouble competing with rivals that follow a more differentiated or lower-cost strategy.

Why is it so difficult to occupy the middle? Think of the differences between a famous artist, who has to sell only a few paintings at very high margins to survive, and a pin

EXHIBIT 4.12
Low-Cost and Differentiation Strategies: Resources and Capabilities

Generic Strategy		
	Cost Leadership	**Differentiation**
Resources		
	Scale-efficient plants	Branding and brand advertising
	Access to capital	Custom design
	Control of overheads and R&D	Special services
	Avoidance of marginal customer accounts	Unique quality features
Capabilities		
	Design for manufacturing skills	Marketing product
	Process engineering skills	Engineering creativity
	Frequent reports	Product R&D
	Tight cost control	Qualitative measurement/incentives
	Specialization of jobs and functions	Strong cross-functional coordination
	Quantitative measurement/incentives	

manufacturer, which must sell millions of pins at very low margins to survive. Now imagine trying to combine both *successfully.*

To be a cost leader, a company must be run like a pin factory. It must be highly efficient; it has to divide the labor and carry out tasks according to detailed instructions; and it has to have many quantitative checkpoints and frequent feedback to ensure that goals are met. Recall the discussion of Taylor and scientific management in Chapter 3. Employees in a low-cost business have to be closely supervised. They must work to schedule on highly mechanized tasks. Their work is closely coordinated with machines, and neither workers nor machines can be allowed to be idle. In a pin factory, the value comes not from the uniqueness of the creation but from its sameness. Deviations are not tolerated; every pin has to be exactly alike.

A differentiated firm is more like an artist's studio than a pin factory. The resources and capabilities needed to be a differentiator involve a high degree of freedom and improvisation. The success of a differentiated firm depends on its employees' creativity. Employees have to be given the chance to experiment, and failure must be allowed. Like the artist, the differentiated firm thrives on individuality.

A cost leader, in accord with the terms used in Chapter 3, needs a mechanistic organization, while differentiation relies on an organic organization. Advertising, book publishing, consulting, and the movies are examples of organizations producing highly differentiated products, while McDonald's and Burger King are examples of organizations producing similar products at low cost.

Low cost is mainly achieved by spreading fixed costs over large volumes and investing in large and technologically sophisticated capital equipment. The firm gains knowledge and experience from doing the same thing many times. The practical implications are very low margins. Market share is critical for sustaining competitive advantage, and to gain market share, the firm must engage in heavy discounting and promotions. The risks associated with this strategy are that the firm may not be able to detect needed marketing or product changes because of its obsession with cost. Because of technological breakthroughs, its plant and equipment might become obsolete, but the large investments needed for modernizing will make it disinclined to change. The firm also may go too far in cutting costs, thereby alienating customers through cheap products and employees because of low wages or poor working conditions. Competitors may be quick to catch up with any cost-saving methods the firm uses.

Product differentiation, on the other hand, is achieved mainly by producing a high-quality product and being responsive to customers. Because differentiation costs money, Porter argues that it is not compatible with low cost. High margins make up for the low volume. The risks associated with differentiation are that customers may not be willing to pay the high price for differentiated features; they may no longer perceive the special features as adding value; competitors may be able to copy the special features; and to maintain advantage, constant innovation, which subjects the firm to great pressure, is needed.

The New Alternative: Best Value

The old orthodoxy was that cost and quality were incompatible. Customers could not have a selection of products that met their specialized needs at a low price. The Model T came in only one color—black. Customers had to either accept a single product at low price or pay for unique features customized to their needs. This belief that the middle position is not sustainable has been breaking down for a number of reasons:[18]

1. Product innovations undermined the low-cost strategy. For instance, the replacement of black-and-white TVs with color TVs and that of transistors with semiconductors showed the futility of chasing large volumes. A company could be the low-cost producer of black-and-white TVs or transistors, but their obsolescence doomed this strategy to failure.

2. Successful companies have shown that they can *combine* low cost and differentiation in attractive, value-for-the-money packages. McDonald's success, for instance, has been built on more than cheap burgers. The food is reliable, the service is fast, and the facilities are comparatively clean. The advertising creates an image that appeals to customers. Similarly, Toyota proved that inexpensive cars did not have to suffer from the maintenance and safety problems of U.S. counterparts such as the Corvair and Pinto. Low-price cars can be built well, be safe to drive, and last for years. Another example is the Swedish retailer IKEA, which has succeeded with its concept of "democratic design"— furniture that is attractive, high-quality, inexpensive, and highly functional.

Flexible and lean production methods are enabling companies to combine the benefits of low cost and differentiation. The new position toward which many companies are moving is not low cost or differentiation but *best value*.[19] The capabilities needed to achieve a **best-value strategy** include team-based product development, closely integrated supply chains, and reliance on total quality management (TQM) principles.

Team-Based Product Development

The sharing and pooling of information and ideas among teams of people traditionally kept apart can make business processes more fluid, efficient, and effective. In a *sequential* product development process, decisions move from one functional group—research, design, manufacturing, marketing—to another, with each function providing input only once.[20] In a *parallel* process, the groups combine to work together as a team, with each providing input at each stage. Thus, issues that arise do not get passed from group to group for consideration, as in an assembly line; the participants can consider many issues simultaneously. If a mistake is made, it can be corrected without having to return to the beginning and start again.

Integrated Supply Chains

In the **just-in-time (JIT) approach** to inventory management, the firm produces only what the customer wants in the quantities the customer actually requires and when the customer needs it. This has led to faster turnover and shorter production lines. There is less material usage, less waste, and fewer defects.

Total Quality Management

Deming's steps to improve corporate quality were like a chain reaction in that each built on the other.[21] These steps consisted of:

1. Improved quality.
2. Productivity improvement.
3. Higher market share.

4. Increased profitability.

5. More jobs.

Under the Deming system, low cost was combined with high quality. Implementing **total quality management (TQM)** means sharing close relations with a few trusted suppliers rather than having power over suppliers, as in Porter's framework. In contrast to Porter, it also means focusing on customers rather than achieving power over them. A company practicing TQM has to reduce the number of components, operations, and suppliers and cut distance and inventory in the flow of goods and services to customers. It also has to intimately understand its customers and dedicate itself to continual, rapid improvement in response time, quality, flexibility, and cost.

The end result of using methods such as these is an ability to develop successful *best-value niches* in the middle ground. Increasingly, companies are positioning themselves in such niches, showing that it is possible to fuse characteristics that Porter had believed to be incompatible. Best Buy with its combination of myth products and commodities is a good example of a company that has found a home in the middle. Dell, too, has been very comfortable operating in this space.

Repositioning

Porter's generic strategies, thus, have been increasingly challenged. D'Aveni argues that Porter's concept of four generic strategies is a static view of strategic maneuvering:[22] A more dynamic model of price–quality advantages would consider how competitors will react and maneuver around the price–quality positions that rivals stake out. It will ask, how do firms change their relative positions over time to create advantage?

According to D'Aveni, Porter fails to sufficiently account for the fact that the positions companies occupy are not stable: Over time, in response to competitive challenges, companies move from position to position.[23]

As argued before, it was fast movement that allowed Best Buy to widen the gap between itself and Circuit City. Best Buy went from a narrow differentiated position to a narrow low-cost one (see Exhibit 4.13).[24] It started as a high-quality stereo store for audiophiles, with

EXHIBIT 4.13
**Best Buy:
From a
Differentiated
to a Best-Value
Strategy**

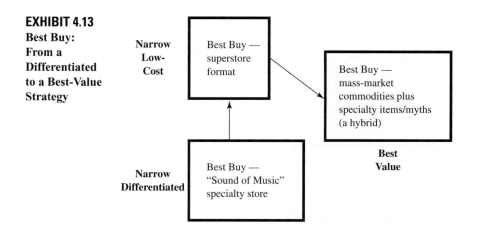

a few stores in Minneapolis/St. Paul, Minnesota, before it moved to its current niche as a low-cost electronics outlet, but it did not stop there:

- Concept One was introduced in 1983 because the company feared extinction. Best Buy expanded its floor space and selection, priced competitively, and created a very exciting store environment. Best Buy wanted to be the "fun place to shop" for the 18- to 25-year-old male.
- In 1989, the company rolled out Concept Two. No longer satisfied with its position as a low-cost leader, Best Buy combined mass-market and specialty retailing. It offered value products in select categories without the selling pressure of a commissioned sales force. Best Buy was in a sense returning to its roots as a specialty store—the Sound of Music. Concept Two was extremely successful, allowing Best Buy to overtake Circuit City in sales, but the run-up in sales was not matched by a concomitant growth in earnings.
- Concept Three was designed to address the earnings problem by positioning the company as even more of a hybrid. Best Buy offered both high-margin myth products and low-margin commodity elements. This strategy mixed low cost and differentiation and moved the company closer to the middle.

Each phase in Best Buy's development was built on the previous one. As it repositioned again and again, the company held on to elements of its old image even while it branched out and developed new ones. Customers liked the stores because they had everyday low prices and were bright, fun, leading-edge places.

Considerable repositioning has occurred in the securities industry as well. As discussed earlier, Schwab moved from its low-cost position as a discount broker to a middle position by offering full services to high-net-worth individuals. At the same time that Schwab was undergoing its transformation, full-service brokers such as Morgan Stanley also were changing (see Exhibit 4.14). Morgan Stanley made its move toward the middle by purchasing

EXHIBIT 4.14
Schwab and Morgan Stanley: From Polar Opposites to the Middle

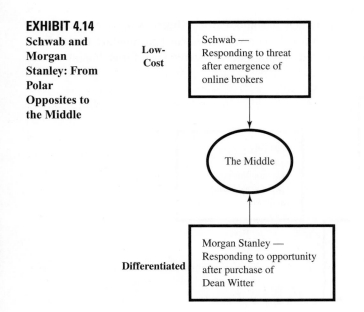

EXHIBIT 4.15
Ivory: From a Differentiated to a Low-Cost Strategy

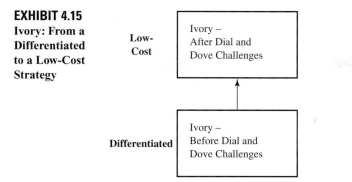

Dean Witter in 1997. It obtained more than 10,000 brokers whose clients were not the high-net-worth individuals to whom Morgan Stanley traditionally had catered. The culture of exclusivity had to give way to a more common appeal as the firm merged two powerful, very different organizations.

Porter himself provides an extremely interesting example of product repositioning: Ivory started as a differentiated soap.[25] In 1879, when more than 300 companies produced crude, inexpensive soaps, Ivory was the first pure and mild brand. It had no harsh ingredients, and it floated. Ivory was heavily advertised, and the company's message was purity ("99.44 percent" pure). Ivory aggressively used comparison ads and the endorsements of chemists and physicians to certify the pure image. Early on, it adopted the image of a baby and the slogan, "If it's mild enough for the baby, it's mild enough for you." Ivory sold at a premium price and commanded a leading share of the market until it was challenged by Dial, the first deodorant soap, and by Dove, the first beauty bar. In response to these challenges, Procter & Gamble decided not to add these features but to reposition Ivory as a basic, good-value soap. Ivory went from differentiation to cost leader (see Exhibit 4.15). It quickly established itself in a leading market position as the simple, no-frills soap that was sold in the package with no shiny paper or garish colors. Procter & Gamble pioneered the idea of bundling bars of soap by selling six bars of Ivory together. Its advertising stressed that Ivory was a great soap and a great value: "We probably should charge more for great soap like Ivory." Contributing to Ivory's low cost was its air bubbles, which not only allowed it to float but also reduced the material needed to manufacture it. It also lacked expensive additives like those in Dial and Dove. Its simple packaging was inherently cheaper, and its long and consistent brand image controlled advertising costs. It also was a traffic builder for retailers, so Procter & Gamble did not have to spend much on trade promotion.

The history of Ivory as well as the other companies discussed negates the idea of a product life cycle in which maturity in whatever space a company occupies—low cost or highly differentiated—is inevitable. These examples show change and continuity among brands. They show brands that are almost alive to consumers with a personality—a set of character traits that consumers immediately recognize because of the brand's or the company's history.

Strategic Groups: Company Segmentation

As the examples suggest, there are many ways to differentiate. The strategist's job is to identify principal variables that distinguish **strategic groups** (see earlier discussion in Chapter 1) where similar strategies are followed.[26] In the pharmaceutical industry, there are price

EXHIBIT 4.16
Forest Labs Changes Strategic Groups in the Pharmaceutical Industry

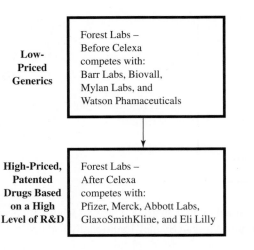

Low-Priced Generics	Forest Labs – Before Celexa competes with: Barr Labs, Biovall, Mylan Labs, and Watson Phamaceuticals
High-Priced, Patented Drugs Based on a High Level of R&D	Forest Labs – After Celexa competes with: Pfizer, Merck, Abbott Labs, GlaxoSmithKline, and Eli Lilly

and R&D distinctions. Companies high on both attributes sell patented medicines, while companies with the opposite tendencies sell generic medicines. These are the two most important strategic groups in the pharmaceutical industry (see Exhibit 4.16).

The resources, capabilities, and competencies needed to compete in these groups are different; thus the barriers to entering them are not alike. Movement from segment to segment is difficult, as doing so requires the acquisition of new resources, capabilities, and competencies. Nonetheless, Forest Labs did make this move. It moved from the generic drug group to the proprietary (patented-drug) group on the basis of its successful antidepressant drug, Celexa. Forest Labs was a very agile company. It started in 1956 as a vitamin and candy company. Then it moved into generic drugs, competing with the likes of Watson Pharmaceuticals. Next it started marketing an angina drug (Tiazac) in Europe. This was followed by its marketing of Celexa, a Danish-produced, high-efficacy antidepressant with few side effects—a move that brought Forest into competition with the large pharmaceutical companies.

Forest Labs moved into this position in a relatively short time. In 2003, it achieved a 9.8 percent market share in the very lucrative U.S. antidepressant market, with sales of Celexa accounting for 70 percent of the company's revenues. Its small size in comparison to the pharmaceutical giants allowed it to make a quick move into a new competitive space. Forest was very focused; it vigorously marketed only a few drugs at a time, and it even started to engage in large-scale R&D in competition with the major drug companies. The drugs in its pipeline are focused on diseases of the elderly, which is sure to be a strong market in the future. A segment, while it can be very competitive within, is supposed to be protected from without by entry barriers, but Forest Labs demonstrated that entry barriers can be breached.

Within every segment, positioning leaves empty spaces for new players. In low-cost, mass-merchandise retailing, Target tries to be more upscale, Kmart tries to compete as the low-cost alternative, and Walmart is in the middle—nonetheless, opportunities still exist for differentiation. Family Dollar went after low-income families by opening small neighborhood stores. It created a new segment based on a different business model, one that matched buyers and products in a novel way: a discount chain that offers customers value via low-cost, basic merchandise in stores less than one-tenth the size of a typical Walmart. The first store opened in 1959 in Charlotte, North Carolina; by 2002, Family Dollar operated 4,693 stores in 41 states and employed more than 25,000 people. Its company expanded solely by relying on retained earnings—it had zero debt. Its stores are in both rural and urban areas, but the company's recent expansion has been concentrated in inner-city, urban neighborhoods. The stores offer a variety of products including clothing, blankets, sheets, towels, household chemical and paper products, candy, and health and beauty aids. All stores are similar in appearance, and they have the same policies (e.g., none accepts credit cards or extends credit). They are low cost and user friendly in a way that Walmart cannot match.

Segmentation by Product or Service

The ability to find new opportunities comes from understanding product attributes not well covered by existing players in the marketplace. The evolution of pain relievers is an interesting example. At one time, there was the high-on-effectiveness, low-gentleness cluster, which consisted of Excedrin, Anacin, and Bufferin. Of these, Excedrin was highest on effectiveness and lowest on gentleness; Bufferin was highest on gentleness and lowest on effectiveness; and Anacin was somewhere in between (see Exhibit 4.17). All three were considered to be an improvement over aspirin. Tylenol had the gentleness space to itself, although it was not perceived to be as effective as the other analgesics.

The existence of these products, however, did not preclude other options; it still left spaces open for additional painkillers and painkilling methods. Some of the pain relievers filling those spaces claimed to be even more effective, such as ibuprofen; some were more specialized, like Celebrex and Vioxx; some were more powerful and required prescriptions, such as Darvon and Darvocet; and some were totally different. Meditation, acupuncture, electrostimulation, massage, acupressure, and relaxation were highest on gentleness, but

EXHIBIT 4.17
Perceptions of Painkillers

Source: Adapted from R. Grant, *Contemporary Strategy Analysis,* 4th ed., 2002. Reprinted with permission of Blackwell Publishing.

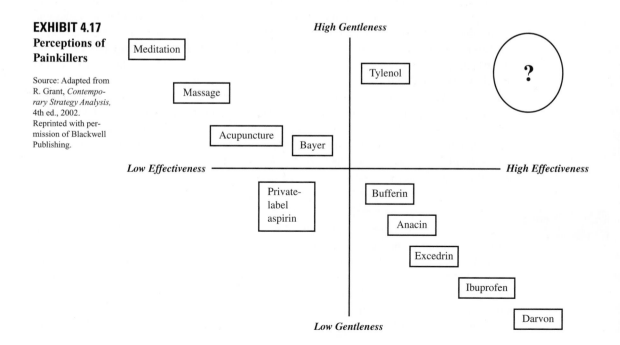

were they really effective in killing pain? The search for the highly effective, extremely gentle pain reliever continues.

A product or service can be segmented in many ways:[27]

- *Industrial buyers* can be divided by industry, strategies that the firms pursue in their industry (low-cost or differentiation), size and type of ownership, decision-making unit or process, order pattern, technical sophistication, and the extent to which they serve the original equipment manufacturers (OEM) or the replacement market.
- *Household buyers* can be divided by demographics, lifestyle, language, and purchasing process and occasion.
- *Distribution channels* can be partitioned into direct distributors, wholesalers, brokers, and other intermediaries, as well as retail, mail order, phone, and the Internet. These channels can be exclusive or nonexclusive, generalists or specialists.
- *Geographic area* can be segmented by locality, region, nation, blocs of nations, continents, weather zones, and other distinguishing features.
- *Attributes* of a product or service can be grouped on the basis of physical size, price level, packaging, promotion, color, appearance, physical feel and other product features, technology, design, inputs or raw materials needed to use the product or service (e.g., an ink cartridge for a printer), actual performance characteristics in comparison to other products or services of its type, or presale and postsale services provided.

There are also many ways to bundle or separate aspects of the product or service mix to create categories. A product's differentiation involves both tangible and intangible aspects. The *tangible* aspects include all the observable product characteristics such as size, color, materials used to make the product, packaging, and complementary services. The *intangible* aspects include unobservable and subjective qualities—image, status, exclusivity, and identity. The total value of a product to the customer is conveyed not just by the functions the product performs but by the entire relationship with the customer.

People often define themselves in terms of what they buy. Those who buy Ivory soap are expressing different views of themselves than are those who buy Dial or Dove. Those who use alternative medicines are making a different statement about themselves than are those who use conventional ones. Those who shop in Target as opposed to Walmart, Kmart, or Family Dollar are also saying something different about themselves. We all know that Harley-Davidson is more than a motorcycle company and Starbucks is more than a coffee shop. People buy from these companies because it provides them with status and identity. The strategist must appeal to this need for status and identification, as it is an excellent source of differentiation.

Summary

After analyzing the external and internal environments, the strategist has to set up an array of alternative moves and analyze their relative benefits. These moves have two components—timing and positioning. Should a firm go first with the moves it is capable of making? How should the managers of a company approach timing? Game theory offers a methodology for dealing with this question: When managers contemplate a move, they have to consider how their rivals will respond and what the payoffs will be depending on the likely responses of the rivals. Moves are not made in isolation. They are carried out in a competitive context in which rivals make countermoves that can neutralize the effects of the moves a company makes. The potential countermoves have to be considered before the corporation acts.

Moreover, a strategist must think not just about single moves in isolation but about series of moves. He or she has to consider how the relationships among the moves and the responses to the moves will affect a company's future performance. Simply put, the moves a company makes must have consistency. They cannot be onetime thrusts, but must be a set of coordinated actions over time. The reason for making strategic moves is to position and reposition the firm so that it is less vulnerable to the competition and better able to stave it off.

Porter posits that companies can move into four basic, or generic, positions. These positions are depicted in a matrix in which low cost and differentiated are the vertical cells and broad and narrow (focus) are the horizontal cells. Porter has argued that sustained competitive advantage can be achieved either by being in a high-volume, low-margin business or by being in a low-volume, high-margin business. He warned that being stuck in the middle was the sure route to sustained competitive disadvantage since the resources, capabilities, and competencies that a company needs to be in a high-volume, low-margin business are incompatible with the ones it needs to be in a low-volume, high-margin business.

Many companies, however, have transcended this dilemma and achieved sustained competitive advantage by combining elements of low-cost and highly differentiated strategies. They use such methods as sequential teams in product development, just-in-time inventory management, and the principles of total quality management to develop unique niches that combine low cost and differentiation. This combination is called a best-value strategy, or a strategy of delivering to customers the best value for their money regardless of where the company stands on the low-cost–differentiated continuum. Increasingly, companies are moving toward the best-value position, and many have thrived by tilting their business in this direction.

Carefully analyzing the competitive space in which a company operates will identify unrealized opportunities. Finding these unrealized opportunities is one of the strategist's most important jobs.

Endnotes

1. R. D'Aveni, *Hypercompetition* (New York: Free Press, 1994).
2. Ibid.
3. D'Aveni's concern is with rivals that can circumvent or overcome entry barriers and the responses incumbents have to make. He deals with changes in the five forces. What if the firm increases its power over suppliers? How will the suppliers react?
4. M. Lieberman and D. Montgomery, "First-Mover Advantages," *Strategic Management Journal* 8 (1988), pp. 441–52; and "First-Mover (Dis)advantages: Retrospective and Link with the Resources-Based View," *Strategic Management Journal* 19 (1998), pp. 1111–25.
5. B. Charkravarthy and V. Kasturi, "Best Buy," Harvard Business School/Strategic Management Research Center University of Minnesota case 9-598-016, revised October 28, 1967.
6. K. Eisenhardt and J. Martin, "Dynamic Capabilities: What Are They?" *Strategic Management Journal* 21 (2000), p. 1107.
7. D. Teece, G. Pisano, and A. Sheun, "Dynamic Capabilities and Strategic Management," *Strategic Management Journal* 18 (1997), pp. 509–33.

8. D. Miller, *The Icarus Paradox* (New York: HarperBusiness, 1990).

9. D. Smith and R. Alexander, *Fumbling the Future* (New York: William Morrow, 1988).

10. S. Oster, *Modern Competitive Analysis,* 2nd ed. (New York: Oxford University Press, 1994). On the Web, a game theory simulator can be accessed at http://broadcast.forio.com/sims/pricing/.

11. S. Makridakis and S. Wheelwright, *The Handbook of Forecasting,* 2nd ed. (New York: Wiley and Sons, 1987).

12. D. Spulber, *Management Strategy* (New York: McGraw-Hill/Irwin, 2004).

13. D'Aveni, *Hypercompetition*.

14. Ibid., p. 99.

15. A. Brandenburger and B. Nalebuff, *Co-opetition* (New York: Currency Doubleday, 1996), p. 61.

16. Ibid., pp. 72–76.

17. M. Porter, *Competitive Strategy: Techniques for Analyzing Industries and Competitors* (New York: Free Press, 1980); and M. Porter, *Competitive Advantage: Creating and Sustaining Superior Performance* (New York: Free Press, 1985).

18. C. Hill and R. Jones, *Strategic Management,* 6th ed. (Boston: Houghton Mifflin, 2004).

19. J. Harrision, *Strategic Management* (New York: Wiley and Sons, 2003), pp. 156–60.

20. M. Schilling and C. Hill, "Managing the New Product Development Process," *Academy of Management Executive* 12, no. 3 (1998), pp. 67–81.

21. W. Deming, *Out of the Crisis* (Cambridge, MA: MIT, 1986).

22. D'Aveni, *Hypercompetition,* p. 14.

23. Ibid.

24. Charkravarthy and Kasturi, "Best Buy."

25. "Michael Porter on Competitive Strategy," Harvard Business School video, 1988.

26. Porter, *Competitive Strategy*.

27. R. Grant, *Contemporary Strategy Analysis,* 4th ed. (Oxford, England: Blackwell, 2002), p. 121.

CHAPTER FIVE

Mergers, Acquisitions, and Divestitures

"The variety of effects that may result from a merger and acquisition is surprising. . . . Mergers may involve firms selling close substitutes (such as Volvo and Scania truck) to complements (HP printers and Compaq computers). Mergers may reduce competition or facilitate collusion, thus increasing prices. But they also may create synergies that reduce cost and ultimately depress prices. . . . Mergers may involve domestic firms (such as Boeing and McDonnell Douglas) but they might involve foreign competitors. Mergers may be highly profitable though more than a few of them have resulted in large losses."[1]

Duarte Brito and Magarita Catalao-Lopes

Chapter Learning Objectives

- Understanding the difference between business and corporate strategy.
- Being cognizant of the different forms of firm organization including horizontal and vertical integration.
- Being aware of the reasons there has been so much merger, acquisition, and divestiture activity.
- Understanding the motivations for this activity, the outcomes of this activity, and what can be learned from it.
- Realizing how such factors as deregulation have speeded up the pace of this activity.
- Becoming acquainted with portfolio management techniques such as the BCG matrix and the GE/McKinsey model.
- Examining vertical integration.

Introduction

This chapter moves our analysis of strategic management from business to corporate strategy. **Business strategy** deals with how the firm competes—should it be low cost, differentiated, or some combination of the two? **Corporate strategy** focuses on the scope of the firm—what business or businesses should it be in? It includes such issues as determining how broad or narrow the field of the firm's business operations should be. With regard to such matters as product, geography, and value chain, should it have a narrow or broad focus?

There are four basic options for changing a firm's scope:

- It can do so through internal ventures and development.
- It can partner with and form alliances with other firms, for example, through joint ventures.
- It can acquire or merge with firms that have the resources, capabilities, and competencies it needs.
- It can eliminate businesses by divesting, liquidating, selling, or disposing of them.

Different Forms a Firm Can Take

These moves can take the firm in a number of different directions (see Exhibit 5.1).[2] The firm can engage in **horizontal integration;** that is, it can increase market share by purchasing companies that are in the same business line it is in. Another option is to diversify. *Dominant-product* firms diversify to a minor degree, but typically no more than about 30 percent. At least 70 percent of their sales continue to come from a single product or market area. *Related-product* firms diversify into new product areas that share market or technological features with the company's existing products.

Vertically integrated firms operate in a number of different parts of the value chain. In **vertical integration,** the firm combines production, distribution, and/or sales in the same company. Large petroleum companies are classic examples: They simultaneously explore for oil, transport it, refine it, sell or use the chemical by-products, and operate retail gas stations.

Conglomerates, or *unrelated diversified* firms, are a collection of discrete businesses operating in the same company. The theory behind this arrangement is that the businesses

EXHIBIT 5.1
Expanding the Scope of the Firm: Five Choices

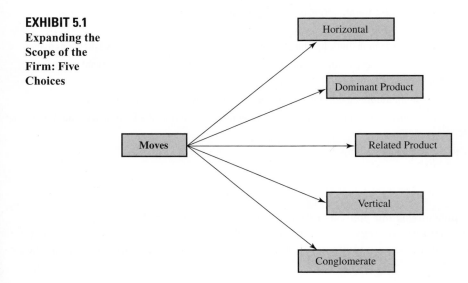

EXHIBIT 5.2
The Main
Tasks of
Corporate
Strategy

Determine the scope of the firm.
  Decide what business or businesses to be in.
  • *Should the portfolio be broad or narrow?*
      Horizontal, dominant product, related product, vertical, or conglomerate
  • *What merger, acquisition, and divestiture (MAD) strategy should be
    adopted?*
Create cohesiveness and direction among the assembled pieces.
  Allocate resources to the different businesses.
  Help formulate their business strategies.
  Coordinate their activities.
  Control their performance.

return more to shareholders by being together than they would if they were separate. Some firms have proved to be much better than others at managing a broad portfolio of businesses. GE, for instance, has a stellar reputation for managing its many diversified businesses; in fact, its distinctive competence may lie in this area.

Once these decisions about a firm's scope are made, the main task of corporate strategy is to create cohesiveness and direction (see Exhibit 5.2). Management must allocate resources to the assembled units and hold them accountable for performance. Portfolio management methods, including those developed by the Boston Consulting Group, McKinsey & Company, and GE, will be examined later in the chapter.

Mergers, Acquisitions, and Divestitures: The Record Thus Far

In making decisions about the scope of the firm, the company must consider mergers, acquisitions, and divestitures. However, the record of firms conducting mergers and acquisitions is not particularly good. While the share price of firms that are sold usually goes up, buyers' share prices often go down, as shown by the data in Exhibit 5.3. Why? The buyer's decision making often is flawed in that it pays too much for firms it acquires or it cannot execute on its designs and effectively integrate the new units.

In a study of acquisitions of greater than $500 million in value from 1990 to 1995, Mercer Management Consulting found a success rate of just 17 percent.[3] A 2002 study by *BusinessWeek* concluded there had been "no improvement in CEOs' deal-making skills since 1995, when *BusinessWeek*'s major survey of mergers in the early 1990s found that half were failures."[4] *BusinessWeek* wrote:

> The M&A (mergers and acquisition) bonanza during those six years (1995–2001) . . . was five times greater than any previous M&A boom in U.S. economic history. Why were shareholders left with such a hangover after the binge? The main conclusions of our study: Fully 61 percent of buyers destroyed their own shareholders' wealth. A year after their deals, the losers' average return was 25 percentage points below their industry peers'. The gains of the winning minority could not make up for the buyers' losses: The average return for all buyers was 4.3 percent below their peers and 9.2 percent below the S&P.[5]

The magazine continued, "An army of consultants and bankers has tried to help CEOs improve their success rate. But they've failed."

EXHIBIT 5.3 **Changes in Share Prices after Mergers**

Source: Reprinted with permission from *BusinessWeek,* October 14, 2002.

Buyer	Industry	Target	Date	Value* (Billions)	Premium†	Returns‡ Seller Initial	Returns‡ Buyer Initial	Returns‡ Buyer 1 Year
America Online	Internet Software	Time Warner	1/00	$165.9	55.8%	11%	1%	17%
Pfizer	Pharmaceuticals	Warner-Lambert	11/99	93.9	29.7	20	−12	1
Exxon	Oil & Gas	Mobil	12/98	77.2	34.7	18	1	−5
Travelers Group (1)	Insurance	Citicorp	4/98	70.0	10.4	8	6	2
SBC Communications	Telecom Services	Ameritech	5/98	61.4	23.1	3	−8	−19
Nationsbank (2)	Banks	BankAmerica	4/98	59.3	48.4	2	4	4
AT&T	Telecom Services	MediaOne Group	4/99	55.8	24.3	18	−6	−4
Bell Atlantic (3)	Telecom Services	GTE	7/98	52.8	3.8	−1	5	6
Viacom	Media	CBS	9/99	40.4	4.0	5	6	32
Qwest Communications	Telecom Services	US West	6/99	40.3	27.5	4	−23	21
Daimler-Benz	Automobiles	Chrysler	5/98	38.6	54.3	16	−6	−30
JDS Uniphase	Communications Equipment	SDL	7/00	38.1	59.7	24	−19	−14
Chase Manhattan (4)	Financial	JP Morgan	9/00	36.3	28.9	1	−16	−10
Chevron	Oil & Gas	Texaco	10/00	35.8	24.8	12	−3	10
Norwest (5)	Banks	Wells Fargo	6/98	33.9	0.9	−3	−11	10

*Value of offer when announced.
†Difference between the offer price and the seller's market price one week before the announcement.
‡Percentage-point difference between company returns and indexes of S&P 500 peers from one week before announcement to one week (initial) and one year after.
Current name: (1) Citigroup, (2) Bank of America, (3) Verizon, (4) JPMorgan Chase, (5) Wells Fargo
Data: Standard & Poor's, Mergerstat, Boston Consulting Group, Inc., Thomson Financial.

These poor results bring up a number of questions:

- Why has there been so much of this activity?
- What are the motivations for and outcome of it?
- What can be learned to make it more likely that mergers and acquisitions will succeed?

A Poor Record of Past Performance

From 1998 through 2000, nearly $4 trillion was spent on mergers and acquisitions—more money than in the preceding 30 years combined.[6] There were blockbuster deals between Pfizer and Pharmacia, Hewlett-Packard and Compaq, and other companies. The deals were concentrated in certain industries. The telecommunications and communications-equipment industries led the way with 5 out of the top 15 deals in the 1998–2000 period. The banking, financial, and insurance industries were not far behind, with 4 out of the top 15 deals. The largest deal, valued at $165.9 billion, was between AOL and Time Warner.

External factors influenced this activity. Competition intensified in the United States and other countries because of deregulation and privatization, rapid technological change, and in some instances industry maturity. Globalization played a part, as did the development of the Internet. With traditional industry boundaries blurring, searching for the right mix of businesses to ensure corporate survival was a trial-and-error effort. Because the environment was turbulent, it made sense for firms to restructure.

Much of restructuring, however, has not been successful. For example, AT&T spent $7.5 billion in 1990 to buy the computer manufacturer NCR, only to dispose of it five years later, taking a $1.2 billion charge, laying off 10,000 employees, and losing $500 million. Many firms, including AT&T, ITT, Hanson PLC, W. R. Grace, Sprint, Tenneco, Sears, and GM, had to reverse steps they had taken. They liquidated assets and broke up portfolios because the mix of businesses they assembled did not work well together.

Bad deals were common. The German automaker Daimler made a mistake when it bought Chrysler, a decision it had to reverse in 2007 when it sold the bulk of the company to private equity firm Cerberus because of large financial losses. Cerberus' acquisition of Chrysler also has been a flop. Ebay overpaid for the Internet telephone service Skype in 2005; it had to take a $1.4 billion writedown in 2007. The Time Warner and AOL deal, which never worked as planned, is generally considered to be the worst combination in history (see Exhibit 5.3). However, the 1965 deal that brought together PepsiCo and Frito-Lay is seen as a success. News Corp.'s purchase of social networking site MySpace shows promise, while the results of its purchase of *The Wall Street Journal* are yet to be seen.

A Shifting Landscape

While who wins and who loses as a result of mergers, acquisitions, and divestitures often is not clear, it is certain that mergers, acquisitions, and divestitures shift the corporate landscape. For example, in Minneapolis-St. Paul:

- Grand Metropolitan Ltd., the large U.K. food conglomerate, acquired Pillsbury; Silicon Graphics acquired Cray; Federated Department Stores acquired Fingerhut; and Conseco acquired Green Tree Financial.
- Grand Metropolitan then sold Pillsbury to General Mills, and with the collapse of Fingerhut's business, Federated divested it. Nearly the same fate befell what remained of Green Tree Financial.
- 3M's spin-off of its magnetic media division (now called Imation) was notable, as was Honeywell's divestiture of Alliant Tech, and Control Data's breakup into a number of parts.
- Mergers included Norwest Bank with Wells Fargo, First Bank with U.S. Bank, Honeywell with Allied Signal, and Northern States Power (NSP) with New Century Energy (NCE).
- United Health, Medtronic, and other companies made steady streams of small acquisitions. United Health became a behemoth in the health insurance industry by means of these acquisitions.
- SuperValu and St. Paul Companies made big acquisitions, with SuperValu buying Albertsons and the St. Paul Companies buying Travelers.
- Cargill acquired fertilizer manufacturer IMC Global, only to spin it off as a separately traded company, Mosaic, in which it held a controlling interest.

Motivations Behind M&As

Though M&As do not always succeed, companies do not desist from engaging in this activity for reasons such as the following:

1. *To expand.* Horizontal expansion may be blocked so companies choose the conglomerate mode. Almost random combinations of activities characterized conglomerate formation in the 1960s. Companies such as ITT epitomized this trend. ITT's portfolio included Hartford

Insurance, Sheraton Hotels, Rayonier Paper, defense electronics and semiconductor manufacturing, auto products, and industrial hydraulic products. Firms formed this type of conglomerate because of strict interpretations of U.S. antitrust laws during the Kennedy administration. Combinations of firms competing in the same markets (horizontal combinations) were not viewed favorably. However, this doctrine has shifted. As long as there is freedom of entry and competition in a particular market niche is not directly eliminated, antitrust authorities are likely to accept the merger or acquisition. A mere expansion in market share does not provide prima facie evidence for a practice that is uncompetitive.

2. *To avoid or halt decline.* Diversification motivated by decline in a firm's core business was a defensive move taken by companies threatened by foreign competition. Examples were U.S. Steel's merger with Marathon Oil and Texas Oil and Gas, and General Motors' purchase of Electronic Data Systems (EDS) and Hughes Aerospace. Unrelated combinations such as these, however, have lost favor. Companies usually do not have the competence to integrate and manage separate businesses about which they know little.[7]

3. *To cut costs.* Many mergers and acquisitions have occurred in slow-growth industries with poor pricing power. A good example has been the oil industry, which was under pressure because of on-and-off weak oil prices. Exxon thus merged with Mobil. Its aim was to cut costs by reducing overhead, closing overlapping gas stations in saturated markets, consolidating exploration and production activities, and increasing buying power. Chevron's merger with Texaco was justified in the same way. Horizontal transactions allowed these companies to consolidate and reduce costs and improve efficiency.

4. *To bring about turnarounds.* Healthy companies sometimes purchase a company experiencing business problems. The buying company's management is convinced it can do a better job than the acquired company's existing management. It tries to take advantage of the acquired company's depressed price.

5. *To gain access to products and technologies.* In growth industries, the aim is often to gain access to attractive products and technologies. In industries such as pharmaceuticals, where it requires 8 years or more to achieve profitability with a new drug and 12 years or more to generate adequate cash flows, acquisitions lower the costs and time of new-product development.

6. *To gain production or distribution capabilities.* A company's managers might believe that they need either production or distribution capabilities to fend off or keep up with competitors. Vertical mergers, for instance, have been common in the entertainment industry for this reason (see later sections in this chapter), but simultaneously managing different parts of the value chain is challenging, and many companies have been unsuccessful at it.[8]

7. *To increase earnings per share.* Some mergers and acquisitions simply have been driven by the stock market. Although other reasons were given, AOL's inflated stock price made possible its purchase of Time Warner. The merger was consummated by means of AOL's high-priced stock, which AOL used to buy a company many times its size. Tyco under Dennis Kozlowski's leadership grew in this manner.

The Role of Deregulation

Another major factor spurring mergers and acquisitions in many industries has been deregulation. The process started in the United States in 1978 with deregulation of air transportation and natural gas. It continued in the 1980s and 1990s with deregulation in railroads, trucking, telecommunications, cable television, financial institutions, and electric utilities. As a result, these formerly protected industries were exposed to competition and market forces. At first, many new firms flocked into the newly deregulated sectors, but then a series of mergers and acquisitions led to consolidation. In telecommunications, for instance, AT&T was broken up into a long-distance company that retained the AT&T name, an equipment company (Lucent), and seven "Baby Bells," or local service operators. Aggressive new entrants such as WorldCom appeared on the telecommunications scene, followed by a host of mergers and acquisitions. WorldCom failed amid a huge financial scandal and was incorporated into MCI. Of the original seven Baby Bells, only a few are left. SBC Communications, one of the seven Baby Bells, ultimately bought AT&T, since AT&T's original business model no longer was valid, and took on its name. The role of deregulation had significant impacts on M&A activity in the airline, railroad, and banking industries as well.

Airlines

Critics claimed that lower rates would prevail in an unregulated environment, so in 1978, under the Carter administration, the Airline Deregulation Act was passed. At the start of 1979, 43 large, certified carriers were in operation. At the end of that year, there were 60 carriers—22 airlines had entered and 5 had exited. The number of carriers continued to grow until 1984, when it reached 86. Market concentration decreased from 1978 through 1985, but then it started to rise sharply and has stayed high above its 1978 level since. Initially, deregulation provided many opportunities for new entrants. Frank Lorenzo created a national airline, Continental, through a series of mergers, reasoning that regional airlines wouldn't survive. The companies he brought together included Peoples Express, Texas International, and Eastern. By 2002, however, all the major airlines were in trouble with the exception of Southwest, which operated under a different business model. The industry consolidated rapidly. Delta's purchase of Northwest in 2008 made it the largest U.S. carrier, and the talk was of still more industry consolidation.

Railroads

Before 1980, the federal government set shipping rates through the Interstate Commerce Commission (ICC).[9] The Staggers Act of 1980 partially deregulated the industry but left the ICC, replaced by the Surface Transportation Board (STB) in 1995, with oversight powers to approve mergers and review shipping prices. Because the railroads were in such a weak financial condition, the STB rejected few applications for mergers. Several reasons existed for the abundance of mergers, but most had as their main motivation the desire to improve revenue and earnings in a slow-growth industry that was struggling to maintain market share against inroads made by other means of transportation (trucks, boats, and planes). After all the merger activity, the railroad industry was reduced to five major players that accounted for 94 percent of all traffic in 1999 (see Exhibit 5.4).

EXHIBIT 5.4
Railroad Industry's Major Players, 1999

Source: H. Sun, "The Sources of Railroad Merger Games," *The Transportation Journal* 39, no. 4.

Company	Total Track Routes (miles)	Revenues (billions)
Burlington Northern Santa Fe	33,500	$ 9.1
Union Pacific	33,400	10.2*
CSX	23,000	6.6*
Norfolk Southern	21,600	5.2
Canadian National	17,000	3.6

*Union Pacific and CSX have nonrail subsidiaries that contribute to revenues.

Banking

Deregulation in the banking industry occurred gradually, starting at the state level in the late 1980s and continuing through 1999.[10] Before deregulation, the most significant piece of federal banking regulation had been the 1933 Glass-Steagall Act, which limited banks' products and prices and disallowed investment banking. Commercial banks could not sell securities or insurance and could not integrate checking and investments. In addition, as late as 1975, no state permitted out-of-state commercial banks to own in-state banks, and only 14 states allowed statewide commercial banking.[11] These regulations protected the commercial banks from competition but also allowed them to become inefficient and suppressed innovation, thus creating fertile ground for competitors.

Investment banks saw the opportunity and responded. In 1972, investment banks offered the first money market mutual funds. In 1974, they started to offer check-writing capability. In 1978, they offered cash management accounts (CMAs). Meanwhile, the product restrictions and geographic limitations imposed on commercial banks by regulation left them vulnerable to bank failures such as those associated with the 1980s savings and loan (S&L) crisis.

To compete with investment banks, the commercial banks found loopholes in the laws. In 1977, Citibank took advantage of such loopholes to do the first-ever mass mailing of credit cards. In 1982, Bank of America tried to enter investment services by purchasing Charles Schwab & Co., a marriage that ended in divorce. In 1986, Citibank got legal approval to set up its own mutual funds. In 1987, the Federal Reserve allowed Citicorp, JP Morgan, and Bankers Trust to underwrite securities. By 1992, all states except Hawaii allowed interstate banking, and all states except Arkansas, Minnesota, and Iowa permitted statewide branching.

Further deregulation came in 1993 when Mellon Bank bought Dreyfus Corp. mutual funds and in 1998 when Citicorp merged with Travelers Group (including Smith Barney Investment Banking). In addition, competition grew on the lending side from such organizations as consumer finance companies, interstate thrifts, GE Capital, and credit cards. Foreign banks were able to enter local markets. By 1997, the commercial banks had lost a significant share of their business, which had dropped from 94 percent of all deposits in 1973 to just 50 percent (see Exhibit 5.5).

The Financial Modernization Act, passed in 1999, allowed the commercial banks to offer a broad range of products, including investment banking, brokerage services, and insurance, and permitted interstate banking. The act enabled commercial banks to compete on a more equal footing with their many competitors. The Federal Reserve reviewed M&A proposals of banks, but denied few of them. Substantial consolidation occurred within the banking industry.

- In 1998, NationsBank merged with California's BankAmerica, creating Bank of America—at the time, the second-largest U.S. bank holding company.
- In 2004, Bank One merged with JPMorgan Chase, creating a banking colossus, the second largest in the United States.

EXHIBIT 5.5
Banking Industry Deposits (in billions)

	1973	1981	1990	1997
Traditional commercial bank deposits and mutual funds	$682	$1,580	$3,450	$3,790
Investment banks money market funds, bonds, and stocks	46	241	1,060	3,790

- Citicorp merged in 1998 with Travelers Group, a financial institution with a broad array of services, and the stock price soared. It ultimately divested Travelers Group. Nonetheless, Citicorp, renamed Citigroup, became one of the largest and most influential banks in the United States.
- Norwest Bank bought California's Wells Fargo Bank in 1998. In 1996, through a hostile takeover, Wells Fargo had acquired a competing California bank, First Interstate. The new Wells Fargo continued to purchase dozens of small financial services firms each year as long as the price was reasonable.

Examples of Good Deal Making

Some companies have had great track records in making these deals, while others do not. Cisco Systems' processes for selecting targets and integrating businesses after the deal are considered to be outstanding. The computer network company buys to enhance its existing lines of business, opens new ones in adjacent markets, or obtains promising technology. There are good examples of deal making despite the many failures, as the following examples show.

The Consolidator

In 1997, Amphenol merged with NXS Acquisition, a subsidiary of the investment bank Kohlberg Kravis Roberts & Co. (KKR), which was best known for its 1989 takeover of RJR Nabisco. The capabilities of KKR's management team provided additional capital and provided Amphenol with the chance to be an aggressive consolidator. Through its acquisitions, Amphenol consolidated interconnect companies, an opportunity that existed because of a fragmented and declining market. The company's acquisitions broadened and enhanced its product offerings and expanded its global reach.

Moving to New Industries

In 1995, SPX designed and made specialty tools, a business that had numerous competitors and low operating margins. To combat the cyclical nature of SPX's business as well as low profit margins, the company searched for customers in new industries. U.S. automakers constituted 37 percent of its revenues. By 2002, they constituted less than 20 percent of the company's revenues. SPX transformed itself through acquisitions. Two of them were very large. In 1998, it bought General Signal, nearly twice SPX's size, and in 2001, it acquired United Dominion flow technology business, a company with revenues roughly equivalent to General Signal's.

Purchasing Talent

The gaming company Activision also aggressively acquired other companies. From 1997 to 2002, it made 14 acquisitions that allowed it not only to diversify its operations, add channels of distribution, and expand its library of titles, but also to develop a new pool of talent among the companies it purchased such as Head Games Publishing, Expert Software, and Elsinore Multimedia.

Broadening of Scope

Insurance company Brown & Brown broadened its scope through mergers and acquisitions. From 1992 to 2003, it acquired 118 small insurance companies, thereby expanding from its base in Florida to include California, Connecticut, Indiana, Michigan, Minnesota, Nevada,

New Jersey, and more. The company's aim was to acquire small, profitable companies to branch out into underutilized, niche markets with high margins.

Buying Competitors

The packaging business in which Ball competed was mature and had low profit margins. Companies in this industry faced intense pricing pressures and the threat of consolidation. To achieve a stronger position, Ball successfully acquired and integrated major competitor Reynolds Metals in 1998, expanding Ball's aluminum can business. In 2002, it acquired Germany-based Schmalbach-Lubeca, the second largest beverage can manufacturer in Europe.

M&As and the Global Economic Meltdown

Waves of M&A activity follow periods when this type of activity slows considerably. The global economic meltdown of 2008 greatly diminished the prospects for mergers and acquisitions. Thousands of deals were delayed or abandoned. U.S. deal volume plunged because of the tightening in credit markets and lack of confidence in where the economy was heading. For instance, Dow Chemical's proposed acquisition of rival Rohm & Haas, which had been considered a sure thing, stalled when the Kuwait government withdrew from a joint venture that would have provided Dow with funding. To pay for the purchase of Rohm & Haas, Dow had to draw down on a billion-dollar short-term bank loan, sell assets it would acquire in the deal, and lay off thousands of workers. Financing of deals during the economic meltdown was difficult.

Often the deals were done out of necessity. An example is Bank of America's forced buyout of troubled investment bank Merrill Lynch. Merrill Lynch had little choice but to go along with the deal. Another example is IBM's bid for Sun Microsystems. Sun had been a high-flying start-up. A major seller of premium-end servers to the financial sector, it struggled after the dot-com bust and had trouble reorienting its business to low-cost servers that relied on Intel and AMD chips. Under duress, Sun approached HP, Dell, and IBM, hoping to be acquired. When IBM decided it could take the risk of trying to rescue Sun, Oracle decided to preempt IBM and buy the ailing company. Though the economic difficulties created such opportunities, many deals did not happen because capital was not available, business prospects were poor, and it was uncertain how the Justice Department would view the proposals. Instead, most companies followed more conservative survival strategies. Rather than trying to expand, they conserved cash, minimized overhead, and reduced their workforces (see Exhibit 5.6). Though restructuring through merger and acquisition might be needed, most companies just cut back.

Pharmaceuticals

One industry that has experienced major restructuring is pharmaceuticals. A drive toward consolidation has been spurred by a decrease in the number of patentable products in the pipeline, though the large drug company Pfizer's purchases of Warner-Lambert in 2000 and Pharmacia in 2003 have not replenished its roster of new drugs. Almost all the major players in this industry have been involved in consolidation or are likely to be. In March 2008, Roche successfully purchased Genentech, a deal that came just after Merck's

EXHIBIT 5.6
Number of
Jobs Cut by
March 2008

Source: Adapted with
permission from *The
Wall Street Journal,*
"Jobless Rate Tops
8%, Highest in 26
Years," March 7, 2009.

Company	Number of Jobs Cut	Percent of Workforce
Caterpillar	20,000	18%
Nissan Motor	20,000	8
NEC	20,000	7
United Technologies	18,000	8
Alcoa	15,000	14.5
Panasonic	15,000	5
GM	10,000	14
Boeing	10,000	6
Pfizer	11,500	10
Sprint Nextel	8,000	13
AstraZeneca	7,400	11
Macy's	7,000	4
Home Depot	7,000	2
Hitachi	7,000	2
Starbucks	6,700	4
HSBC	6,100	1.9
Intel	6,000	7
Goodyear Tire	5,000	7
Microsoft	5,000	5
Eastman Kodak	4,500	18
Motorola	4,000	6
Corning	3,500	13
Texas Instruments	3,400	12
Nortel Networks	3,200	10
Time Warner Cable	1,250	3
General Dynamics	1,200	1.3
Harley-Davidson	1,100	11
Electronic Arts	1,100	11
Saks	1,100	9
AMD	1,100	9
Walgreens	1,000	0.6
Seagate Technology	800	10
Cummins	800	2

agreement to acquire Schering-Plough. Earlier in 2008, Pfizer had taken over Wyeth. The other large drug companies—Eli Lilly, Bristol-Myers Squibb, AstraZeneca, Sanofi-Aventis, and Johnson & Johnson—were not sitting on the sidelines and were likely to be main actors in the next round of consolidation (see Exhibit 5.7).

Consolidation in the pharmaceutical industry could mean lower costs for drug companies as they combined research and sales efforts and laid off workers. However, an industry dominated by exceptionally large firms raised questions about the future of smaller drug and biotech companies. Were they in line for takeover attempts by the large firms?

The prospect of health care reform by the federal government also motivated the large pharmaceutical firms to consolidate, believing they would be better able to bundle products and have more power in price negotiations with the government. Questions remain, however, of whether the creation of larger and larger drug entities is in the best interests of society.

EXHIBIT 5.7 **Drug Industry Consolidation**

Sources: Credit Suisse; company reports; Bloomberg. Reprinted with permission from *The New York Times,* March 12, 2009.

Drug Industry Consolidation

A series of mergers has winnowed the drug industry to a few major players.

DATES DEALS WERE ANNOUNCED

'93	'95	'97	'99	'01	'03	'05	'07	'09

American Home Products   Wyeth (renamed 2002)

American Cyanamid

Pfizer

Warner-Lambert

Pharmacia   Pharmacia & Upjohn

Upjohn   Monsanto was spun off as an

                                    agricultural products company.

Monsanto   Monsanto

Wellcome

Glaxo   Glaxo Wellcome   GlaxoSmithKline

SmithKlineBeecham

Synthélabo

Sanofi   Sanofi-Synthélabo   Sanofi-Aventis

Rhône-Poulenc   Aventis

Hoechst

Merck

Schering-Plough

Zeneca   AstraZeneca

Astra

Sandoz   Novartis

Ciba-Geigy

Roche

Genentech (Roche bought most of the company in 1990, but has announced a deal to buy the rest)

Sources: Credit Suisse; company reports; Bloomberg   The NEW YORK TIMES

Why Do M&As Fail?

Mergers and acquisitions fail for at least eight reasons.

1. *Price too high.* A huge problem is paying too high a price for an acquired company. Due diligence has to occur before the acquisition to ensure that the buyer knows what it is getting, but even with due diligence, serious mistakes often are made. The banks discussed

previously often paid too high a price for other banks. Westinghouse paid far too much for CBS in 1995. This acquisition contributed mightily to the company's ultimate breakup and demise.

2. *Products or services less than expected.* The purpose of mergers and acquisitions may be to gain access to sought-after products, services, or technologies, but managers of acquiring companies often do not assess the target company carefully enough to ensure that the products, services, and technologies they are obtaining have sufficient value. This task is often difficult to perform adequately in the time allotted. In merging with Electronic Data Systems (EDS), for instance, GM expected to get from EDS the ability to automate its factories, but EDS lacked this kind of experience and was of no real help to GM in this area.

3. *Lack of marketing leverage.* Acquiring companies often expect that an acquisition will provide marketing leverage. The acquirer may believe that the new products it has acquired can be sold to its existing customers. However, the acquirer tends to overestimate the cross-selling potential and to underestimate the need to retrain its sales force to sell the new goods.

4. *Few benefits from the overlapping of core competencies.* When a rapidly growing company uses its high-price stock to make acquisitions, it can be vulnerable to careless mistakes. For example, it can easily go beyond its core competency and buy a firm that contributes little to what it does best. Since the acquisition may lead to an immediate increase in earnings per share, this type of foolish acquisition is hard to resist.

5. *Cultural problems.* A major difficulty in almost every M&A is combining divergent corporate cultures. Divergent cultures and management styles present significant barriers to achieving success. These differences can impede the process of consolidation and cost cutting, result in increased unhappiness among employees, and diminish productivity. The previously mentioned General Motors–EDS merger did not work because it combined radically different cultures. GM's elaborate bureaucracy and strong unions clashed sharply with EDS's fiercely independent employees.

6. *Unfriendly mergers and acquisitions.* Unfriendly takeovers add to the problem of merging diverse cultures. When anger and resistance are prevalent, it is hard to integrate the component pieces.

7. *Failure to retain key personnel.* For most acquisitions, it is important that the buyer retain the key personnel in the acquired company. The failure to retain key personnel is particularly a problem when the takeover is hostile and the corporate cultures clash, but even in friendly mergers, management has to keep valuable people. When these people leave, it is much more likely that the merger or acquisition will fail.

8. *Failure to achieve a turnaround.* Acquirers often believe they can bring about a rapid turnaround in the acquired company's performance. However, the managers of the acquiring firm often overestimate their ability to solve the problems of the acquired company. Unforeseen problems may arise such as the discovery of unacceptable accounting procedures. The merger also may alienate the acquired company's customers. These factors often are not taken into account by the overconfident management of the acquiring firm.

Why Do Mergers Succeed?

Each merger and acquisition is different and has to be assessed on its merits. To increase the chances for a successful acquisition, certain key issues should be addressed beforehand:

- Does the acquirer's management team know enough about the acquired company's businesses to competently run them?
- Are the businesses of the acquired company more attractive than the businesses in which the acquiring company is engaged?
- Are the costs of entry so high that they will destroy the added income the acquiring company hopes to gain?
- Is it really possible to establish synergies between the new and old businesses?

The synergies **(economies of scope)** that might be established are critical elements in successful M&As. Synergies include:

- Sharing of tangible resources (research labs, distribution systems) across multiple businesses.
- Sharing of intangible resources (brands, technology) across multiple businesses.
- Transferring functional capabilities (marketing, product development) across multiple businesses.
- Applying general management capabilities to multiple businesses.

Synergy is crucial, but it may be very hard to achieve.

Mergers of Equals

Mergers of equals are more likely to succeed than mergers of dissimilar firms. Exhibit 5.8 compares two utilities that merged in 1999. They had a relatively easy time with their merger. As the data indicate, the companies were quite similar. Management estimated net cost

EXHIBIT 5.8
A Premerger Comparison of NSP and NCE

	Northern States Power (NSP)	New Century Energies (NCE)
Total revenues (1998)	$2.82 billion	$3.61 billion
Net profits (1998)	$282 million	$342 million
1998 growth rate in number of customers	1.4%	2.2%
Allowed rates of return	MN: 11.47% (1993)	CO: 11.0% (1993)
	WI: 11.3% (1996)	TX: 15.05% (1996)
1998 rate of return	11.3%	13.8%
Markets		
Electricity generating fuel mix	84% of total sales	75% of total sales
Coal	44%	48%
Nuclear	25%	0%
Hydro and other	4%	3%
Natural gas	0%	30%
Purchased electricity	27%	19%
Natural gas	16% of total sales	23% of total sales
Total full-time employees (1998)	7,492	6,375

savings over 10 years of about $1.1 billion as a result of combining operations. These potential expense reductions were the result of carefully identifying duplicate corporate and administrative functions that could be eliminated by consolidating and integrating the companies. Substantial cost savings also were derived from the scale economies of combining production units.

Effective Management

Ultimately, M&A success depends on how effectively the newly merged and acquired companies are managed. Some companies are very good at this. Their ability to do deals and manage acquired firms is a core competency. This is true of Cisco, as mentioned earlier, and of SPX.

In successful M&As, top management's role is critical. In theory, the top executives in a company, those in corporate headquarters positions, create value by acquiring new businesses, restructuring inefficiently managed businesses, and allocating capital and labor among businesses. The executive team transfers skills and capabilities to divisions. It shares activities, establishes linkages, and determines the logic of integration. The synergies it creates have to consist of more than just sharing corporate services such as finance, legal, taxes, research, public relations, and investor relations. They must also consist of sharing tangible and intangible resources and functional capabilities and applying general management tools and techniques.

In practice, large, complex organizations often are rife with conflict between the corporate office and the divisions over strategic and operational issues. Headquarters is inclined to favor uniformity but differences might create advantages. Managing the interrelationships among divisions requires intricate systems that push top executives and people in the divisions to the limit and stretch what they can do effectively. For instance, top management may decide to superimpose functional and geographic divisions on top of product and market divisions and create matrix structures. These systems may not work well or may not work as intended. Exhibit 5.9 summarizes the theory-versus-practice issues in the role of top management.

Over the past century, management's corporate strategy role has moved in four directions largely in response to changes in the external and internal environments of businesses at the time.

1. *Expansion.* Starting in the early 20th century, with the growth of the typical firm's products and geographic scope, the value chain got bigger, but administrative costs did not go up. Declining administrative expenses were made possible by advances in transportation, communication, and information. They were also a consequence of developments in management

EXHIBIT 5.9
Top Management's Role: Theory and Practice

In Theory	In Practice
Creates value	Is often in conflict with divisions over
Acquires new businesses	strategic and operational issues
Restructures inefficiently	May try to impose uniformity despite
managed businesses	advantages of differences
Transfers skills and	May be pushed to limit by complex
capabilities to divisions	systems for managing interrelationships
Establishes linkages	
Determines logic of integration	

sciences in such areas as accounting and finance. Organizational capabilities grew. The modern firm with several distinct functions such as accounting, finance, marketing, and operations took shape. These helped with the management of much larger, more complex entities.

2. *The M-form.* A new type of structure for the firm, called the **M-form,** came into being. This structure improved efficiencies. At the top was a tier of high-level executives who made strategic choices. They interacted with shareholders and allocated resources to separate, independent business units, each with its own management that made everyday decisions. Thus, the executives at headquarters offices were not overly involved in the day-to-day activities of the firm's separate business units. Instead, they held each unit's management accountable for its profitability and performance as measured by such quantitative indicators as market share.

3. *Portfolio management.* In the mid-1970s, many theorists championed an important extension of the M-form, which was known as **portfolio planning.** Portfolio-planning models helped large, complex organizations manage their separate business units. These models focused on the direction, coordination, control, and profitability of the different business units. More will be said about portfolio models in the next section.

4. *Contraction.* By the late 1970s, however, serious questions were raised about how efficient the M-form and portfolio-planning models really were. A large, complex corporation run in this way could not keep up with small, nimble competitors. It lacked the flexibility to deal with growing market turbulence, deregulation, and technological change. Many management specialists advocated contraction in the size and scope of the firm to provide it with speed, flexibility, and responsiveness. The trend shifted to a preference for a more focused organization.

Despite this change, portfolio models in vogue in the mid-1970s continued to be used by many companies. The two most commonly used portfolio models were derived from the BCG matrix and the GE/McKinsey model.

The BCG Matrix

The Boston Consulting Group (BCG) created one of the best-known systems for portfolio management. Under the BCG system, a company divides its businesses into **separate business units (SBUs)**—closely related businesses or groups of businesses that can be subjected to strategic analysis. Then a company's top executives, perhaps with the assistance of consultants, evaluate the performance of the SBUs and help in drafting strategies for them. The method of evaluation is a form of **SWOT analysis** (strengths, weaknesses, opportunities, and threats analysis). The consultants and executives examine the internal strengths and weaknesses of each SBU, compare them with external opportunities and threats, and then allocate resources based on this analysis. Business units are classified as follows (see Exhibit 5.10):

- SBUs that are high on internal strengths and high on external opportunities are considered *stars.* The strategy for these SBUs is to invest in them and increase their share of the firm's overall business.

- SBUs that are high on internal strengths but low on external opportunities are considered *cash cows.* The strategy in this case is to hold onto them and maintain them to extract the cash needed to invest in more promising businesses.

EXHIBIT 5.10
SWOT Analysis

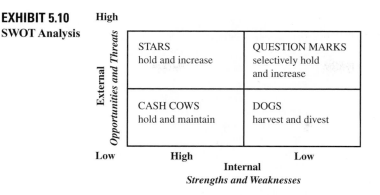

SBUs that are low on internal strengths but high on external opportunities are *question marks*. The strategy here is to selectively hold onto them, invest in the most promising, and increase their share of the company's overall business. The money to invest in them comes from cash cows, since question marks are the source of the company's future stars.

• SBUs that are low on both internal strengths and external opportunities are considered *dogs,* and the strategy is to harvest and divest them.

The main issue is how to determine whether an SBU is high or low on these dimensions. BCG came up with a very simple solution to this problem: A company is high on internal strengths if its *relative market share* is high; it is high on external opportunities if its *industry growth rate* is high.

This method of sorting companies, however, is problematic. There have been companies with high market share, such as General Motors, that were low on profitability, and there have been companies with low market share, like mini mills in the steel industry, that were high on profitability. The low-cost strategy, which is used to build high market share, might not translate into a profitable strategy if an industry is very competitive and prices are declining. Niche strategies that involve differentiation and focus but low market share can be profitable ones.

The GE/McKinsey Model

Working with the consulting firm McKinsey & Company, General Electric developed a different approach to assess internal strengths and weaknesses and external opportunities and threats. Recognizing that internal strengths and weaknesses are more than just market share and that external opportunities and threats are more than just market growth, this approach examines an array of factors (see Exhibit 5.11). The strength of the GE/McKinsey model is its realism; the weakness is that it depends on qualitative judgment to determine internal strengths and weaknesses and industry attractiveness.

In a firm with numerous SBUs, each one wanting to claim a portion of overall corporate resources, this allocation method opens up the possibility of bitter bureaucratic infighting and power struggles. Unless it is managed carefully, this type of portfolio management can be very difficult to use.

EXHIBIT 5.11
GE/McKinsey
Model:
Evaluation
Criteria

Business Unit: Internal Strengths and Weaknesses	Industry: External Opportunities and Threats
Market share	Market growth rate
Sales force	Market size
Marketing	Cyclicality
Customer service	Competitive structure
R&D	Barriers to entry
Manufacturing	Industry profitability
Distribution	Technology
Financial resources	Inflation
Image	Regulation
Breadth of product line	Social and environmental issues
Quality/reliability	Political and legal issues
Managerial competence	

Portfolio planning models offer several advantages, including the ability to see the big picture in a single diagram on which each SBU is positioned, and the ability to apply the same method to many types of businesses. Portfolio models might be a good starting point for more sophisticated analysis. They can be augmented, but then they lose an important advantage, their simplicity. They have many problems. They reduce to a minimum the factors that determine internal strengths and industry attractiveness; they do not eliminate subjective judgment; and they are ambiguous. In addition, they depend on how a market is defined, and in an environment in which markets and industries are rapidly changing, market definition is difficult to determine.

A huge issue with portfolio planning models is that they do not consider synergy, or the interdependencies among SBUs. The dogs in portfolios might be wagging the stars' tails. Without the dogs, the stars would be poorer performers. Corporate performance is a team effort. In well-managed companies, SBUs are more than separate entities with their own profit and revenue streams. They share resources, link capabilities, leverage competencies, and achieve synergies. The corporation as a whole, and not its individual units, develops sets of skills that have the capacity to open opportunities for the firm.

Breaking Down the Corporate Hierarchy

In the 1990s a number of new trends in headquarters' role came to the forefront. During this period, GE showed that a large diversified conglomerate could be very profitable and deliver high returns to shareholders if it was well managed. GE took a series of steps to reinvent the company. It "delayered" the organization, going from 9 or 10 layers of hierarchy down to 4 or 5. It decentralized decision making whenever possible so low-level managers had the discretion to respond quickly to emerging issues. It reformulated strategic planning, changing it from a formal, document-intensive activity to a series of face-to-face discussions. It tried to redefine the CEO's role from that of checker, inquisitor, and authority to one of facilitator, helper, and supporter. To some employees, this redefinition was believable; to others, it was not. Jack Welch, the CEO at the time, laid off vast numbers of employees in restructurings and became known as "neutron Jack."

Welch reasserted the importance of the coordinating role played by top executives in the company. The purpose of top executives was to break down boundaries so ideas flow freely and innovations are common. Top executives should function as change agents and be driving forces of renewal. As part of the effort to continually reinvent GE, Welch held open-ended "workout" sessions with employees at all levels to hear their concerns and respond to them.

Other firms went even further in breaking down the corporate hierarchy. The Swiss-Swedish firm ABB, in some markets a competitor of GE, is also a leader in power and automation technologies. The ABB Group operates companies in hundreds of countries and employs thousands of people. It radically decentralized its operations to rely on bottom-up management. With a corporate staff of less than 100 people, individual country subsidiaries were encouraged to make their own decisions. The firm was divided into many small- and medium-sized businesses, which negotiated relations among one another without central direction. Each business had its own balance sheet by which it was judged. For a long time, ABB was successful with this model, but it ran into trouble for a variety of reasons, including old asbestos-related suits, that were unconnected to this initiative.

Is Vertical Integration the Answer?

A key question for a large diversified firm is whether it should move up or down the supply chain and become vertically integrated. Vertical integration in industries such as pharmaceuticals were once common, but management soon realized quickly that it was not a good way to achieve sustained competitive advantage. Both Lilly and Merck purchased distribution arms (PCS Health Systems and Medco Containment, respectively), but both companies quickly sold these units.

Vertical integration raises a variety of questions. What is more efficient—specialist firms linked by market exchanges, or firms combined under a common ownership? In many industries, firms unite on a project basis in the market. The woolen industry involves independent spinners, weavers, and merchants coming together to produce final goods for sale to consumers. The remodeling industry involves builders, plumbers, electricians, and painters working together on a project basis. Why should all these activities come under the purview of one firm?

In deciding whether to combine or leave activities separate, managers must compare external market transaction costs to internal administrative costs. Which are greater? High market transaction costs are good reasons for uniting activities in one firm, while high administrative costs are good reasons for keeping these activities in separate entities. The external transaction costs of operating in the market have to be compared with the internal administrative costs of operating inside the firm.[12] Within a firm, managers cannot just command employees to do their bidding. They incur monitoring and incentive costs when they try to ensure employee compliance. These costs may be greater than the costs of transacting in the market. Also, the information a firm's top executives receive from their subordinates may not be better than the information they receive from outside the firm. Employees may misrepresent situations. So, why have them as employees? Hire them on an as-needed basis.

The cost of uniting disparate elements in the firm includes the hassles of dealing with potentially recalcitrant employees who have to be motivated to do the job right. These costs increase when the firm engages in vertical integration and attempts to combine dissimilar stages in the production process such as manufacturing, marketing, and distribution in the same firm.

Between pure market transactions and vertical integration, there are a number of hybrid-like options:

- A firm can have *long-term contracts* and partnerships with suppliers.
- It can have *franchising* agreements with independent or semi-independent distributors rather than incorporate them in the firm.
- It can create *joint ventures.*

These arrangements may compensate for the limits of internalization and for the limits of market exchange. In each instance, the issue is how to best design the arrangement. The parties have to be able to answer questions such as how to allocate risk and what are the incentives to work together. These alliance-like options have gained considerable attention in management circles in recent years and frequently are resorted to rather than mergers and acquisitions. They may be a preliminary stage, a trial period, in what later becomes an outright merger and acquisition.

The Entertainment Industry

To better understand the pluses and minuses of vertical integration, it is useful to look at the entertainment industry.[13] This industry has converged toward a single model that combines production of content with multichannel distribution (see Exhibit 5.12). Companies attempt to sell content in many ways, for example, through movies, TV shows, books, theme parks, and increasingly Internet channels (Time Warner, AOL). Some companies have bought distribution channels (Disney purchased television network ABC) (see Exhibit 5.13); others

EXHIBIT 5.12
Vertical Integration: Entertainment Industry

Content		Distribution	
Resources	**Creation**	**Delivery**	**Retail**
Actors	Television production	Broadcast television networks	Local affiliates
Writers	Movie production	Cable television networks	Local cable companies
		Movie distribution	Local theaters

EXHIBIT 5.13
Vertical Integration at Disney

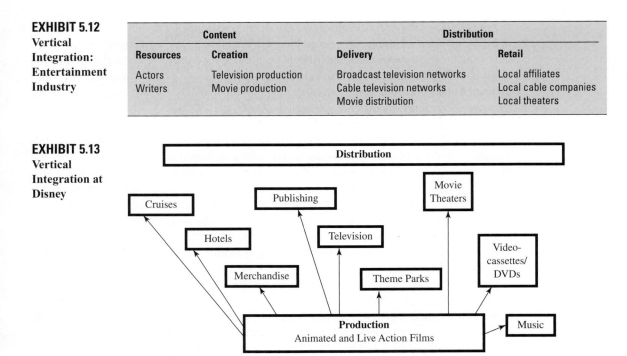

have built their own networks (News Corp. started Fox); still others did both (Viacom built UPN and purchased CBS). A new trend has been to combine content with the added distribution possibilities of the Internet.

In the entertainment industry companies are involved in vertical integration through direct ownership as well as many alliances via long-term contracts and onetime "spot-market" transactions. The old studio system tied actors to studios for long periods. In today's industry, actors sign contracts to do "*x* number of pictures" with a studio. Production companies can be either independent or owned by integrated entertainment companies. In either case, production is sold to the highest bidder, not necessarily to the company that produced the content. Local television affiliates and movie theaters sometimes are bound by contract, sometimes entirely independent, and sometimes owned by an entertainment company. This last situation is common in large metropolitan areas, where the major companies want close links to viewers. Agents and other facilitators play a role in bringing together the parties in the value chain.

Vertical integration can mean lower risk (regardless of where the profits are, the companies have a foothold) and lock in distribution for high-risk production. But production companies supply all networks and networks access all suppliers, so the motive for consolidation is as much to gain bargaining leverage as to lock in distribution. All companies are aiming for synergies, cross-selling to end users and cross-platform-selling to advertisers. Companies have tried to acquire complementary assets (e.g., Viacom was strong with a young audience, while CBS was strong with an old one). Nonetheless, much of the consolidation in the industry has not lived up to its billing. It is arguable if Time Warner, Disney, and News Corp. are better off after their major acquisitions. Viacom has decided to divest and separate into two units, Viacom and CBS. After years of mergers and acquisitions, divestitures may be the next major trend in this industry.

The Rationales for Vertical Integration

Before government regulation in the 1950s, the large Hollywood studios had been vertically integrated. A few large studios owned most production and worldwide distribution. This system was broken up by government regulation. It was not until the late 1980s that the federal government again allowed companies owning studios (TV production units) to also own TV broadcast networks (distribution).

Several rationales have supported vertical integration. One reason has been the convergence of computing, telecommunications, information, and entertainment. Convergence has created a hierarchy in which content, the scarcest commodity, is the most valuable resource. Content is a high-overhead, high-risk, and low-margin business. The cost of making and marketing movies continues to increase; yet the likelihood of success is more and more a matter of guesswork. The odds are no better in TV production. Thus, a rationale for joining production and distribution is to guarantee outlets for a firm's production. Captive outlets provide a built-in output for content. Networks cut costs by owning and/or supplying their own prime-time programming. Networks are understanding of their own production units, but there are limits, because production companies cannot force bad shows on networks and hot networks can demand high prices for airing shows.

Another rationale for vertical integration is that it enables big entertainment companies to sell content, that is, to market the same character or idea in many ways. The content of the entertainment companies can originate anywhere—movies, TV, music, publishing, merchandising, theme parks, and Internet sites. It can be repeatedly recycled in new formats to maximize returns. For this to work, synergy must exist along the value chain: Different parts of the business have to be aligned so that they add value to each other.

Each revolution in distribution and transmission gave companies with content (production) more outlets for their creative products. Compared with network TV, cable not only gave customers more distinct viewing options but also provided the owners with revenues from both subscriptions and advertising like print journalism. The evolution has progressed from broad mass audiences via TV networks, to aggregations of specific audiences (children, news, movies, comedy) via cable, to individual interests via direct satellite services and digital cable, to the potential of markets of one and entertainment on demand on Internet sites such as YouTube.

Conclusions on Vertical Integration

Though the entertainment industry offers good examples of the potential for vertical integration along the value chain, the results have not lived up to expectations. A number of conclusions about vertical integration therefore may be reached:

- It may not always make sense to think about acquisition of distribution.
- In theory, there are many potential advantages, including risk reduction (regardless of where profits move, a company is in a position to gain), but these advantages are hard to achieve.
- If distribution is purchased, it makes sense not to lock it into in-house production; rather, distribution should be used as a bargaining tool (ends dependence, provides credible threat to go elsewhere).
- On the other hand, an advantage of acquiring distribution is that it provides closeness to customers. This may translate into the possibility of cross-selling, developing new products, differentiating existing products, and catering to individual customer needs. And catering to individual needs can yield higher profit margins than selling an undifferentiated commodity.
- Once acquisition of distribution occurs, however, synergy may be hard to achieve. Management of the complementary assets is a huge challenge, one that is still a challenge for the large entertainment conglomerates.

Summary

The reasons for mergers and acquisitions are many. They include getting around antitrust laws that limit a firm's expansion, dealing with decline in a corporation's core business, coping with slow growth, trying to achieve turnarounds, gaining access to attractive products and technologies, building in distribution or production capacity when they are lacking, and taking advantage of high stock market valuation in a bull market.

Deregulation and privatization have played a major role in the restructuring of many industries and have led to numerous mergers and acquisitions. In airlines, railroads, and banking, the number of firms has shrunk. Some firms have coped with this situation much better than others.

Merger and acquisition winners have a few characteristics in common. They are good at dealing with the cultural problems that emerge after a merger or acquisition has been completed. They don't overpay for the companies they buy. They make sure they know what they are getting. They operate well in the postmerger or acquisition environment, achieving marketing leverage and other synergies. They make sure to retain the key personnel of the merged or acquired company. And they strive to gain the benefits from complementary core competencies. Mergers of equals, we have argued, are more likely to succeed than mergers of vastly different companies. Still, it is necessary for management to plan carefully before engaging in any merger or acquisition. Synergy is the key, but achieving it is far from easy.

Theories of managing the large, diversified organization have gone from expansion to policies of contraction and focus. Portfolio management tools like those BCG and GE/McKinsey developed were once very popular. They divided firms into separate business units and viewed the units as independent entities. Although they are still popular today, firms more and more are looking for boundary-free arrangements where capabilities are linked, competencies leveraged, and synergies achieved.

The vertical integration decision is a complicated one, since in many instances it may make more sense for the firm to buy the goods and services it needs in the market rather than to produce them itself. The firm's top executives have to decide where the firm's comparative advantage lies and concentrate in this domain rather than spreading the company too thinly. The market transaction costs of vertical integration have to be compared with the administrative costs of internalizing an additional function in the firm. The complicated nature of the vertical integration decision is apparent in the entertainment industry, where most of the large acquisitions and mergers of recent years have not worked as well as expected.

Endnotes

1. D. Brito and M. Catalao-Lopes, *Mergers and Acquisitions: The Industrial Organization Perspective* (Leiter, Netherlands: Kluwer, 2006).

2. R. Rumelt, *Strategy, Structure, and Economic Performance* (Boston: Harvard Business School Press, 1986).

3. A. Fisher, A. Michels, and J. Antony, "How to Make a Merger Work," *Fortune,* January 24, 1994, pp. 66–70. Consultant McKinsey & Company, in a 1994 study, found that only 23 percent of mergers examined over a 10-year period generated returns in excess of the costs incurred in the deal. Also see, D. Ravenscraft and F. Scherer, *Mergers, Sell-Offs, and Economic Efficiency* (Washington, DC: Brookings, 1987). Ravenscraft and Scherer, in a study of the postacquisition performance of acquired firms, found that profit levels and market shares on average did not grow.

4. "Mergers: Why Most Big Deals Don't Pay Off," *BusinessWeek,* October 14, 2002.

5. Ibid., pp. 60–68.

6. The 1990s saw even greater amounts of activity than the 1980s. In 1988, the decade's peak year, $246.9 billion was invested in M&As. In 1995, the total transaction value was more than $450 billion; in 1996, more than $470 billion; and in 1999, a staggering $1.4 trillion (the current record). See *BusinessWeek,* October 14, 2002.

7. Rumelt found that concentrating on a single field was more profitable than moving boldly into uncharted territory. He blamed unrelated diversification on management fashion and argued that related diversification was a better strategy.

8. Rumelt warned against this type of merger.

9. Sources on the railroad industry include Alfred Marcus, *The Adversary Economy;* Mercer Management Consulting, *The Impact of Deregulation;* and H. Sun, "The Sources of Railroad Merger Gains," *Transportation Journal* 39, no. 4, pp. 14–26.

10. Sources on the banking industry include R. Eisenbeis, "Mergers of Publicly Traded Banking Organizations Revisited," *Economic Review* 84, no. 4 (1999), pp. 26–37; J. Jayaratne and P. Strahan,

"The Benefits of Branching Deregulation," *Regulation,* Winter 1999, pp. 8–16; A. Kover, "Big Banks Debunked," *Fortune,* February 21, 2000, pp. 187–94; R. Kroszner, "The Economics and Politics of Financial Modernization," *Economic Policy Review* 6, no. 4 (2000), pp. 25–37; and B. Shull and G. Hanweck, "A New Merger Policy for Banks," *Antitrust Bulletin* 45, no. 3 (2000), pp. 679–711.

11. In the 19th century, branch banking had been regulated to ensure easy access by customers and to prevent local market concentration.

12. O. Williamson, *Economic Institutions of Capitalism: Firms, Markets, Relational Contracting* (New York: Free Press, 1991).

13. Sources on the entertainment industry include Marc Gunther, "TV's Rerun from Hell: Paradise Lost," *Fortune,* February 5, 2001, pp. 28–30; "Television Takes a Tumble," *The Economist,* January 20, 2001, pp. 59–61; J. Angwin and M. Peers, "The New Media Colossus," *The Wall Street Journal,* December 15, 2000, pp. B1, B7; Stephen Battaglio, "TV Networks Are More Than Just Survivors," *Fortune,* September 18, 2000, pp. 56–57; J. Lipman and B. Orwall, "Who's Left at the Media Ball?" *The Wall Street Journal,* September 8, 1999, pp. B1, B4; Marc Gunther, "Viacom: Redstone's Remarkable Rise to the Top," *Fortune,* April 26, 1999, pp. 130–37; "A Brand New Strategy," *The Economist,* November 19, 1998, special section; and Frank Rose, "There's No Business Like Show Business," *Fortune,* June 22, 1998, pp. 86–98.

Globalization

"Conventional wisdom argues that domestic competition is wasteful:
It leads to duplication of effort and prevents companies from achieving
economies of scale. . . . Domestic rivalry, like any rivalry, creates pressure
on companies to innovate and improve. Another benefit . . . is the pressure
it creates for constant upgrading of the sources of competitive advantage.
Ironically, it is also vigorous domestic competition that ultimately pressures domestic companies to look at global markets and toughens them to
succeed in them . . . local competitors force each other to look outward to
foreign markets to capture greater efficiency and higher profitability. And
having been tested by fierce domestic competition, the stronger companies
are well equipped to win abroad."[1]

Michael Porter, The Competitive Advantage of Nations

Chapter Learning Objectives

- Appreciating that strategic management has a global dimension.
- Understanding the parallels between global and domestic strategy.
- Being aware of Porter's "diamond" and how it can be used to help formulate a global strategy.
- Understanding comparative national growth rates and structural differences among nations.
- Recognizing the importance of local adaptation when a firm enters foreign markets.
- Being aware of the reasons for global expansion and some of the choices for global management, such as licensing, franchising, and greenfield operations.

Introduction

Along with decisions about positioning, and decisions about corporate strategy, decisions about global moves are among the most important ones the strategist makes. This chapter examines these moves. It explores why firms operate internationally. At first glance it seems that operating abroad only adds to the costs of doing business—extra communication and transportation costs, extra costs of training staff and moving individuals to different countries, and the expense and time required to learn about diverse cultures and languages.

In addition, barriers against gaining access to key businesses and other contacts must be surmounted. Local firms have built-in advantages: They know the situation better than any foreign firm could. Their understanding of the domestic market and business conditions is better than that of foreign firms, which may make culturally insensitive decisions and take awkward actions. A firm that is considering doing business abroad must have a rationale and logic for how it can compensate for and overcome the liabilities and disadvantages that arise from its foreignness.[2] There must be some special product-market opportunity that it can exploit or a unique set of resources, capabilities, and competencies that it can configure and then apply that domestic firms cannot match.

This chapter considers a number of reasons firms operate abroad. The focus is on life-cycle factors in mature industries where companies tap successful domestic models for export. An excellent example is the global soft-drink industry, in which Coca-Cola and PepsiCo have waged war with each other for more than half a century for worldwide dominance.[3] With the average American consuming huge numbers of carbonated soft drinks per year, Coca-Cola and PepsiCo have little room for market growth in the United States. To stimulate new streams of revenue, they have taken their mature U.S. products and spread them across the globe. In the process they have tried to learn from the foreign experience and infuse some of those lessons back into their U.S. operations, thereby giving their domestic businesses added vitality. After discussing the importance of globalization to a firm's strategy, this chapter analyzes why firms expand internationally, some of the choices they have in doing so, and some of the issues they must confront.

Reasons for Globalization

Given the difficulties firms have in entering foreign markets, why do they do it? In today's world, the scope of the firm extends beyond national boundaries. Inputs—human as well as physical resources—come from all over the world. Potential as well as actual customers are found in every country. In most industries, the competition is not just domestic, but international.

Firms operate internationally for a number of reasons:

- They may be seeking to secure better sources of *raw materials and energy*. Inputs such as bauxite, rubber, and oil can be best secured in global markets.
- They may want to obtain access to low-cost *factors of production* such as labor.
- They may be attracted to certain countries because of the *subsidies* those countries provide.
- They may be seeking new *markets* for their products. They can better exploit their technological advantages or a brand name if they diffuse their products or services globally.
- Domestic markets may no longer be able to absorb *production at a minimum efficient scale*. To get the production costs of a unit low enough to be competitive, companies have to produce millions of units per year, not thousands. They can find markets this large only if they operate globally. The costs per unit produced would be too high if companies sold just to the local market.
- They may be motivated by *life-cycle factors*. Domestic markets become saturated. As they mature, firms look abroad for new opportunities.
- They may be seeking opportunities for *economies of scope* (synergy) and for *learning*.

Economists once assumed that the factors of production were relatively static among nations, but in today's world, capital, technology, and labor readily move from country to country and comparative advantage shifts rapidly.

Product Maturity: Soft Drinks

One means of warding off product decline is globalization. U.S. consumers can devour only so much soda, so many hamburgers, and so much pizza. Coca-Cola recognized this problem long ago. About two-thirds of sales and 80 percent of its profits come from its foreign sales. The hypercompetitive environment in the United States has forced Coca-Cola to look favorably on opportunities abroad.

In the United States, Coca-Cola and PepsiCo have been locked in a duel that involves the pressures of high-cost, celebrity-based advertising and the difficulties of maintaining access to shelf space in supermarkets, keeping fountain business in restaurants, and developing vending business. To keep costs down, both companies have had to carefully manage their relations with bottlers and suppliers of aluminum cans and raw materials such as sugar. The inroads that Coca-Cola and PepsiCo have made on smaller soft-drink companies have limits. Restrictions exist on the two companies' abilities to introduce new products and further differentiate their existing ones.

As baby boomers age, they show signs of weariness with soft drinks. Bottled water, juices, and so-called new-age beverages have taken domestic share away from both Coca-Cola and PepsiCo's core cola and cola-related products. Gigantic outlets such as Walmart and other mass distributors have demanded huge discounts, plus they have developed their own in-house labels to compete with Coke and Pepsi.

With the average American consuming up to 18 ounces of carbonated soft drinks per day, only so much more product can be sold in the United States. PepsiCo keeps making inroads on Coca-Cola's U.S. market share, and the latter has recognized that it has to look abroad for new business, where it has greater brand recognition than PepsiCo.

However, PepsiCo cannot allow Coca-Cola to win market share abroad uncontested, so it has followed Coca-Cola. Although behind Coca-Cola in nearly every market, PepsiCo has made the effort to be a formidable global competitor (see Exhibit 6.1).

EXHIBIT 6.1
Soft Drinks: Selected International Market Shares, 1999

Country	Annual Growth,%, 1992–1999	Coca-Cola, %	PepsiCo, %
United States	2	44	31
Germany	−3	56	8
United Kingdom	7	43	12
Spain	3	60	16
Italy	0	45	8
France	3	60	8
Mexico	2	70	19
Brazil	12	51	7
Chile	5	81	4
China	8	34	16
Philippines	9	70	18
Japan	−1	55	11
South Korea	−2	54	13

EXHIBIT 6.2
Industry Life Cycle

Source: Adapted from Michael Porter, *Competitive Strategy* (New York: Free Press, 1980), p. 158.

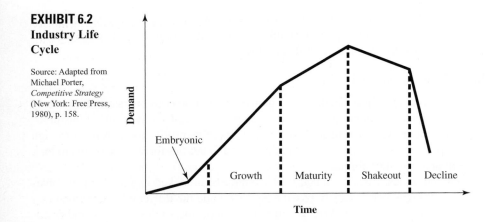

Industry Evolution

As products mature, industry structures change in fundamental ways.[4] The evolution of industry structures is a critical element in the formulation of a company's global strategy. Initially, there is rapid growth as buyers rush to a market once a product proves successful. The penetration of the potential buyers, however, is eventually reached, causing rapid growth to level off (see Exhibit 6.2).

In the **embryonic stage** when a product is just getting off the ground, there are likely to be *few exports*. Prices tend to be high, and margins and profits low. Production runs are short and require skilled labor. Specialized channels are needed for distribution, and relatively few companies are in the industry. Usually, a high-income or sophisticated purchaser has to be persuaded to buy what is still a relatively poor-quality product that has design and development problems. There are many product variations, no standards, and frequent design changes. Companies face high advertising and sales costs to persuade buyers to make a purchase.

In the **growth stage,** *exports pick up*. Although products continue to have technical and performance differences, efforts to improve product reliability start to pay off. There is a widening group of buyers and a shift to mass production and distribution. Prices go down and profits up. Competitors enter the industry in increasing numbers.

As **maturity** sets in, *exports grow even more* to pick up slack. At home, there are few new buyers; most are repeat buyers. Competitors struggle for the same customers. Uniform quality is assumed. Competitors must make small but regular changes in what is a standard product. Overcapacity develops. To extend the life cycle, companies segment the market into more and more categories. They provide deals to customers to gain market share and compete bitterly with regard to price and factors such as packaging.

With lower profits the norm, there is a shakeout among the competition. Firms in mature industries find it hard to be innovative because of investment in existing capabilities and acceptance of conventional industry models. A firm has to be creative to reconfigure the value chain and redefine products and markets.

If exports cannot pick up the slack, **decline** sets in. In the decline stage, there is less and less product differentiation. Spotty product quality reemerges. There are falling prices and margins and fewer competitors. The process of commoditization makes once attractive industries much less attractive.

Although life-cycle models are useful, one cannot assume a common, predetermined pattern of development in every case. The duration of these stages varies from industry to industry. Some industries skip maturity and pass straight from growth to decline. Some industries revitalize after periods of decline. Technology-intensive industries, where the pressures to innovate are constant, may hold on to features of emerging industries, while industries providing basic necessities such as food, housing, and clothing may attain maturity but never fall into decline.

Companies affect the evolution of the life cycle through innovation and repositioning. The actual evolution of industries takes many paths. A way to avoid decline is to tap successful domestic models for export—to find abroad the conditions that first led an industry to be vibrant and growing.

Changes in domestic demand over the product life cycle lead firms to operate internationally. A product becomes highly standardized, competitors enter the business, and firms compete more on the basis of price. Whether it is U.S. products sold in foreign markets or foreign products sold in U.S. markets, products that are common at home are seen as exotic abroad. Away from the home country, the products become premium, deluxe goods that command higher margins; they have more snob appeal. Thus, the product life cycle drives companies to seek markets abroad.

Global Analysis

In recognition of the growing significance of international business to strategy, the five-force framework (see Chapter 2) has been reformulated to take globalization more into account.[5] The **diamond framework,** shown in Exhibit 6.3, affects the competitiveness of nations and regions as well as firms. Factor conditions represent the inputs to production or suppliers, which are global in nature. Demand conditions represent customers, who are also found in every corner of the globe. Firm strategy, structure, and rivalry represent competition within an industry. This element in the diamond incorporates new entrants and substitutes as well as existing competitors, and it, too, is not confined to national borders. Related and supporting industries, an added element, are complements.

EXHIBIT 6.3
Porter's Diamond

Source: Taken from Michael Porter, "The Competitive Advantage of Nations," *Harvard Business Review,* March–April 1990, p. 79.

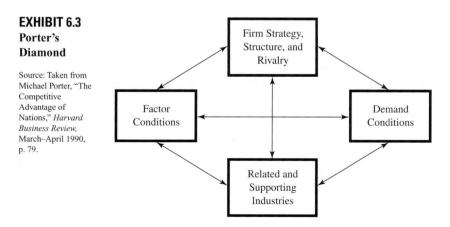

This reformulation of industry analysis recognizes that the firm needs allies, especially when operating internationally. Without allies, the firm cannot succeed globally; these allies are found everywhere the firm competes. The attractiveness of an industry is determined by global as well as domestic conditions.

Where to Invest

In making choices about how to manage a firm's global holdings, competitive conditions in nations, not only in industries, must be considered. The diamond can be used for this purpose. Which regions or countries are most ripe for global expansion? How much should it invest in various regions?

An Example: Soft Drinks

An example would be soft drinks, in which market Coca-Cola and PepsiCo continually face the question of where, among the nations of the world, they should invest to expand the sales of their beverages. These companies have to be sensitive to changing consumption patterns, but understanding demand conditions is not enough. They must understand the factors of production, the competition, and the strength of related and supporting industries. Which regions should be the focus of Coca-Cola's and PepsiCo's attention? Which of their brands have the most promise in different regions (see Exhibit 6.4)? Which investments should they make in different countries?

While North America is the largest soft-drink market, sales there are saturated and growth possibilities limited. The drinks with the most potential are not cola but alternative beverages such as juices, sports drinks, and bottled water. For carbonated beverages, the fastest growing consuming nations are in Asia, Eastern Europe, and the Middle East.[6]

Of these regions, Asia has high potential for carbonated beverages. Because the Asian nations are very populous and their economies rapidly expanding, consumption in Asia is projected to overtake that of North America. Pakistan, indeed, is predicted to have the highest percentage growth rate; India is likely to make sizable volume gains with the spread of affluence; and Indonesia, Vietnam, and China also have strong potential.

Before investing in any of these countries, Coca-Cola and PepsiCo have to appraise the conditions that might affect future demand growth.[7] Not all of these are favorable.

- Pakistan has been a hotbed of Islamic extremism, which might increase anti-American feelings.
- Though forecasts suggest that the gross domestic product (GDP) of India, the longest-functioning democracy in the region, will grow at a fast pace, bureaucracy has crippled foreign companies that have tried to operate in India.
- Indonesia, site of the 2002 Bali terrorist bombings, is a promising nation, but security drawbacks exist.
- Vietnam is rampant with corruption, and the business environment needs improvement.
- Though China's economy is freer each day, officials often still make it difficult for multinational corporations to operate.

EXHIBIT 6.4
**Soft-Drink
Market in
the World:
2004–2008**

Source: Reprinted by
permission of
Euromonitor
International, © 2009.

Regions (% breakdown)	2004	2005	2006	2007	2008
Asia Pacific					
Coca-Cola Co.	20.6%	20 %	19.5%	19.5%	19.7%
PepsiCo	4.5	4.5	4.6	4.7	4.9
Australasia					
Coca-Cola Co.	44	43	42.9	41.6	40.2
PepsiCo	7.2	7.5	7.3	7.2	7.5
Eastern Europe					
Coca-Cola Co.	18.8	18.8	18.4	18.1	18.1
PepsiCo	8.5	8.7	8.7	8.7	13.3
Latin America					
Coca-Cola Co.	39.9	39.4	38.5	38.9	38.8
PepsiCo	11.1	11.2	11.2	11.1	10.9
Middle East and Africa					
Coca-Cola Co.	34.7	33.5	32.9	31.9	30.9
PepsiCo	12.1	13.7	13.8	13.5	13.2
North America					
PepsiCo	26.9	27.1	26.8	26.2	25.5
Coca-Cola Co.	25	25.4	24.5	25.1	24.9
Western Europe					
Coca-Cola Co.	21.7	21.6	21.9	21.9	21.9
PepsiCo	5.8	6.2	6.1	6.2	6.3

Brands (% breakdown)	Company	2004	2005	2006	2007	2008
Coca-Cola	Coca-Cola	10.4%	10.1%	9.9%	9.8%	9.7%
Pepsi	PepsiCo	3.8	3.9	3.8	3.6	3.5
Diet Coke	Coca-Cola	3.1	3.1	3	2.7	2.4
Gatorade	PepsiCo	2	2.2	2.3	2.1	2
Fanta	Coca-Cola	2	2	1.9	2	2
Sprite	Coca-Cola	1.7	1.7	1.7	1.7	1.7
Tropicana	PepsiCo	1.2	1.1	1.1	1	1.1
Minute Maid	Coca-Cola	0.9	0.9	0.9	1	1
Diet Pepsi	PepsiCo	1.1	1.1	1.1	1	0.9
Coke Zero	Coca-Cola	—	0	0.2	0.5	0.7
Mountain Dew	PepsiCo	0.8	0.8	0.8	0.8	0.7
7-Up	PepsiCo	0.6	0.6	0.6	0.6	0.6
Georgia	Coca-Cola	0.8	0.8	0.6	0.6	0.6
Glacéau	Coca-Cola	—	—	—	0.4	0.5
Powerade	Coca-Cola	0.4	0.5	0.5	0.5	0.5

The Chinese government rejected Coca-Cola's 2009 attempt to acquire Huiyuan, which has about a 33 percent share of China's juice market, claiming the takeover, which would have been the largest ever for a foreign company in China, would dampen competition and raise prices. The deal would have been Coca-Cola's largest internationally, second only to its takeover of Glaceau, Energy Brands, in 2007.

The Chinese decision to block Coca-Cola's acquisition was alleged to be in retaliation for U.S. opposition to China's National Offshore Oil Company's failed bid to take over Unocal in 2005. New aggressive antimonopoly laws dampen foreign investment in China.

In making foreign investment decisions, judgment is needed. No country is likely to provide the perfect environment for expansion. Hedging strategies can be used to balance the risk of operating in one country against the risk of operating in another.

Does Globalization Pay?

The globalization option consists of taking a successful domestic model and spreading it to fast-growing markets in other parts of the world. When a domestic market is saturated and mature, the only real choices are to (1) innovate domestically, with new products and/or services that expand the customer base or to (2) reproduce a successful model abroad. Global expansion, however, is rarely smooth. The commitment of Coca-Cola and PepsiCo to quenching the world's thirst has been met by controversy after controversy from opposition from conservative religious groups to tainted water in India. To what extent can these companies prevent these controversies from raging?

The integration of the world's economy has opened many opportunities to expand sales and operations, but these opportunities are accompanied by novel hazards. Various strategies exist to mitigate and overcome these hazards, yet the hazards often undermine the success of global expansion. Some companies have been very successful in extending their global reach, while others have not.

Successful Globalization

Here are some examples of successful globalization.[8]

- By 1998, the U.S. market for products Amphenol sold to the cable television industry was saturated; about 70 percent of U.S. households already had subscribed to cable programming, a number that was not growing. Because satellite technology had become a potent substitute for cable in the United States, growth would have to come from abroad; in Europe the subscription rate for cable was only 31 percent. Amphenol capitalized on the growth of overseas cable programming; by 2001 its international sales of coaxial cable exceeded domestic sales. By 2002, 24 percent of the company's sales were Asian. Its movement into Europe and Asia allowed it to tap markets less affected by the North American downturn.

- To combat domestic overcapacity and to increase market share, Ball Corporation first entered the global arena in 1974 with a joint venture. Through acquisitions and joint ventures, the company then expanded its geographic reach to China, Brazil, Hong Kong, Thailand, and the Philippines. In 1997, it acquired 75 percent of M.C. Packaging in Hong Kong, making its subsidiary the largest beverage can manufacturer in China, but after poor results, it exited the China market. It closed Chinese plants that were not profitable, though it continued to have strong ties to Thailand, Taiwan, and the Philippines. Ball then acquired minority or majority ownership in packaging companies in Canada, Europe, Asia, and South America and in late 2002 purchased Germany-based Schmalbach-Lubeca.

- Before SPX Corp.'s acquisition of the Canadian company United Dominion Industries, 86 percent of its sales came from the United States, 7 percent from Europe, and 7 percent from other countries. With the acquisition of this company it had operations in 21 countries. It then proceeded to increase its sourcing outside the United States, and from 2000 to 2002, its international revenues grew more than 350 percent. By 2002, Europe accounted for 20 percent of its sales, and the rest of the world 13 percent.

Unsuccessful Globalization

However, not every company has had such good results.[9]

- Snap-on hoped to expand product lines and compete internationally, but the global acquisitions in which it engaged did not succeed. It offered products in over 150 countries, but growth was slow and the market for its products shifted downward. Globally, it was spread very thin. It operated in 115 countries and generated sales in 150, but sales outside the United States and Europe were only 5 percent of its total sales and its global businesses were not positioned for strong future growth.

- About half of Parametric Technology Corp.'s employees were located in the United States, with the other half operating in foreign countries, including Canada, France, Germany, and Japan. Despite its global presence, Parametric had serious problems relating to its customers. Customers found the company to be distant. It was ill equipped and unresponsive to their needs to integrate the engineering software it sold.

- Through its acquisitions, Campbell Soup Co. had developed a global focus, selling products in 120 countries and often tailoring the products to specific foreign markets, such as dry soups in Europe. The company moved aggressively to take advantage of overseas opportunities, building an extensive dry soup concern in France, which it used to leverage growth in the rest of Europe. Campbell Soup also acquired several other leading producers of soups, including Erin Foods and McDonnell's in Ireland and Velish in Australia. It bought the Arnott's brand in Australia, a leading snack foods company, and strengthened its presence in the snack market with the acquisition of Snack Foods Limited, the number 2 salty snack company in Australia. However, Campbell's global expansion did not pay off and it failed to make up for growing domestic weakness and loss of U.S. market share.

Globalization's Success Factors

Surprisingly, the empirical evidence on whether global expansion results in positive or negative net benefits is mixed. Some studies show that globalization leads to enhanced performance, while others find no relationship or a negative tie to performance. What the studies show is that firms face the greatest costs at globalization's earliest stages. However, these costs may be overcome with *experience and learning,* but they may grow again at globalization's later stages when conditions again change.

Whether global expansion results in positive or negative net benefits depends on answers to a number of questions. Does global expansion allow a firm to hedge economic risk? Can it benefit from differences in economic cycles? One country's GDP may be on the rise, while another's is slowing. Does global expansion yield increased flexibility? Does it bestow useful managerial and technical knowledge and competence?

The positives must outweigh the negatives. Political and economic risks from operating in foreign countries are likely to be greater than those encountered when operating domestically. The costs of coordinating and communicating with foreign subsidiaries are likely to be high. As the locus of control diffuses among the subsidiaries, the home office is required to exert great effort and expend resources to maintain control. These costs often lead to foreign subsidiary underperformance.

Which Regions in the World?

Pursuing global expansion depends on determining which regions in the world are most attractive.[10] By 2050, the distribution of the world's people will be quite different than it is today. In Europe, the population is expected to decline by about 9 percent, while in Africa it is expected to grow by 120 percent. Within regions there is likely to be heterogeneity. Throughout the world, the movement from countryside to city is expected to continue. By 2020, there are expected to be more than 30 mega-cities, many of them in developing countries.

If the past provides a guide to the future, the pace of change will be rapid. There were 1 billion Internet users in 2007. By 2011, there are likely to be 2 billion. Prosperity has spread unevenly. It has been accompanied by social and economic ills, population dislocations, sickness, poverty, and debt. Today, about a quarter of the world's population lives in poverty, and as many as 800,000 people are malnourished. In many parts of the world, markets are underdeveloped; and it is not clear how to develop them, whether through micro-finance, products tailored to help the poor, or outright aid.

The United States continues to be the world leading economic power, but will this trend continue? How quickly will the lagging economies catch up and how? Who will set the standards for future economic growth? Will it be Asian countries or those in North America? In 2007, 8 of the world's 10 largest companies (ExxonMobil, Citigroup, General Electric, Bank of America, Freddie Mac, Altria, Walmart, and Microsoft) were headquartered in the United States. By 2008, only four of the firms on this list were headquartered in the United States (ExxonMobil, General Electric, Chevron, and Microsoft). The other companies represented a variety of foreign countries—Holland, England, Russia, France, and China.

The U.S. economy has shown that it has weaknesses. Early-stage venture capital has declined. More R&D also has been moving outside the United States. Worldwide, technology alliances between foreign-owned firms and U.S.-owned companies have mushroomed. China and India accounted for 31 percent of global R&D employees in 2007, up from 19 percent in 2004.

The Comparative Development of Nations

In the 21st century, nations throughout the world are starting to catch up with the major industrial powers. Many factors affect the comparative growth rates of nations.

Labor, Capital, and Technology

According to economists, labor, capital, and technology are the main factors that account for differences in national economic growth rates. *Labor* consists of weekly working hours, while *capital* is increments in investment minus depreciation. Labor can be augmented by improvements in educational quality and work intensity, by increased capital, and by better technology. These can offset a decline in working hours and in this way increase productivity (see Exhibit 6.5).

Productivity also is affected by differences in educational quality.[11] Germany, for instance, is known for its high-quality scientific and technical education and specialized training. It has distinctive industrial apprenticeship systems that few countries can match. Japanese workers are known for their skills in subjects such as mathematics and for their discipline, willingness to work hard, and group orientation. Japan has a large pool of well-trained engineers and excellent in-house company training programs. Japan's strengths in elementary and secondary education and in-house training more than compensate for weaknesses in its colleges and universities. Great Britain has a truly outstanding tier of

EXHIBIT 6.5
Contribution of Labor, Capital, and Technology to Economic Growth

Source: Alfred A. Marcus, *Business and Society* (Homewood, IL: Irwin, 1993), p. 303.

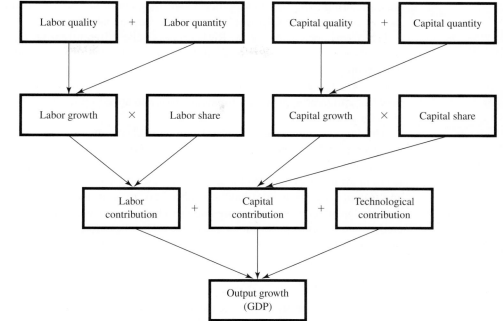

people who are noted for their creativity, inventiveness, and independent thinking and for their capabilities in areas such as pure scientific research. However, the educational system lags that in other countries. Technical colleges have had a very low status, and there is no well-developed apprenticeship system. The United States possesses very high-quality schools at the top, but the percentage of students with technical majors in U.S. universities is low. Public elementary and high schools in the United States have had difficulty providing training in the sciences, mathematics, and languages. Deep-rooted concerns about the U.S. educational system have received much attention.

Investing in capital can partially make up for workforce quality. Economists have found that the most significant predictor of economic growth is the accumulation of capital, measured by investment in GDP. Capital augmentation does not just come from the replacement of old capital with new. It also results from the experience and the knowledge that employees gain on the job and from the recombining and retrofitting of existing capital.

The Austrian economist Joseph Schumpeter argued that technical change also plays a very important role.[12] New capital replaces old ("creative destruction") in waves as particular sectors (e.g., textiles, steel, railroads, automotive, chemicals) dominate the world economy at certain intervals only to be replaced by other sectors (pharmaceuticals, telecommunications, computers, and biotechnology).

Two kinds of technological change occur. **Process technologies** enable firms to improve their ability to make goods and services, while **product technologies** are improvements in the goods and services that are marketed to buyers. Historically, Japanese firms excelled at process technologies, and U.S. firms excelled at new-product innovations. Americans, for instance, invented the videocassette recorder, but the Japanese lowered the costs of manufacturing—improved the process—so they could sell VCRs at low cost. Without Japan's contribution, VCRs would not have become a viable business.

U.S. firms once managed the R&D process quite differently from Japanese firms, but they have since copied much of what the Japanese do: deliberately creating excess information and sharing it among horizontally and vertically linked groups outside and inside the firm; regularly consulting vendors and subcontractors during the development process; and overlapping development phases to speed up market entry and gain early consumer information.

The Japanese consumer provides Japan with an advantage.[13] The Japanese demand for compact, portable, quiet, light, multifunctional products comes from the crowded living conditions and small plants, offices, and warehouses that exist in Japan. These conditions led to innovations in the use of materials, energy, and logistics. Pioneering in space-saving and just-in-time production has been necessary to meet the demands of Japanese consumers. Japan's consumers also are known to be sophisticated and quality-conscious, especially when it comes to consumer electronics. They have forced Japanese firms to be more innovative and to produce to more exacting standards, thus generating advantages in the global marketplace.

Open Economies

Economists consistently emphasize that open economies, those engaged in global trade, perform better than those sheltered from global competition. Since 1970, international trade has *doubled* as a share of the total world economy. This change has occurred for many reasons, including advances in technology, lower transport costs, and more liberal trade policies.

Economists argue that increased world trade has allowed nations to concentrate on the things that they do best (their *comparative advantage*), while trading for those things that they do less well. The gains from such specialization have been mutual; as each nation concentrates on what it does best, its trading partners consume a larger bundle of goods than they could produce by themselves.

In the end, global production, marketing, and distribution lead to the more efficient production of goods and services. Scale economies achieved in global operations yield reductions in per-unit operating costs. More competitive global markets promote competition in local markets, prodding local competitors to upgrade and providing consumers with more choice. In open economies, consumers are able to buy a wider variety of goods at lower prices.

In some countries, the domestic markets are not large enough to support cost-efficient firms, but this does not matter when the trade sector grows and becomes part of global commerce. Countries such as Singapore, Thailand, the Philippines, South Korea, Taiwan, and Indonesia have large trade sectors and have benefited from them. The more open countries have seen much higher growth rates in their real GDP per capita.

The U.S. trade sector also has increased. The largest trading partners of the United States are Canada, Mexico, and Japan. Yet, the United States trails many other nations on the extent to which its economy is intertwined with economies of other nations.

In different countries, increased exposure to global commerce has evolved in different ways. France's economic performance, for instance, rests heavily on its policy of international engagement.[14] The strategy that France had employed after World War I—political isolation and economic exploitation of its traditional adversary Germany—failed. Thus, France's goal after World War II was to integrate as much as possible with its European neighbors to make war impossible and enhance its own prosperity and that of all of Europe.

France became a charter member of the General Agreement on Tariffs and Trade (GATT) in 1947. The following year, it became a member of the Organization for European Economic Cooperation (OEEC). It committed in principle if not always in practice to the concept of free trade. In 1950, France called for the creation of a European common market. The 1957 Treaty of Paris created the European Economic Community (EEC), which prohibited tariffs, quotas, and subsidies that restricted or distorted trade between member states. Like other nations in the EEC, France was heavily exposed to foreign direct investment. Overall, France experienced the salutary effects of international market exposure in the post–World War II period.

South Korea's growth also has involved heavy exposure to international markets, but the South Korean government assumed control over the private sector with the purpose of creating significant export-led growth.[15] Inflows of foreign credit came to South Korea from financial institutions such as the World Bank and International Monetary Fund. Few other countries have had such a high dependence on foreign trade as South Korea. The only comparable nations are Hong Kong, Singapore, and Taiwan.

Both Taiwan and South Korea made enormous strides in the post–World War II period, but they did so in quite different ways. Their progress is interesting when compared to that of their neighbors, the People's Republic of China and North Korea, both of which started at similar levels but did not go nearly as far in this period because they were sheltered from global market conditions.

Taiwan and South Korea had few resources, little arable land, and high population densities. Both countries pursued export-led growth policies, but Taiwan was much less aggressive in protecting its domestic industries and relied more on the free market. It used a highly educated, technically trained (more than one-third of Taiwanese students in higher education study engineering), and enterprising workforce to make its advances and financed its companies through equity markets. These companies were mostly lightly leveraged and small. In comparison, South Korea's large conglomerates, known as the *chaebol*, were highly concentrated and heavily leveraged firms (e.g., Samsung, Hyundai, Lucky-Goldstar, Daewoo). The top 10 constituted about two-thirds of the South Korean economy.

Exhibit 6.6 provides a full list of elements involved in enhancing a nation's economic performance.

Parallels Between Global and Domestic Moves

Globalization holds out the promise of higher growth rates and expanding demand, but the promise of globalization is neither automatic nor guaranteed. For firms, the global arena may involve less head-to-head combat than in the domestic market. All competitors can experience strong growth in revenues and profits. The fighting is not a zero-sum game over a fixed pie. However, globalization presents formidable obstacles. Traditional substitutes must be overcome (in Asia, for instance, the drink of choice is tea, not cola). The infrastructure for expansion may be weak, and there may be opposition from the host government. Distribution channels may be missing or inadequate.

In going global, firms face strategic challenges at both the business level and the corporate level. Companies' global moves must parallel their domestic business and corporate strategy moves.

EXHIBIT 6.6 Elements in Enhancing a Nation's Economic Performance

Labor Productivity	Capital Accumulation and Innovation	The Cost of Capital	Resource/Sectoral Factors	Government Factors	World Market Orientation
Value of leisure time	Extent of investment	Ability of firms to generate retained earnings	Energy intensity	Industrial policies	Closed/open character of economy
Work intensity	Age of capital: replacement of old with new (modernization), Investment in short-lived vs. durable	Savings	Natural resource intensity	Inward orientation or export-led	Government protection of infant industries/promotion of exports
Educational quality		Government programs to expand savings	Sectoral elements (industrial vs. service sector vs. specialization in primary and secondary products)	Response to market signals	
Experience and knowledge gained on the job (learning by doing)	Recombination and retrofitting of existing capital	Individual propensity in population to delay gratification		Control of financial sector	Knowledge of foreign markets
Employment contracts (short-term vs. lifetime)	Ability to innovate in use of capital	Debt	Emphasis on labor-intensive or capital-intensive industries	Benefits offered exporters	Language and capabilities among managers to enter foreign markets
Payment schemes (straight salary vs. salary + bonus)	R&D spending in the firm	Availability and use of foreign financing, foreign aid, and assistance from the World Bank and IMF		Control of trade policy	Extent of involvement in foreign markets
Unions and relative wages	R&D spending in society as a whole	Conditions imposed by banks in financing and refinancing loans		Import barriers	Import-intensive (raw materials)
The work ethic	Extent of engineers in the population	Types of financial institutions and their soundness		Import substitution	Export-intensive (finished products)
Cultural factors such as the Confucian and Protestant ethics	Technical education	Legal climate for lending		Extent and type of regulation	Imitation capabilities
	Ability to exploit scale economies from large-scale projects	Acceptance of equity ownership by banks		Commitment to private sector	Introduction of foreign technology
	Development of an entrepreneurial/managerial class with the requisite motivations and skills to start projects and sustain economic development	Equity market and bond market development		Government ownership	Absorption of foreign know-how
	Risk-taking propensities in population	Pressures exerted by these markets for short-term payoffs		Ratio of government expenditures to GDP	Ability to move into markets opened by others
	Availability of venture-capital opportunities	Return on investment (actual/expected) needed for loans and capital market investment		Extent of government deficits	Exchange rates
	Requisite flexibility in use of capital			Political stability	Availability of foreign exchange
	Capability of managers to shift resources to most profitable applications			Social solidarity and political cohesion	Competitive devaluations/inflation
	Skill development among managers			Distribution of income	
	Training and awareness of managers			Democracy	

Business Strategy

With respect to business strategy, a company's global expansion can be organized in a way that accentuates a low-cost, highly differentiated, or best-value position:[16]

- A **global product-market strategy** has a single dominant design or business model; this approach takes advantage of economies of scale and is a highly efficient, low-cost way to expand internationally.
- A **multidomestic product-market strategy** adapts and modifies a product or service to each separate country or region. It extracts high margins and charges a premium price for delivering customized products and services that meet the needs of individual markets.
- A **transnational product-market strategy** combines global design and local responsiveness. To achieve best value, it both exploits scale economies and adapts to local conditions.

When cost pressures are high and pressures for local responsiveness are low, companies can use uniform global strategies. When cost pressures are low and pressures for local responsiveness are high, multidomestic strategies can be followed to adapt to the needs of each local market. The former is similar to a low-cost business strategy, and the latter is similar to a differentiated strategy. If cost pressures are high and the pressures for local responsiveness are also high, companies might be forced to move toward the middle and carry out transnational strategies that have some elements of global homogenization and some of local adaptation.

For Coca-Cola and PepsiCo, the decision would be whether they should sell the same products everywhere or adapt them to local conditions. The advantage of global strategies is the ability to build low-cost positions by exploiting economies of scale, economies of scope, and experience-curve effects. The advantage of multidomestic strategies is the ability to earn higher margins by customizing products and marketing to local needs. Transnational strategies try to combine the advantages of low cost and differentiation and provide the best value for the money on a global basis.

In going global, a firm may have to meet the pressures for both low cost and local responsiveness. Low cost might be best achieved by a single brand produced in a uniform way for all markets everywhere, thus reducing design costs, lowering manufacturing costs, and achieving greater efficiencies. However, given the existence of different infrastructures, distribution patterns, and government demands, it may not be possible to achieve uniform policies throughout the world. Local acceptance is likely only by accommodating local tastes and adapting to traditional practices. Accommodating local needs, however, is costly and difficult, as the following example indicates.

Entering Japan

A U.S. firm entering another market must be sensitive to differences it will experience. Its success will depend on its ability to adapt to these differences. The expansion of fast-food companies into Japan is a good example.[17] At the start of the 1990s, the fast-food business in Japan was rapidly expanding. People were spending a larger portion of their incomes on eating out. Although Japan was the second largest consumer market in the world, it was an alien place to many U.S. franchises. The Japanese people were friendly to the Americans, but many U.S. businesses that tried to move into Japan failed.

The key to Kentucky Fried Chicken's success (KFC was then owned by PepsiCo) was adapting to Japanese conditions. The company married "modern business practices with Japan's century old traditions." Its success depended on many elements, such as:

- *Adapting to local customs.* The head of KFC operations in Japan, an ex-IBM employee, was willing to adapt to local customs. At business gatherings, he would say a few words in Japanese no matter how difficult it was for him. He understood that he had to socialize, network, and form personal bonds with KFC's franchisees and other business partners. In Japan, business relations are built on trust, a handshake, and a glass or two of sake. He was an outgoing person, enjoyed the sake, was proud of his "fiberglass liver," and liked attending geisha parties.

- *Delegating authority.* The KFC head in Japan also understood that he had to delegate real authority to his Japanese staff. His executive vice president was a 27-year-old local man, whom he immediately hired to be his peer and with whom he shared an office and developed a friendship. He gave this man the opportunity to expand the business with him. Usually in Japan an employee cannot climb to the position of chief operating officer until the age of 40, but KFC Japan's second in command had a large say in decision making from the outset.

- *Training for life.* At KFC in Japan, employees did not "work" for the company but "belonged" to it. Since employees were going to stay with the company for their entire careers, the head of KFC Japan believed the company could invest heavily in training. The training was not only in methods but also in the spirit of the company. Employees started each day with a pledge to serve customers promptly, be polite, maintain the stores in spotless condition, and pay attention to hygiene. They took these company slogans very seriously. They were shown behind-the-counter technique and drilled until they got it right. For instance, when an order was taken, they had to remember that a packer was behind them and they had to repeat the order to the packer. They had to use both hands when giving the product to the customer, and they had to say very politely, "Here you are."

- *Locating stores effectively.* The location of new stores was chosen carefully because overhead was high in comparison to that in the United States. A new store could cost the equivalent of $400,000 to build and equip and $28,000 a month to maintain, so it had to generate at least $85,000 a month in revenue. A logarithm was developed to predict business per month based on foot traffic, population density, and other factors.

- *Sizing stores appropriately.* The first stores that KFC built in Japan were exact replicas of its U.S. stores. As KFC Japan's chief operating officer remarked, they were like "full-size Cadillacs." In Japan's crowded and narrow streets, they were not appropriate, so they had to be redesigned. To suit local conditions, everything was reduced to one-third the size of a U.S. KFC store, but the smaller stores were expected to do three times the business of their U.S. counterparts.

- *Changing the menu.* The menu was adapted to Japanese tastes, with additional items such as smoked chicken, yogurt, and fish and chips being available. French fries replaced mashed potatoes, and the coleslaw was less sweet than the U.S. version.

- *Having display samples.* Japanese consumers demanded display samples that were exact replicas of the food they ate. These were designed, built, and showcased in each store.

- *Displaying statues of the colonel.* The head of KFC Japan found old life-size statues of the "Colonel" in a U.S. warehouse. He placed them on the sidewalk in front of each store to show the authenticity of the product.

- *Advertising to Japanese customers.* A Japanese agency developed the TV advertising campaign, which cost $5 million annually. The advertisements stressed the product's association with America and its "aristocratic elegance." They also showed satisfied, smiling faces the world over. The appeal was not good basic food at a reasonable price but unusual, distinctive food from Kentucky (the theme song was "My Old Kentucky Home") that came from the Colonel's home kitchen. The associations with the product's noble and fine features allowed KFC Japan to earn higher margins.

- *Having a committed partner.* Mitsubishi, the trading company, was a half owner of KFC Japan and was the main supplier of the meat. It invested heavily in KFC Japan to expand the market for chicken, in which it had also invested. Mitsubishi was patient with KFC Japan, allowing it to miss profit projections while it built market share. Mitsubishi had a longer-term time horizon than the U.S.-based KFC. It had less pressure from investors and financial analysts.

- *Co-opting local competitors.* Usually, there were many Japanese competitors in the neighborhoods where KFC stores opened—sushi and noodle shops and local butchers that sold smoked chicken on the side. KFC Japan mounted public relations efforts whenever it opened a new store. Before opening the store, representatives from KFC Japan would tour the neighborhood, giving gifts and discount coupons, introducing the store supervisor, and asking for support. All of this was done to prevent local opposition and to combat the feeling that outsiders were not welcome.

- *Using local rituals.* A centuries-old Shinto ritual with a Buddhist priest was performed at a store's inauguration ceremonies. The prayers were derived from seventh century texts, and on an altar were items such as the branch of a tree, sake, rice cakes, and dried squid, all of which were prescribed by Shinto law.

- *Fighting off U.S. competitors.* All the care KFC Japan took did not prevent other U.S. firms from trying to follow in its footsteps. Church's Fried Chicken soon entered the Japanese market and claimed that its quality and service were better than those of KFC, its chickens were larger and juicier, its slices were bigger, and its product's taste was better because its chicken was marinated and fried, rather than pressure-cooked, and therefore crispier.

To make its business succeed in Japan, KFC had to overcome many obstacles.

Corporate Strategy

Just as there are parallels between a company's global and business strategy, so too there are parallels between its global and corporate strategy. The methods of global expansion run the gamut from concentration on a single line of business and/or a single phase in the product life cycle to broad diversification across numerous product lines and/or many phases in the product life cycle.

In establishing a global strategy, a company can purchase foreign firms to facilitate its expansion—it can use mergers and acquisitions as its means of gaining a foreign foothold—or it can start new, wholly owned subsidiaries (greenfield operations).[18]

One option is **exporting production** and relying on foreign firms for marketing and distribution. A company does not even have to set up production facilities in the foreign country, but, rather, can outsource to foreign firms what it cannot do itself. The risks are high transportation costs, trade barriers that may keep the firm's products out of local markets, and problems that may arise from relying on foreign marketing and distribution agents.

Another option is **licensing** the product to foreign firms. The foreign firms make the product in their own country and handle arrangements for marketing and distribution. The parent company reduces its risks but also loses some control. The foreign firms to whom it licenses the product may appropriate the company's technologies. The company also has less ability to coordinate its international holdings and achieve operational efficiencies.

Franchising is still another option, in many ways similar to licensing. The company disseminates its business methods and models, providing franchisers with a brand identity and a business image, which they then might have to adapt to local conditions. In return, the company gets a percentage of the profits. The franchisers have to do most of the day-to-day work and bear most of the business risk. The disadvantages are that the parent company gives up control, a franchisee may not live up to the quality standards the company has set for itself, and the company is less able to coordinate its foreign operations and achieve economies of scale and scope if it does not manage them itself.

A company achieves maximum control if it establishes its own **greenfield operations** in the foreign country. With this approach, it can control everything from production to marketing and distribution. It is better able to protect its technology from appropriation by a foreign partner, and it is in a better position to engage in global strategic coordination and to achieve operational efficiencies. However, greenfield operations are very challenging if the company does not have prior foreign experience or experience in a particular country. The costs and risks are great.

Coca-Cola and PepsiCo have had to decide whether to fully own their foreign subsidiaries, to contract out the functions of these subsidiaries, or to rely on intermediate means for accomplishing the same purposes. Coca-Cola and PepsiCo could buy local bottlers or establish their own. These choices are endemic to foreign expansion.[19]

Entry into a foreign market can be via export, where the company focuses solely on production and distribution and sales are *outsourced* to foreign concerns. Or a company can achieve access by *internalizing* nearly every phase in the value chain from production to delivering finished goods to consumers. In between the extremes are *intermediate forms of entry* such as licensing, franchising, and joint venturing. Regardless of what a company does, its foreign expansion involves working with other firms. Should Coca-Cola and PepsiCo license to local soft-drink companies, acquire the local brands and bottlers, develop franchise-type relations or joint ventures with them, or set up greenfield operations? However they proceed, they must protect themselves from the risks of working with local partners. Managing a joint venture is apt to be difficult. A partner can exploit the partnership for its own ends, appropriate the company's technologies, or prevent the company from coordinating international operations for the company's benefit.

To protect the company, safeguards have to be built in. The key safeguards are those preventing the loss of critical technology and ensuring the freedom to coordinate diverse global holdings without interference from an alliance partner. Many joint ventures dissolve. The two parties leave with bitterness, each feeling that the other side has exploited it.

Globalization's Challenges

Global strategies have parallels in business and corporate strategies, but globalization also has unique challenges: imbalances in the global economy, insecurity, youth violence, and government incapacity.[20]

Economic Imbalances

The U.S. trade sector has grown more rapidly than total output and its growth has been exceedingly rapid, but this growth has been uneven, with imports surpassing exports. From 1975 to 2000, imports rose from 7.5 percent of GDP to 14.9 percent, while exports grew from 8.3 percent of GDP to 11.2 percent of GDP, which means the United States has had a rising trade deficit. With regard to capital goods, the United States does not have a deficit; rather it is a net exporter. But the nation does have huge deficits in consumer goods such as electronics, autos, and energy, where U.S. dependence is growing.

An important accounting formula requires current account transactions to equal capital account transactions.[21] Because the balance of payments has to even out, a rising trade deficit is not necessarily negative. A healthy growing economy offers attractive investment opportunities and generates an inflow of capital. This inflow is a net plus. It stimulates the economy, just as the availability of foreign goods at low price helps to keep inflation in check.

After 9/11, a slowdown in business investment occurred in the United States, and GDP declined an estimated 1 percent per year between 2001 and 2003. Policy makers put their feet on the accelerator, propping up the U.S. economy and creating a real estate boom, which came crashing down in 2008, resulting in conditions unseen in the world since the Great Depression of the 1930s. U.S. global debt, which helps maintain the U.S. economy, is held in a relatively few hands. In 2007 foreign holdings were mostly in Japan (21 percent), China (20 percent), Taiwan (6 percent), and Korea (5 percent). These nations provided U.S. consumers with money in the form of credit, which they mainly used to buy goods and services from Asia. As a consequence, the Asian economies grew rapidly and U.S. consumers were better off because they had more goods to choose from, most offered at lower prices than otherwise would be the case. This bargain was at the core of the world economy. Asia was the world's workshop and the United States was its shopping center. A key question was how long this situation could continue. How stable was it?

Insecurity

Another important issue was global security. Consider Walmart. Its aim has been to become a trillion-dollar enterprise by about 2012, with less than 60 percent of its growth coming from domestic markets and more than 40 percent from foreign markets. Another example was 3M. Already, more than two-thirds of 3M's sales came from abroad. If global security were to deteriorate, the flow of goods, money, and people in the world would be impaired and companies like Walmart and 3M would have less chance to grow at the rates at which they were aiming. A decline in security would increase their costs of doing business. Global supply chains and operations might have to be shifted, alliances and partnerships ended, entry into countries delayed or deferred, trade not entered into, marketing and product development cut back, and the sourcing of raw materials and labor might be jeopardized.

Violent Conflict

Violent conflict would have serious effects on the global economy.[22] Violence decimates populations, diminishes human and social capital, and destroys physical infrastructure—roads, power and communication systems, transport links, public and private buildings, and essential physical assets. Corporations must spend heavily to protect both people and property. Violent conflict can damage corporate reputations if corporations are implicated. It destabilizes governments, reducing their capacity to fight corruption and making them less able to guarantee contracts and more likely to impose exorbitant taxes. Because of violent conflict, governments can be overthrown and replaced by regimes that might renegotiate the terms under which companies operate.

Though violent conflict adds to the dangers of doing business and raises the likelihood that revenue streams will be curtailed or eliminated, corporations have not stopped increasing their activities in many violent-prone nations. For firms in extractive natural-resource-based industries, such as mining, oil and gas, hydroelectric engineering, and forestry, the benefits appear to outweigh the costs. Firms facing maturity in their domestic markets also may be attracted to violence-prone nations; because fewer companies invest in these nations, a firm can earn monopoly or near-monopoly returns.

Firms can take a number of steps to mitigate the dangers of operating in violent-prone nations. They can rely on the early warning systems provided by consultancies whose work is supplemented by multilateral organizations, governments, academic research institutes, and nongovernmental organizations (NGOs). These organizations offer many services, including the rating of countries based on underlying structural conditions that may lead to violence. A list of the underlying structural conditions generally includes variables representing human development, social solidarity (such as religious and ethnic heterogeneity), economic development, and government capacity. To the underlying structural conditions, they may add accelerators and/or triggers and catalysts, such as suicide bombings, that ignite a crisis or conflict.

Another mechanism companies can use to mitigate the dangers of violence is to hedge their bets. Based on the consultancies' ratings and their own assessments (many firms have their own assessment capabilities), companies may decide to invest in a guarded or step-by-step fashion, diversify, find partners, or impose high hurdle rates often expressed in financial terms as discount rates that are used to calculate projects' net present value or payback periods. To tailor strategies to reflect their individual profiles, firms also consider such factors as their size, familiarity with the local environment, status of their partners, influence of stakeholders, and their experience levels. Projects in more violent-prone countries then will have lower net present values compared to similar projects pursued in less violent nations and therefore will be less likely to be pursued. Companies also frequently buy insurance to hedge the dangers. But a random element still exists with regard to the occurrence of violence that cannot be predicted with great precision.

Youth Violence

Since the role of young and educated people is an important indicator of tendencies toward violent conflict, their role must be better understood. Young and educated people can be divided into two main groups.[23]

Gracious Living

What one group of educated young people aspires to may be called *gracious living*. This group is optimistic and entrepreneurial. It favors the opening of societies and the introduction of cosmopolitan ideas from throughout the world. People in this group believe in freedom, choice, and competition and seek affluence, though they may be concerned that this affluence cannot or will not be widely shared. More so than their parents, they are willing to live for the moment and to take on debt. They are affected by advertising, the media, and popular entertainment and cultural symbols such as Disney. Their dominant orientation is materialistic, though they may be aware of materialism's costs, such as increased pollution.

This group can be found in the rising sectors of India, China, Brazil, Chile, and Mexico, and they are located throughout the world wherever there is hope that individual efforts can lead somewhere, that self-improvement is possible, and that societies can rise based on the initiative of individuals.

Disappointed and Disillusioned

Another group has a far different orientation—and this group may be labeled *disappointed and disillusioned*. These young people also tend to be educated, compared to others in their society, and relatively well off. They are serious, intent, and motivated, perhaps even more so than the young people that fit in the category of *gracious living*. But they also are resentful and they tend to believe that they have no future; there is little hope that things can get better. Their strong collective identities focus on ties to religion and ethnicity. They revisit group memories of injustice. Many live in countries that were once occupied by colonial powers. They resent having lost national and/or religious power or glory. Many of them conclude that armed struggle and violence are acceptable.

Young people who fit in this category more often are found in the Mideast and Africa, but they exist throughout the world including in Sri Lanka, the Philippines, Indonesia, Colombia, Bolivia, and Venezuela. Some of them have migrated to the developed nations, and they can be found throughout Europe and the United States. Many have nothing but contempt for Western values. They are repulsed by the individualism, materialism, freethinking, loose sexual morals, and self-indulgence.

The Challenge of Youth

Companies may be able to make a difference by motivating and guiding youth to productive activities. Examples exist of companies engaged in this activity. For instance, Nokia and the International Youth Foundation (IYF) have launched a global youth development initiative to strengthen the life skills of young people and prepare them for the future. By 2008, Nokia had invested $26 million in 24 countries and directly benefited more than 330,000 young people.

Companies must help spread a message of confidence and hope rather than despair and pessimism. The combined message of skills, opportunity, and hope is displayed in "bottom of the pyramid" advocacy of such writers as Prahalad and Hart.[24] More experiments of this nature must be tried.

Government Incapacity

If instability overtakes the world, the benefits of globalization become more difficult to realize.[25] Thus, the governments of the world must make the effort to educate the young and harness their drive, energy, creativity, and ambition. However, the nation-state as a system for world governance is a relatively recent phenomenon. Sentiment in its favor reached its apex after World War II and the creation of the United Nations. The original 50 nations that composed the U.N. have since grown to include more than 190 states. This system of nation-states has largely taken over from the empires—British, Austro-Hungarian, Russian, Turkish, and French—that carved up much of the world in the 19th century. The modern states of Germany and Italy were forged toward the end of the 19th century. The German and Italian languages and their national identities took shape then. Neither had the final form they have today. In the 19th century, the elements that formed modern Germany and Italy were small republics, tiny kingdoms, vassals of empires, principalities, or extended city-states.

The conflict between empire and nation-state as an organizing principle was an important backdrop to both the First and Second World Wars. Out of the ruins of both of these wars many nations were given their independence and many new states were created. Countless aspirations centered on people having a nation-state of their own, but not all people were satisfied, such as the Kurds and Armenians, for instance.

No one now doubts the centrality of the nation-state system today, but as recently as 100 years ago, when this system was still in formation, many people did. A key element in state legitimacy is that the state possesses the sole legal means for quelling violence within the territories it governs. Citizens, in fable if not fact, cede their right of self-preservation and self-protection to the state to benefit from the peaceful conditions it can impose. Life for most people would be nasty, short, and brutish were it not for the protection afforded by the state. In many parts of the world, however, rather than creating peace, stability, and order, the nation-state has subjected its citizens to wars, persecution, and tyranny.

The state's rise often is accompanied by the type of violence and civil wars it is supposed to suppress. Consider the U.S. Civil War, which was the most violent event in U.S. history, leading to more casualties than any conflict in which the country has been involved before or since.

Many competing institutions are in conflict with today's nation-state and test its capacity to maintain people's loyalty. Within some nation-states are irredentist movements—Basque, Quebecois, and so on—that can cause states to collapse. Witness what happened to Yugoslavia, which was a far cry from the peaceful dissolution of Czechoslovakia.

Outside the state, many institutions compete with it. Non-state and super-state actors abound, some of them threatening to the state and some supportive. They range from Al Qaeda to multinational corporations. They include NGOs such as Greenpeace and the World Wildlife Fund and supra-government organizations like the United Nations, the World Bank, and the World Trade Organization. The global media giants—Reuters, CNN, the BBC, SkyNews, Al Jazeera—may be headquartered in a particular country, but their allegiances are transnational. The nation-state is far from being the undisputed force in the world that it was once thought it would be.

Summary

Every aspect of strategic management has a global dimension: corporate performance, the firm's decisions about expansion and entering new markets, the external and internal analyses managers carry out, the business-level moves they make relating to timing and product positioning, and the corporate-level moves they make relating to mergers, acquisitions, and divestitures.

The five forces and the macroenvironment have global dimensions. Thus, Porter modified the five forces to take this into account. Porter's diamond is based on factor conditions (suppliers); demand conditions (customers); firm strategy, structure, and rivalry (competitors, substitutes, and new entrants); and related and supporting industries (complements). It explains the competitive advantage not only of firms but also of nations and regions.

The global macroenvironment must be scrutinized with respect to what it reveals about elements in the diamond. International parallels can be drawn to business strategies—low cost, differentiated, and best value—and to corporate strategies—the make-or-buy decision and choices about vertical integration.

One main issue in globalization is the direction of a firm's expansion—which nations or regions of the world make the most sense? To determine the answer, the firm must examine the stability of nations being considered. Nations such as Pakistan, India, Indonesia, China, and Vietnam are populous and their economies are growing at a much more rapid rate than the economies of advanced developed nations; however, these countries may be subject to political repression, corruption, insufficiently free markets, and violence.

Developed nations are mature markets. They may be saturated with the product a company provides and thus less capable of long-term growth. Often, life-cycle factors such as maturity drive companies to expand internationally despite the difficulties of globalization. But companies expand globally for many reasons, such as seeking new markets, better resources, greater efficiency, and/or less risk or countering a competitor's move.

Among the factors affecting the comparative growth of nations are labor, capital, technology, and market exposure. It is critically important for a company to adapt to local customs when entering a country. The nature of this adaptation has many dimensions, from delegating authority to local managers to having local partners and following local customs. A company can enter foreign markets in a variety of ways including direct export, franchising, licensing, greenfield operations, or joint ventures.

Many challenges continue to affect globalization. The ones discussed in this chapter include economic imbalances, violent conflict, the aspirations of young and educated people, and government incapacity.

Endnotes

1. M. Porter, *The Competitive Advantage of Nations* (New York: Free Press, 1990).
2. S. Zaheer, "Overcoming the Liability of Foreignness," *Academy of Management Journal* 38, no. 2 (1995), pp. 341–64.
3. David Yoffie, "Cola Wars Continue: Coke and Pepsi in the Twenty-First Century," Harvard Business School Case 9-702-442, revised July 30, 2002.
4. M. Porter, *Competitive Strategy* (New York: Free Press, 1980).
5. M. Porter, *The Competitive Advantage of Nations.*
6. www.softdrink.ca/tp100f2e.htm.
7. See "Country Briefings," *The Economist,* www.economist.com/countries/Economist.

8. A. Marcus, *Big Winners and Big Losers; The 4 Secrets of Long-Term Business Success and Failure* (Upper Saddle River, NJ: Wharton School Press, 2006).

9. Ibid.

10. A. Marcus, *Strategic Foresight: A New Look at Scenarios* (New York: Palgrave MacMillan, 2009); see the Afterword with M. Amin.

11. Porter, *The Competitive Advantage of Nations.*

12. J. Schumpeter, *Capitalism, Socialism and Democracy* (New York: Harper, 1975) [orig. pub. 1942.]

13. Porter, *The Competitive Advantage of Nations.*

14. W. Adams, *Restructuring the French Economy* (Washington, DC: The Brookings Institution, 1989).

15. A. Amsden, *Asia's Next Giant* (New York: Oxford University Press, 1989); and "Taiwan and Korea: Two Paths to Prosperity," *The Economist,* July 14, 1990, pp. 22–29.

16. C. Bartlett and S. Ghoshal, *Managing across Borders: The Transnational Solution,* 2nd ed. (Boston: Harvard Business School Press, 1998).

17. "The Colonel Comes to Japan," Enterprise Series, Learning Corporation of America Video.

18. J. Shaver, "Accounting for Endogeneity When Assessing Strategy Performance: Does Entry Mode Choice Affect FDI Survival?" *Management Science* 44, no. 4 (1998), pp. 571–86.

19. O. Williamson, *Economic Institutions of Capitalism: Firms, Markets, Relational Contracting* (New York: Free Press, 1991).

20. Marcus, *Strategic Foresight.*

21. A current-account deficit must equal a capital-account surplus and current-account surplus must equal a capital-account deficit. Current-account transactions consist of: merchandise trade *(import and export of goods),* service trade *(import and export of services),* income from investments, and unilateral transfers *(gifts to and from foreigners).* While capital-account transactions consist of: direct investments by foreigners in the United States and by U.S. citizens abroad and loans to and from foreigners. The official reserve transactions of all governments have to equal zero.

22. A. Marcus, M. Islam, and J. Moloney, "Youth Bulges, Busts, and Doing Business in Violence-Prone Nations," *Business and Politics* 10, no. 3 (2008), Article 4.

23. Marcus, *Strategic Foresight.*

24. C. Prahalad, *The Fortune at the Bottom of the Pyramid: Eradicating Poverty Through Profits* (Upper Saddle River, NJ: Wharton School Press, 2006); and S. Hart, *Capitalism at the Crossroads* (Upper Saddle River, NJ: Wharton School Press, 2007).

25. Marcus, *Strategic Foresight.*

CHAPTER SEVEN

Innovation and Entrepreneurship

"What good will it do to follow the rules when some companies are re-writing them? . . . Shackled neither by convention nor by respect for precedent . . . [the rule breakers] are intent on overturning the industrial order. They are the malcontents, the radicals, the industrial revolutionaries. Never has the world been more hospitable to industry revolutionaries and more hostile to industry incumbents."[1]

Gary Hamel, professor, Woodside Institute

Chapter Learning Objectives

- Explaining the factors needed for successful innovation and entrepreneurship.
- Examining barriers to innovation and suggesting how to overcome these barriers.
- Understanding how to identify opportunities for innovation and entrepreneurship.
- Being aware of the role leading-edge industries and environmental challenges play in innovation and entrepreneurship.
- Distinguishing risk from uncertainty and exploring different types of uncertainty.
- Seeing innovation and entrepreneurship as a long-term process.

Introduction

All the moves discussed so far in this book (positioning; mergers, acquisitions, and divestitures; and globalization) require some degree of innovation and entrepreneurship. Without innovation, they would be easy to imitate. Without entrepreneurship, they would have great difficulty getting off the ground. But how much innovation and entrepreneurship are involved in these moves? Firms generally are conservative, and for good reason. Few new undertakings yield positive returns. Even fewer become highly profitable. Honestly calculating the expected costs and benefits beforehand is almost certain to diminish the ardor for innovation and entrepreneurship.

Though most firms go to great lengths to ballyhoo innovation and entrepreneurship, few are really good at these activities. The number of failures is many times the number of

EXHIBIT 7.1
Managing Innovation and Entrepreneur-ship: All the Pieces Must Be in Place

Source: Based on Anne Adams, Chris Kingsley, and Pam Smith, "Managing Complex Change," *Community Youth Development Journal,* 2001, www.cydjournal. org/Brandeis/ smith_0322.html.

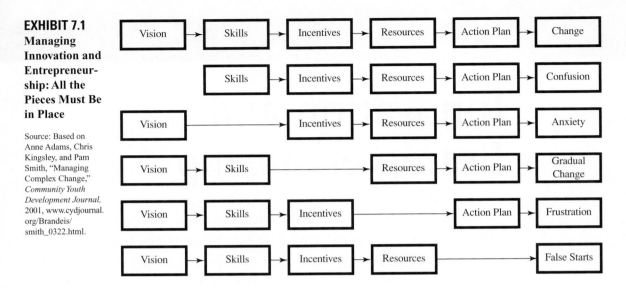

successes. Venture capitalists say that of 30 projects they typically back, only one lives up to expectations. Even highly successful venture capital firms do not have many hits. They back companies that barely make a go of it and others that go nowhere. Innovation and entrepreneurship are risky. The factors for success are hard to assemble (see Exhibit 7.1). Even one missing element can undo a sound project.

This chapter explores the factors needed for successful innovation and entrepreneurship. It examines the barriers and provides suggestions on how to overcome these barriers. The test for the strategist is to recognize the risks and uncertainties and understand the moves that can be taken to cope with them. This chapter begins by examining the difficulties of succeeding in new business ventures and then scrutinizes the commercialization process. It requires both discovering new opportunities and exploiting them, with discovery being easy in comparison to making new ideas a commercial success.

Challenges of Succeeding in New Business Ventures

Plenty of good business ideas exist.[2] A list of ones that have been successfully exploited includes Trader Vic's, which mixes a gourmet deli and discount retailer; the disposable camera, which spread the use of 35-millimeter film; and Internet banks, which were open all hours. Having a good idea, however, does not guarantee a successful business venture. Failure often is not in coming up with the idea, but in making it a profitable business. As important as having the idea is commercializing it.

Success Stages

Propelled by increases in sales, new ideas are supposed to evolve through stages of introduction, growth, and maturity.[3] In the initiation stage, the founders decide to start an enterprise that has the capacity to exploit an idea; in the start-up phase, they should be able to develop new products and services based on the idea; and in the takeoff phase, the ventures they create should get off the ground and sales should grow rapidly.

But after an idea is initially hatched not all business ventures pass smoothly through these stages. Some show promise but fail to take off. Others take off but hardly expand. Moving from idea generation to takeoff and from takeoff to sustained growth, that is, when a business can sustain itself without large outside infusions of capital, requires critical mass and momentum. Most new ventures never get to this point or the process can unfold over a very long time with great frustration on the part of the founders, their exiting the scene, and turnover among those active in continuing to promote the idea.

Some businesses move from origin to takeoff to sustained growth in just a few years, while others may take a half century or more.[4] Average time for moving from initiation to sustained growth has been estimated to be 29 years with the standard deviation being 15 years. Founders and entrepreneurs have to be persistent and have considerable commitment if they are to succeed.

Commitment

Commitment is especially needed between takeoff and sustained growth, since it is in this time frame that founders often leave the scene and give up. Their interest wanes and they may lose patience. Reasons for abandoning a venture include few customers, technological glitches, waning financial support, and/or negative cash flow. Founders do not always have the skills, determination, or will to overcome such setbacks. New players must be found to take the venture to the next stage. If they are not found, abandoning a business between initiation and takeoff may doom it even if it has intrinsic promise.

The end point does not have to be success or failure Prolonged gestation (see Exhibit 7.2) is a state of neither complete takeoff nor complete failure. What prolonged gestation means is that it takes many more years for a business to gain momentum than the founders anticipated. Though the business is not meeting expectations, the founders or their successors stick with it and maintain their commitment. Often they are stubborn dreamers who cling to their ideas despite the fact that the odds seem stacked against them.

Overcoming Barriers

Many obstacles stand in the way of the full takeoff of even the most promising business idea. A promising idea may be just an **invention,** the creation of a promising notion in a laboratory.

EXHIBIT 7.2
**Prolonged
Gestation for a
New Business**

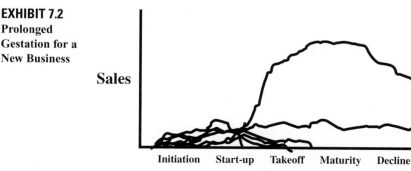

EXHIBIT 7.3
Invention
versus
Innovation

Invention	Innovation
Creation of idea in laboratory	Idea put into widespread use
Test of principle	Commercial exploitation
Act of technical creativity	
Concept suitable for patenting	

A test takes place in the laboratory of the idea's principles. The idea's technical viability is then proven. The originality of the inventors is demonstrated. Their invention may be suitable for patenting. However, **innovation** entails actually delivering on the idea's promise. Without creating distinctive value that meets customers' needs, the idea is just a concept, nothing more. Innovation is putting promising business ideas into widespread use; it is the effort to commercially exploit an idea and ensure its broad application (see Exhibit 7.3). For a new idea to gain widespread acceptance in the marketplace, a number of critical elements are needed: (1) entrepreneurs who have insight into the idea's potential and who are determined to make it a commercial success; (2) innovative companies that package the idea, market it to customers, and offer it as an attractive business proposition; (3) investors who see the commercial potential and back the promising venture, often at great risk to themselves, before it is profitable; and (4) typically, as well, government support in the form of either subsidy or the creation of rules, standards, or infrastructure that are favorable to the idea.

Entrepreneurs

Entrepreneurs are people who typically try to exploit new ideas. As industries mature, products become commodities, economic competition drives rates of return to low levels, and companies start to resemble one another, entrepreneurs enter the scene. They help to set events in motion that disrupt the status quo and render it obsolete. Envisioning new combinations among the factors of production that will increase efficiency or increase sales, they experiment with unproved possibilities that show promise. Attracted by the excitement of doing something new as well as the perception of a possible high rate of return, they invest energy and capital into innovative endeavors. Characteristic endeavors include not only introducing new products or better versions of existing ones, but expanding markets geographically as well as demographically and creating novel production processes and organizational or management methods and business models.

Entrepreneurs often think of themselves as people with superior insight, who can see the future before others, but the future might not turn out as they expect. On the basis of what works and what does not, they adjust to circumstances.

As Exhibit 7.4 shows, many types of people have taken on the role of entrepreneur. In recent years, a large percentage of entrepreneurs have been women. Other entrepreneurs are well-connected individuals who have access to the money of investors—people in investment banks or venture capitalists. Still other entrepreneurs are classic inventors, people who may lack degrees or other credentials and find it hard to work in large organizations. This type of entrepreneur is not likely to be interested in managing a business if it becomes big; thus, he or she might be a serial entrepreneur who goes after one business opportunity after another and then sells these ventures to larger companies.

EXHIBIT 7.4
Types of
Entrepreneurs

Stubborn dreamers
  Stick tenaciously to vision despite odds (less than 1 in 10 new ideas bears fruit)
  Sometimes exhibit foolhardy optimism to overcome natural inclination to caution
Leaders of small companies
  May not have access to capital, workforce, or other resources to complete the task
Refugees from large corporations
  Have solid business experience, which may mean more success
Women
  Numbers are increasing
Classic inventors without conventional credentials
Well-connected individuals
  Access to investment banks and venture capitalists

Dean Kamen is an example of this type of entrepreneur. A college dropout, Kamen holds more than 150 U.S. and foreign patents, many of them for innovative medical devices. While still a young man, he invented the first wearable medical infusion pump, which rapidly gained acceptance in diverse medical applications. In 1976, he founded Auto-Syringe, Inc., a medical device company, to manufacture and market the pumps, but at age 30, tired of managing what was becoming a big business, he sold AutoSyringe to Baxter. Since then, he has worked on a number of business ideas for larger companies, a dialysis machine for Baxter and a patient mobility system for Johnson & Johnson. He also has been the developer of the Segway, the world's first dynamically stabilized, self-balancing human transporter guided by the rider's natural motions.

Kamen is just one example of a kind of entrepreneur. Other entrepreneurs tend to be refugees from large corporations who have solid business experience, but whose efforts to pursue various business opportunities were frustrated in the corporations for which they worked. Entrepreneurs often are people who have been laid off by large corporations. Entrepreneurs by necessity and not by choice, they are people whose prior business experience in a large corporation can increase their likely chance of success.

No matter what the origins of an entrepreneur, the difficulties of the role are great. They include dealing with the competition; accessing capital; the requirement to hire, train, and provide benefits (including health care) to a dedicated cadre of workers; and the need to understand government taxes and regulations that impinge on their venture's success. These obstacles to success in entrepreneurial endeavors deter many. Those who start new businesses must try to minimize the risks. Thus, they often commence their businesses in niches they already know well from previous experience, take on seasoned partners, obtain advice from well-regarded financial backers, or begin as franchisees of larger firms that provide them with proven business models.

In taking on risk in anticipation of high rewards, there is no simple formula for success. Each endeavor that an entrepreneur starts is a bit idiosyncratic. Each differs somewhat and is likely to involve a degree of improvisation. Simple planning is not likely to work out well. Linear movement toward a well-defined goal will not happen. Entrepreneurship requires adaptation and learning. It depends on creaptivity, intuition, and the ability to make on-the-spot choices without lots of formal analysis. However, it is possible to exaggerate the extent to which entrepreneurs are not deliberative and rational and to glorify and romanticize their nonlogical, seat-of-pants decision making. To the extent that they apply and employ known methods, these tend to be experimental ones. They use what amounts to the scientific method to test hypotheses and learn from their experience. Entrepreneurs also often rely on bricolage; that is, they make do with the means or resources at hand, rather than having all the means and resources they need. Different entrepreneurial ventures combine different qualities such as these in different ways, with persistence perhaps being the only constant as a trait entrepreneurs must cultivate.

Innovative Companies

Although small companies employing fewer than 500 people account for a large proportion of entrepreneurial activity, the role of large corporations also is central. Large corporations that face declining growth and profit margins in their mainstream businesses will try to accommodate and make room for entrepreneurial activities. Structural measures to enhance corporate entrepreneurship include corporate venture funds, spinouts, incubators, and business development centers. Corporate entrepreneurs, however, must overcome many obstacles as they remain agents embedded in corporate rules, routines, and a dominant corporate logic, as opposed to small venture entrepreneurs who can create new rules, routines, and a new dominant logic for their ventures.

Being proactive in an uncertain environment and being motivated to change the status quo requires alertness to opportunities on the part of the employees of a large firm. The sources of new opportunities are numerous. They include new knowledge and enabling technologies; observed inefficiencies; incongruities between reality as it is and ought to be; and changes taking place in an industry and its market structure and in society, demographics, politics, and regulation (see Chapter 2). The fast pace of change in emerging economies such as Brazil or India also opens up entrepreneurial opportunities, provided that firms want to and are capable of exploiting them (see Chapter 7).

Innovation involves the implementation of entrepreneurial ideas. Generally there are thought to be two kinds of innovation. *Incremental innovation* improves firm skills, structure, designs, production processes, and plant and equipment, while *disruptive innovation* undermines firm skills, structure, designs, production processes, and plant and equipment. Measures of innovation may include R&D as percentage of sales, new product introductions, and basic innovations in business models, but these measures do not fully capture some firm's innovative activities. These companies have what might be called an innovation culture; their strategy itself is innovation.

For established companies that have had past business successes, innovation poses a challenge. Companies must balance *exploration* (the search and discovery for future opportunities, experimentation, discontinuous innovations, risk taking, autonomy, and creativity) with *exploitation* (incremental change, learning, routines, process management, implementation, execution, quality, and efficiency). Exploration and exploitation require different organizational structures, systems, skills, styles, and processes. Unfortunately, in many firms exploitation often drives out exploration. For many companies, it is hard to carry out the two activities—exploration and exploitation—simultaneously (see Chapter 1). Small firms or small units or groups within large firms, therefore, tend more often to be the home for entrepreneurship than large firms or large units or groups within large firms that already have well-established business models.

Two companies that have been known for their innovation are 3M and Sony. 3M innovations extend from low-tech Post-it Notes to futuristic synthetic ligaments. The company aims to grow by introducing new products. In a typical year, 3M might launch more than 200 new products. Like 3M, Sony has tried to be a consistently innovative company, producing many successes from the transistor radio to the camcorder, compact disc player, Trinitron television, and Walkman. But it also has had failures, including the Betamax videocassette format, which lost out to Matushita's VHS, and the MiniDisc music player, which lost out to digital portable MP3 players such as the iPod. Sony's ability to constantly innovate differentiates it from companies such as Atari, which invented the video game but had no successful follow-ups. Unlike companies such as Casio, Samsung, and Sanyo, which try to copy products made by others and sell them cheaply, Sony aims for new-product introductions. Its goals are to release thousands of new products per year, both improved products and products that open new markets. Sony employs large numbers of scientists and engineers in its workforce, and it spends up to 6 percent or more of its yearly revenues on product research and development. Like 3M, it has had annual employee expositions at which scientists and engineers exhibit what they are doing. Sony's innovation is distinctive in that it gives to its products a special feel by maintaining a strong design center, which employs many artists as well as engineers.

The founder and chair of the company, Masaru Ibuka, articulated Sony's vision as being "never to follow others." The company's employees are supposed to be open-minded and optimistic and have wide-ranging interests. The company shifts them among product groups and tries to instill in them the ambition to create new products. Talented young people are given key positions in product development teams. These newcomers have the freshness of vision to create new products, while experienced engineers find better ways to manufacture existing products. Sony always has concentrated on the consumer market, a market that was once largely ignored by U.S. electronics firms, which mainly worked on military and space applications. Its distinctive capability was packaging the latest technology into small, inexpensive items that consumers found easy to use.

Not everyone in a company is an innovator, but Gary Hamel argues that in every company there are some "revolutionaries."[5] These people are likely to be found among the young and among newcomers at the bottom of the corporate pyramid, where there is more diversity. They are often to be found on the margins, for instance, in foreign operations, where groupthink is less prevalent. Closed-minded decision making at the top stifles them. For managers who wish to jump-start innovation at a firm, it may be necessary to remove people from their usual setting. For instance, holding off-site meetings with a group of recognized creative, critical thinkers may fire employees up emotionally and make their innovative initiatives contagious.

Internal cultures that support innovation tend to encourage personal growth and risk taking. In such cultures, top management supports innovation, and there also are organizational champions below. Teamwork and collaboration are encouraged. For innovation to succeed, hierarchies cannot be so overwhelmingly strong as to suppress it. The approval process for starting work on new ideas must be at least partially decentralized. The focus should be on learning, and employees should be given some time to pursue individual projects. In contrast, rigid bureaucracies, authoritarian leadership, and harsh penalties for failure tend to discourage innovation. However, an innovative company might have to tighten up its approach to market an innovation before its competitors do. It is one thing to generate new ideas and another to make them into successful business endeavors.

Investors

In addition to the factors previously mentioned, new ventures need money. They have at least five sources upon which to rely for their funding:

- Entrepreneurs can use *personal fortunes and contacts* to get them started.
- *Commercial banks* provide loans. In developing countries, where stock markets are weak, they tend to be a very important source of venture formation.
- *Venture capitalists* may take an equity position in a business.
- If an idea shows considerable promise, an *initial public offering* (IPO) of the stock may be issued to raise funds. Working with an investment bank, the firm will draw up a prospectus and present it to potential investors.
- *Large corporations* also can invest in new ventures. They can spend retained earning on R&D and market research and provide people within them the opportunity to develop new entrepreneurial ventures.

These are not exclusive sources of funds for new entrepreneurial ventures. Often more than one of these methods is used on innovative ideas.

However they are funded, innovators need to have patient backers, but funding sources tend to ebb and flow depending on many factors, including the overall state of the economy. The economic downturn at the end of the first decade of the 21st century has not been hospitable to new ideas. If backers are not patient, they can kill ideas that are just starting to show promise.

Regardless of the source of the funding, innovators will need a convincing **business plan.** Whether they will follow it precisely is another thing, but to get funding they must have one. The plan describes the business. It has an external analysis that covers such essentials as suppliers, customers, and competitors; an internal assessment of the budding organization's capabilities and its functional plans; an implementation schedule; an end-game strategy that indicates when the business will be profitable; financial projections; and a risk analysis.

The founders of new businesses must carry out many tasks. They must establish record-keeping systems to track revenues and expenses; set up contracts with suppliers; price, advertise, and market the product or service; get feedback from early customers to improve quality; acquire a physical location and needed furnishings, machinery, and equipment; manage and staff the business's employees; develop efficient operating processes; and understand legal requirements. To secure continued funding, they have to prove to potential investors that they can carry out these and other tasks well. The proof is in their performance.

Entrepreneurs fail for many reasons. Among the most common are inadequate customer relations and a lack of market knowledge and market planning.[6] Inexperienced management may lack the requisite skills to conduct these activities. Because there may be more than one round of funding, continuously demonstrating these skills to the venture's backers is a key to maintaining the flow of resources to start-up enterprises.

Government

Governments play a large role in determining whether entrepreneurial endeavors will succeed. For instance, they may help fund the activity. The rationale for this involvement is that the payoff to society—new jobs and new industries—is greater than that to any individual investor or company. Innovation and entrepreneurship would be underfunded without government involvement. Rational individuals and firms would forgo the effort because they could not appropriate all the benefits.

All major industrial nations have policies to encourage business start-ups. Germany, Switzerland, and Japan once used mainly bottom-up, market-driven approaches, while the United States, United Kingdom, and France relied more on top-down approaches closely associated with the military. The U.S. government's post–World War II technology policy nurtured more than 700 national labs that supported basic research for both military and civilian purposes. The government also funded research in many U.S. universities and private labs. The United States tended to be a leader in basic research, but it started to lag behind other countries in applications. Since the research effort did not result in enough commercial products, Congress showed less willingness to pay for it. Instead, it increased financing for the commercialization of already promising technologies.

The federal labs started to switch from basic to applied research. Many now have cooperative R&D arrangements with private companies. The National Institute of Standards and Technology's (NIST) Advanced Technology Program (ATP) now gives grants to companies that develop promising but risky technologies. The amounts it gives are relatively small. The companies have to be able to convince NIST that the ideas have technical merit and practicality and that they can be exploited commercially. The Commerce Department also has a strategic partnership initiative in which innovative companies that produce new technologies have the opportunity to meet potential customers. The Pentagon, though, is the largest funder of research in the United States, the results of which have had a positive impact on the civilian sector. The funding by the Defense Advanced Research Products Administration (DARPA) is for dual purposes, both military and commercial. The Internet largely was a DARPA success.

Technological Opportunities

All the classical economists of the late 18th and early 19th centuries, including Adam Smith, David Ricardo, and John Stuart Mill, recognized technology's importance in innovation and entrepreneurship. Technology leads to increasing mechanization and gives rise to an efficient division of labor, which improves productivity and permits the efficient accumulation of capital. Thomas Malthus's pessimism that population growth would lead to increasing misery as the world's population expanded more rapidly than the food supply was largely overcome because of technological successes.

Technological developments provide new ideas for innovation and entrepreneurship. However, finding the right technological opportunities for starting new businesses is not easy. To forecast technological change, entrepreneurs must anticipate breakthroughs early.[7] The means of doing so include trend analysis, monitoring expert opinion, and constructing alternative scenarios.[8] Entrepreneurs also can immerse themselves in leading- or cutting-edge technologies. The strengths and weaknesses of these approaches to technological forecasting are worth assessing.

Trends

Trends in one area often forecast trends in another (e.g., military jet speeds foretell commercial jet speeds). Entrepreneurs can extrapolate, for instance, the number of components needed to manufacture one product to estimate the number needed to manufacture a similar product. But trends have to be analyzed with caution. Simple extrapolation can be deceiving if it does not account for the impact of one trend on another, fails to consider how the human response to trends can change their direction, and has no room for surprises. Economic forecasts are good at predicting the future on the basis of the past as long as the future resembles the past in important ways. However, radical breaks occur (e.g., the 1973 Arab oil embargo, the fall of Communism, the 9/11 terrorist attacks, and the economic meltdown at the end of the first decade of the 21st century), which few economists predicted.

Experts

Expert opinion can be used to forecast change, but even experts make serious mistakes. The British Parliament established a committee of experts at the end of the 19th century to investigate the potential of Thomas Edison's incandescent lamp. It found the idea "unworthy" of attention.[9] During World War II, a panel of experts selected by the federal government did not believe that an intercontinental ballistic missile could accurately deliver its payload 3,000 miles away.[10] The Rand Corporation, a think tank in Southern California, devised the **Delphi method** to aggregate the beliefs of experts about particular issues. Each expert is asked to predict important events and to clarify the reasons she or he believes the events are likely to occur. Successive requestioning in light of the answers sharpens the results obtained, but even this method is flawed and has been found to be not particularly accurate.

Alternative Scenarios

Often, when the future is uncertain, the best coping method is to construct alternative scenarios (see Chapter 2).[11] Companies may create a series of possible sequences of future events that include the uncertainty (see Chapter 2). Shell Oil Company, for instance, forecast three different energy scenarios in 1972. It assessed immediate (2 years), mid-range (10 years), and long-range (25 years) implications based on the scenarios. This exercise forced Shell's managers to think through what they would do if unfavorable circumstances should arise and thus provided them with the opportunity to better manage future contingencies when they came.

Entrepreneurs must monitor the environment for signals that may be the forerunners of significant changes. To do so, they have to clarify which indicators to follow. Then they have to understand how to interpret the information. A free society produces an immense amount of information. Professional conferences, technical papers, and the media all yield data that vie for a manager's attention. What to focus on and what to ignore—what is the "true" signal and what is the "noise"—is a perpetual problem.

Leading-Edge Industries

Technological change, according to Schumpeter, is like a series of explosions, with innovations concentrating in specific sectors, so-called **leading-edge industries,** that provide the momentum for growth.[12] These leading sectors propel the economy forward. Entrepreneurs should monitor them carefully. In these leading-edge industries, they are likely to see the opportunities for profit. They then can vigorously exploit the possibilities inherent in these sectors.

EXHIBIT 7.5
Innovation
Waves

Period	Technological Advances
1782–1845	Steam power, textiles
1845–1892	Railroads, iron, coal, construction
1892–1948	Electrical power, automobiles, chemicals, steel
1948–present	Semiconductors, consumer electronics, aerospace, pharmaceuticals, petrochemicals, synthetic and composite materials, advanced telecommunications and the Internet

The pioneers in a leading-edge sector typically are followed by a swarm of imitators. The combined activity of the pioneers and their followers generates boom conditions. Soon, however, there are so many imitators that prices fall and bust follows. Lagging sectors fall behind, their time passes, and they wither and die or are kept afloat by government subsidy and bailout. To spur a revival, new innovation is needed. Schumpeter calls this process "creative destruction."[13]

According to the Russian economist Kondratiev, economic progress occurs in waves, each of which lasts about half a century.[14] Each wave has periods of prosperity, recession, depression, and recovery. These waves are connected to specific technological innovations (see Exhibit 7.5).[15] The first wave after the Industrial Revolution (1782–1845) saw major innovations in steam power and textiles; the second (1845–1892) in railroads, iron, coal, and construction; and the third (1892–1948) in electrical power, automobiles, chemicals, and steel. The prosperity of the post–World War II period was built on innovations in semiconductors, consumer electronics, aerospace, pharmaceuticals, petrochemicals, and synthetic and composite materials.[16] A dynamic growth phase existed from 1945 to 1973, but from 1973 to 1993, the growth rates in advanced industrial nations slowed. Rather than innovating, companies tended to reduce their manufacturing costs by making incremental adjustments and exporting jobs to foreign countries where labor costs were lower. Starting in 1993, the Internet and advances in telecommunications started another wave of industrial innovation. From where will future waves of innovation come? This is still uncertain.

Postindustrialism

The current era has been called one of **postindustrialism.**[17] Postindustrial societies differ from industrial societies in a number of ways. In the economic sphere, there is a move from goods to services. Professional and technical people become preeminent, and theoretical knowledge is central. Control of technology and technological assessment are primary activities. It has been argued that in a postindustrial society "wealth in the form of physical resources" steadily declines in value and significance, and "the powers of the mind" are "ascendant over the brute force of things."[18]

In industrial societies, economic activity revolves around the manipulation and movement of "massive objects against friction and gravity."[19] Industrial societies are built on physical labor, natural resources, and capital. In postindustrial societies, human beings are masters not of "material resources but of ideas and technologies."[20]

The microchip symbolized this "shift of the worth of goods from materials to ideas," as the material costs of the product are only about 2 percent of its total production cost.[21] The most valuable part of this technology is the idea for its design. In postindustrial societies, the information component of what is produced increases and the material component decreases.

EXHIBIT 7.6
Next
Innovation
Wave

Extension of Human Sensory Capabilities and Intellectual Processes

- Genetic engineering
- Advanced computers and telecommunication
- Robotics
- Artificial intelligence
- Alternative energy—solar, fuel cells, etc.
- Advanced materials—molecular design, new polymers, high-tech ceramics, fiber-reinforced composites

The rise of the mind as a source of wealth is among the most important forces of which to take note. The next wave of innovation may extend human sensory capabilities and intellectual processes into such areas as genetic engineering (biotechnology), advanced computers, and robotics (see Exhibit 7.6).

Biotechnology

Robert Shapiro, former CEO of Monsanto, maintained that the movement from industrial to postindustrial society was among the most important factors enabling biotechnology.[22] This movement could bring into existence a more **sustainable society,** one where people's basic needs for food and a healthy environment would be better met. For instance, instead of being sprayed with pesticides, plants will be genetically coded to repel or destroy harmful insects. This is a much smarter way of doing business because up to 90 percent of what is sprayed on crops is wasted.

Shapiro innovated within the company he led and worked to change Monsanto's direction so that it would be committed to making "smarter" products that reduced chemical use. Monsanto developed a bioengineered potato that defended itself against the Colorado potato beetle; Bt cotton, which kills and repels budworms; and Roundup herbicide, which allows farmers to kill weeds without plowing, thereby preserving the topsoil (a practice called conservation tillage). Roundup does not harm crops; it sticks to soil particles and does not migrate into groundwater; it degrades into natural products such as nitrogen, carbon, and water; and it is nontoxic to animals. By 2000 more than half of the U.S. soybean crop and more than one-third of the corn crop involved bioengineered products. Scientists were able to protect crops such as corn, soybeans, cotton, potatoes, and tomatoes from pests. They were also working on taking genes from fish that swim in icy water and injecting them into strawberries to enable the strawberries to resist frost.

In addition to its agricultural applications, biotechnology promises advances in other fields:

- *Nutrition.* Scientists may be able to extract genes from one species (e.g., a Brazilian nut) and put them into another species (the soybean) to increase the protein level to make the soybeans more nutritional. They are trying to make soybeans taste better and to remove some of the saturated fats to improve soybeans' health benefits.

- *Pharmaceuticals.* Scientists may be able to introduce genes into rice that will enable it to produce beta-carotene and thus combat the vitamin A deficiency common among people who rely on rice for sustenance. They also have been developing vaccines for hepatitis B, diarrhea, and other diseases that can be incorporated into the cells of a banana or a sweet potato and thereby distributed to people in developing nations who might not otherwise be protected against these diseases.

- *Industrial.* Ultimately, the aim is to make industrial materials such as plastics, nylons, and other petrochemical by-products from genetically modified plants. These plants would replace world reliance on highly polluting hydrocarbons.

The potential benefits that might ensue are large. Scientists and entrepreneurs hype the chances of success, but there are difficulties deciding which products should come first. What deserves rapid commercialization? What does not?

Government has played a large role in the use of biotechnology for pharmaceuticals. Five federal agencies have some jurisdiction and guidelines are unclear. While waiting for regulatory approval of a product, companies have to develop manufacturing facilities that they cannot run at full capacity and sales forces that cannot yet market the product. Many companies therefore have moved to non-pharmaceutical applications or they have had to ally themselves with large drug and chemical companies that are experienced in dealing with regulators and marketing. Large manufacturers are needed to help the smaller biotech companies shoulder the risks.

Monsanto made a huge early investment in biotechnology, but it was disappointed when Wisconsin's governor banned a bovine growth hormone (BGH) that Monsanto had developed to boost milk production in the early 1990s. The ban was supported by dairy farmers, who were supposed to be the product's main customers. BGH is a protein similar to one cows produce naturally. When injected into cows twice a month, yields increase by 10 to 20 percent. Farmers, however, opposed BGH, fearing a milk glut would lower prices. Consumers' anxieties about artificial foods and retailers' fears that people would not buy milk from cows injected with BGH also prevented the product from being widely used.

Many environmentalists criticize genetically engineered food as being "Frankenstein" in quality. Though the evidence is speculative, they warn against eating these foods. European governments have imposed regulations calling for separating of approved and unapproved strains, requiring labeling, and preventing the sale of some products. European companies Novartis and Aventis, which were once very active in biotech R&D, left the industry because of the controversy.

Still, competition in the biotech industry is intense. DuPont views genetic engineering as a means of using its R&D capabilities to deal with global challenges such as hunger and aging. It has financed research in the life sciences with the profits from its mature businesses, such as nylon and polyester. It reset its corporate portfolio to carry out this strategy, selling a large petrochemical company, Conoco, and buying a controlling interest in a seed company, Pioneer Hi-Bred.

Meanwhile, the prospects of biotechnology go up and down. DuPont and Monsanto remain the major players in the industry. Monsanto has formed partnerships with Cargill to develop animal feed and Mendel Biotech to develop technologies for controlling genes. Industry start-ups include Sangamo Biosciences, which was working on gene switches, and DNP Holding Company, which was working on banana rot and cancer-protecting substances in tomatoes. Monsanto and DuPont compete over which products to commercialize first—corn for chicken feed, soy oil for healthy hearts, or feedstocks for bioengineered chemicals. Whether this industry fulfills its promise depends on whether it can gain public acceptance and overcome regulatory hurdles, especially in Europe.

EXHIBIT 7.7
Environmental
Challenges as
Opportunities

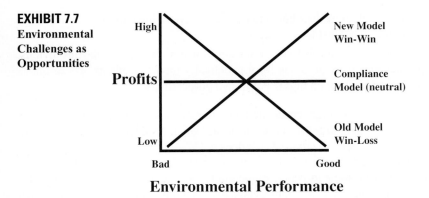

The Environment as a Business Opportunity

To what extent are the environmental problems that society faces serious business opportunities? At one time, these issues were regarded primarily as a threat to business. However, if extracting more economic value from fewer natural resources and raw materials can improve existing products and services and lead to the development of new ones, these challenges can be the catalysts for innovation and entrepreneurship. Win-win solutions would mean that both the environment and society would be better off (see Exhibit 7.7). While the conventional view is that environmental challenges impose costs on business, slow productivity growth, and hinder global competitiveness, a revisionist view sees them as the driving force for entrepreneurship and innovation.

Many firms already have profited from meeting environmental challenges. Environmental considerations have played a central role in their capital investments, new-product development, and optimization of production processes. They have played a central role not only in pollution-sensitive industries, such as petrochemicals and electric power, and in basic manufacturing industries, such as auto, steel, paper, and cement, but also in high-tech industries, such as semiconductors. Intel and Google, for instance, are among the most well-known companies for their environmental investments.

For many companies, excellence in protecting the environment is creating opportunities for competitive advantage. These companies not only are lowering costs and achieving cost leadership by pursuing environmental efficiency, but they also are pursuing a differentiation or focus strategy based on developing "green products" for niche markets. An example is 3M.[23] This globally diversified manufacturer sells thousands of products and services worldwide. Among its more notable consumer products are Scotch Tape, Post-it Notes and Flags, Sandpaper, Scotch-Brite Scour Pads, and Scotchgard Protectors. 3M has been one of the first firms to recognize the importance of environmentally responsible operations. In 1975, it adopted an environmental policy, which said it would:

- Solve its own environmental problems; prevent pollution at the source whenever and wherever possible;
- Develop products that have a minimum effect on the environment; conserve natural resources through reclamation and other appropriate methods; and
- Meet and maintain government regulations; and assist government agencies in environmental activities wherever possible.

EXHIBIT 7.8
Enhanced
Efficiency via
Pollution
Prevention at
Novartis

	Inputs	Finished Products	Waste
1979	100	30%	70%
1988	100	62%	38%
2000	100	75%	25%

Though 3M does not use the term *strategic environmental management,* it is a good description of what the company has done. Its goal is to develop solutions that are both good for the environment and the corporate bottom line.

In 1975, 3M created the 3P (Pollution Prevention Pays) program, which encouraged employees to prevent pollution rather than treat it after it is generated. Under the leadership of its chief environmental officer, Joe Ling, 3M was an innovator in pollution prevention (often referred to as P2), developing the first successful industrial program that committed the company to source reduction by means of product reformulation, process modification, equipment redesign, recycling, and reuse. Today, 3M makes many products and product components that not only help to reduce pollution but also assist in energy conservation and renewable energy generation.

Michael Porter has written that pollution is a form of inefficiency that demands of firms that they lower their costs: It is an indication of unneeded scrap, harmful substances, and energy that is not completely used, and creates no value for customers.[24] Competitive advantage, therefore, can be reached by developing environmental competencies in areas such as pollution prevention (P2) and in developing new energy-efficient products and services. Novartis, for instance, started a successful P2 program in 1979. Then called CibaGeigy, the predecessor company created 30 units of finished products and 70 units of waste for every 100 units of inputs, but by 2000, because of extensive efforts to prevent pollution, it produced 75 units of finished products and 25 units of waste for every 100 units of inputs (see Exhibit 7.8). Companies must rely on **material-balance models** to achieve this type of progress. They have to add up total production inputs and try to minimize them, carefully examining production processes to ensure that they are maximally efficient and do not waste inputs (see Exhibit 7.9), with the goal being to increase usable products and decrease waste.

Many U.S. companies have started *P2 programs.* They have inventoried their wastes, evaluated the impacts, and implemented successful programs. A successful P2 program requires that the company pay attention to product and process design, plant configuration, information and control systems, human resources, R&D, the suppliers' role, and the corporate organization. A P2 team must be assembled, a method for measuring progress determined, process flow diagrams and material balances prepared, and tracking systems for materials set up. Operational and material changes have to be considered, including material use substitutions and process and production changes. For such programs to succeed, employee involvement and recognition are needed.

Environmental Innovation

A high-value environmental strategy does not just involve pollution prevention; it also entails developing new products and services. Consider such examples as the following:

- Ringer, a producer of alternative pesticides and lawn and garden products, developed innovative products.[25] However, the products were high-priced and worked more slowly

EXHIBIT 7.9
Material-
Balance Model

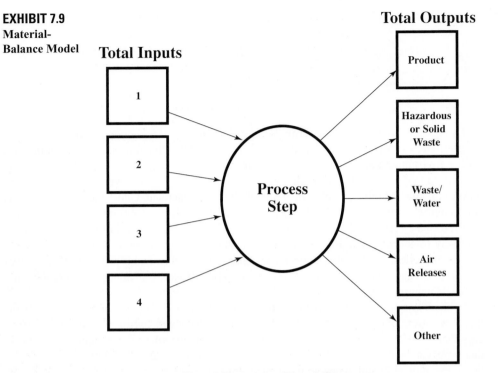

Total Outputs

Total Inputs

1

2

Process
Step

3

4

Product

Hazardous
or Solid
Waste

Waste/
Water

Air
Releases

Other

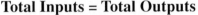

Total Inputs = Total Outputs

than conventional ones. Faced with dedicated and resourceful competition from such companies as Scott, the company had problems gaining market acceptance and becoming profitable. After struggling during most of the 1990s, it went bankrupt.

- Osmonics, in contrast, successfully manufactured and sold filtration devices and equipment that were used to recycle materials in manufacturing processes and in this way played a role in pollution prevention in industries as diverse as electroplating and dairying. Though Osmonics had its ups and downs, it succeeded as an ongoing business and ultimately was purchased by General Electric.[26]

- Another example is Deluxe Printing, which won awards for the development of a new ink system called PrintWise.[27] Unlike soy inks, which rely on petroleum-base products and solvents, PrintWise is a pollution-free, vegetable-base ink that uses water. To succeed, Deluxe had to revolutionize the industry as well as transform itself. Never before had it manufactured or sold ink, yet it now had to sell PrintWise to its major competitors. Like Ringer, Deluxe relied on a high-price strategy, one that its customers were not willing to accept. Although the company's core check-printing business was in decline, the challenges it faced in the ink business were difficult and it sold PrintWise to a French company.

- Still another example is Alliant Techsystems, a world leader in the manufacture of munitions. With cuts in Pentagon spending at the beginning of the 1990s, Alliant Tech faced layoffs and downsizing and it began to search for new business opportunities. At its

Joliet, Illinois, plant, it developed unique methods for recycling out-of-specification explosives and began to seek customers worldwide for this business, especially in former Soviet bloc nations, which had huge stockpiles of antiquated munitions, some dating to the 1905 Russian–Japanese war. Alliant Tech profited handsomely from recycling and selling the explosives and metals for civilian uses.

Though there are these examples of success, the path to success in environmental innovation is a hard one to climb. The pricing has to be right—this is critical—but so too does product quality and service. An environmental entrepreneur, like any entrepreneur, must create real value for its customers. It also has to have a good handle on distribution. The competition can be deadly if not everything is in place for business success. This is the lesson to be learned from examples like Ringer and Deluxe.

Low-Emissions Vehicles

Another instance worth examining has been in the development of low-emissions vehicles. New-product introductions to address pollution problems have been slow in coming. Throughout the 1990s, companies in the automotive industry struggled to commercialize these products. Early research into the feasibility and development of alternative vehicles to reduce pollution and petroleum dependence started in earnest during the gasoline shortages of the 1970s. By 1990, electric cars were seen as a potential answer to growing pollution woes, particularly in cities such as Los Angeles, which was plagued by smog. They were designed primarily in response to new clean-air legislation enacted in select states. In September 1990, California had new laws tightening emissions standards and mandating that 2 percent of all new vehicles sold produce no exhaust. Zero-emission vehicles (ZEVs) would necessarily be electric—no other alternatives met the California standard. However, electric cars were not without their problems: They required that coal, oil, or natural gas continue to be burned to produce the electricity that would power them.

General Motors was a pioneer in developing these vehicles, researching a variety of environmentally friendly cars. However, cumulative sales figures for General Motors' alternative vehicles were low. GM switched technologies, moving from an emphasis on electric vehicles to fuel-cell technology in the mid-1990s.

Instead of all-electric cars, Honda and Toyota marketed hybrids that were part electric and part gas powered. Honda was the first to sell a hybrid, its Insight two-seater. By 2002, Honda had a hybrid version of the Civic. However, Toyota's Prius hybrid, introduced in the United States in 2000, proved to be far more popular than either Honda hybrid. In 2006 Americans bought more than 350,000 of these cars. GM never caught up. At the 2009 Detroit auto show, a main attraction was its battery-powered Volt, but the battery in the Volt was a huge 6 feet tall and 400 pounds and the price of the car, more than $30,000, was considered to be out of line with the value it provided.[28]

The 2009 Obama administration stimulus package included $2 billion in grants for electric car research and $25 billion in low-interest loans for green vehicle purchases. Though an all-electric car has some advantages over conventional vehicles, a key drawback is the range per charge of currently available batteries, which is no more than 150 miles. Plug-in hybrids therefore use an internal-combustion engine to supplement and extend the vehicles' range. The government's goal is to have a million plug-in hybrids on U.S. roads by 2015, but this will amount to only 4 percent of total vehicles that will then be on the roads.

If the electric car industry is to succeed, a new, multibillion-dollar battery industry is needed. It purportedly would generate thousands of U.S. jobs. The state of Michigan has in place a program to provide millions of dollars in tax credits to battery makers that locate there. However, U.S. battery manufacturers lag far behind Asian companies such as NEC, LG, and Sanyo. These are the companies that currently supply Toyota and Honda. U.S. battery manufacturers also are behind the Chinese firm BYD, in which Warren Buffett is a major investor. The Asian companies have substantial experience in mass-producing batteries, which U.S firms lack. The South Korean company LG Chem has the contract to supply batteries for GM's Volt. Batteries for a planned Ford plug-in hybrid will come from a French–American joint venture called Johnson Controls/Saft. Electric car companies are likely to locate near battery suppliers to save on shipping. They also are likely to locate in places where gas prices are high, which means that the industry will not be centered in the United States. The small battery companies head-quartered in the United States, such as Enerl, A123, Quantum Technologies, Altair Nano-technologies, Tesla Motors, and ActaCell (backed by Google), are good at battery design, not production. Their revenues are low, and they have had but limited agreements to work with the major auto producers.

Rechargeable lithium ion, the same kind of battery in a cell phone, is the battery of choice, but producing it in the massive numbers required by a large-scale electric auto industry still will be expensive. Most of the lithium mined comes from Bolivia and there are supply limits. In 2008, a battery for an all-electric car cost anywhere from $8,000 to $30,000. However, prices can drop with additional production experience. The cost of the batteries currently is so high because the batteries have to endure adverse road conditions (snow, sleet, rain, heat, potholes, vibration, crashes, dirt, and debris). Also, they must be repeatedly charged and recharged. They have to last up to 10 years.

A way to drive down prices is to have customers lease the batteries from a third party. The Israeli start-up, Better Place, has proposed to do this. Its business model is to own and maintain the batteries and sell subscription plans for their use. It expects to operate like a cell phone company, but it will sell miles instead of minutes. In countries where gasoline prices are high, it believes that the lifetime costs of owning and operating an electric car will be similar to that of owning and operating a gas vehicle. Better Place is creating conveniently located charging spots that in a few minutes are able to use a robotic arm to replace an old battery with a new one. It has built charging stations in such places as Japan, Israel, Denmark, and Northern California.

Critics have challenged the idea that these schemes for creating an electric car industry are realistic.[29] Are the chances for economic gain for real? If green products do not work well or cost more, consumers will reject them—that is, unless the government definitively reshapes the rules in the favor of these new products. Perhaps cap and trade carbon limitations will have just such an impact.

Obstacles to Exploiting New Technologies

Many ideas, however promising, fail to find widespread application. Of all projects businesses undertake, only an estimated 1 in 10 succeeds, depending on the industry and the circumstances.[30] Failure is common, and the reasons for it are not easy for managers to control.

Economists distinguish between conditions where the odds of success are known with certainty (e.g., flipping a coin), which they call **risk,** and conditions where the odds of success are not known with certainty, which they call **uncertainty.** This classification is a matter of degree. The art of assigning statistical probabilities is just that—an art. When the odds are known with certainty, the situation is insurable, but technical innovation is an uninsurable phenomenon. The odds of success cannot be stated with precision.

Better management does not necessarily reduce the failure rate. Managers cannot always manipulate the situation to their liking or produce the results they desire. After the fact, it may be easy to say why success or failure occurred, but before the fact, it is not easy to know what to do.

Risk

Most managers have powerful reasons for keeping risk to a minimum. They therefore are not likely to endorse innovation enthusiastically. In deliberating about whether to undertake an innovator's project, they have to consider both technical and commercial feasibility. They have to estimate:[31]

- The probable development, production, and marketing costs.
- The approximate timing of these costs.
- The probable future income streams.
- The time at which the income streams are likely to develop.

All these calculations are fraught with uncertainty. The only way to reduce uncertainty is to undertake safe projects. Thus, businesses tend to concentrate on innovations where success is easy. The bias is toward simple, well-trod areas, since fundamental research and invention involve greater uncertainties.

Businesses typically establish new generations of existing products, introduce new models, and differentiate a product further rather than creating different products and new product lines. They reduce uncertainty by licensing others' inventions, imitating others' product introductions, modifying existing processes, and making minor technical improvements (see Exhibit 7.10). An automobile with a new type of engine, for instance, is less likely to be introduced than an auto with simple modifications of existing engines.

Uncertainty

For a new product to be launched, managers must have an optimistic bias. Engineers who design new products in companies, for instance, are known to make optimistic estimates of development costs even when they have strong incentives to be more objective in their appraisals. Without optimistic estimates, they would not be given approval to conduct the projects.

EXHIBIT 7.10
Minimizing Risk

- Focus on simple, well-trod areas.
- Establish new generations of existing products.
- Introduce new models.
- Differentiate product rather than create different ones.
- License others' inventions.
- Imitate others' product introductions.
- Modify existing processes.
- Make minor technical improvements.

As hard as it is to estimate technical success, it is just as difficult to predict market success. Market launch and growth in sales are more distant in time, and conditions in the future vary. The reactions of competitors to the threat of new products are unknown. Achieving an advance understanding of the costs, given changing economic circumstances, is difficult. Predicting a product's life span and dominance, given the threat of technical obsolescence, is also difficult.

The empirical evidence appears to confirm that early estimates of future markets have been wildly inaccurate.[32] Even with successful products, the developers did not recognize the extent to which they would be successful. Four types of uncertainty that affect new-product development are worth examining: technical, business condition, market, and government.

Technical Uncertainty

Even after prototype testing, pilot plant work, trial production, and test marketing, technical uncertainty is likely to exist in the early stages of innovation and entrepreneurship. The question typically is not whether a product will or will not work; rather, the issues at this stage are what standards of performance the product will achieve under different operating conditions and what the costs will be of improving performance under these conditions. Unexpected problems can arise before a product reaches the market, in the early stages of a promising commercial launch, and after product introduction, as the examples below illustrate.

Before a Product Reaches the Market Unexpected problems affected the pharmaceutical company Syntex even before its new product Enprostil reached the market.[33] Syntex needed a new product because the patent on its major moneymaker, an anti-inflammatory drug called Naprosyn, was about to expire. It thought it had come up with a new ulcer drug, Enprostil, that not only eased the pain of ulcers but also lowered cholesterol. With millions of people worldwide suffering from ulcers, drugs that treat the problem yield substantial profits. However, the individual who pioneered Enprostil's development spotted a dangerous side effect of the drug: blood clots that might produce new ulcers. Test-tube clotting suggested the drug might pose a risk of heart attack or stroke. Enprostil had trouble winning FDA approval.

The Early Stages of Production Serious setbacks also can occur in the early stages of a promising commercial launch. For instance, Weyerhaeuser Company sought to become an important player in the disposable diaper market with its Ultrasofts product.[34] Ultrasofts had superior features—a clothlike surface and superabsorbent pulp material woven into the pad to keep babies dry. Consumer tests showed that parents favored it two to one over competing brands. The advertising and promotion campaign offered coupons that saved parents $1 per package for trying the product. Procter & Gamble and Kimberly-Clark, which together had 85 percent of the disposable diaper market, responded with aggressive cost-cutting and promotion campaigns to keep customers loyal.

Early in production, manufacturing problems occurred in Weyerhaeuser's Bowling Green, Kentucky, plant. The system that sprayed the superabsorbent material into the diapers malfunctioned and started a fire. Weyerhaeuser had to raise prices to retailers by 22 percent to cover its unexpected expenses. The retailers responded by refusing to give the product adequate shelf space. Weyerhaeuser withdrew the product from the marketplace.

After a Product Is on the Market   Serious setbacks also occur when a product is on the market.[35] Market share and profits had been falling for GE's appliance division. GE was making refrigerator compressors with a 1950s technology that took three times as long as the process used by Japanese and Italian manufacturers. GE committed $120 million to build a factory to make a newly designed compressor. The new compressor was lighter and more energy-efficient than the old model. It was identical to the one GE used in air conditioners except for two parts made of powdered metal as opposed to hardened steel. Powdered metal was more easily made to the extreme tolerances that were needed and it was cheaper than steel. Evaluation engineers told the designers that powdered metal had not worked in air conditioners, but the designers discounted their views. The test data that senior executives saw showed no failures, and the arguments of technicians who observed excessive heat were ignored. Field testing was limited to about nine months, instead of the usual two years, because managers wanted the product on the market immediately.

GE scrapped its old compressors and proudly declared that an American company could still take the lead in world manufacturing of an energy-efficient refrigerator. Consumers bought the refrigerators with the new compressor in record numbers, with GE increasing its market share by 2 percentage points, its best showing in years. However, after about a year on the market, some compressors began to fail, and GE, which had sold the refrigerators with five-year warranties, decided it had to recall and replace them.

Business Conditions When a Product Is Introduced

It is not only technical uncertainty that affects the introduction of new products. General business uncertainty also is a factor. It had a negative effect on General Motors when the company was bringing its Saturn automobile to the market.[36] Saturn's introduction at a time of poor economic conditions and overcapacity in the industry meant disappointing sales. When the car was introduced in the early 1990s, consumer demand for high-quality, small cars with good gasoline mileage was faltering. Saturn dealers had been handpicked to offer exceptional customer service, but they were given near-monopoly status and thus had little incentive to offer deep discounts to stimulate sales in case of an economic downturn. The labor–management relations GM had established at the Saturn facility were different from those the company practiced elsewhere. Workers basically accepted less pay but had more control over the production process. Managers and workers in other GM divisions complained that the company's commitment to Saturn drained resources from projects that might have had a greater payback.

The Saturn expansion was occurring while GM was cutting back elsewhere. Touted as a top-quality U.S. small car, the Saturn did not incorporate technology that was more advanced than Japanese technology, and production costs were not lower because the expense of building the new production facility had been so high. The promised automation in the production process ("a totally computerized, paperless operation") failed to be completely realized. For about the same amount that GM had spent setting up the Saturn facility ($2 billion), Honda had established a plant in Ohio that produced twice the number of cars (a half million as opposed to about 250,000 Saturns).[37] Honda expanded in stages, adding capacity, as demand required it, and more sophisticated production techniques, as workers were capable of dealing with them. GM, with its all-or-nothing approach, was devastated by the changing business conditions of the early 1990s when Saturn was introduced.

Market Uncertainty

Pioneering new technologies carries great uncertainties in terms of knowing what consumers want and providing it to them in a timely fashion. Models of innovation that start with scientific and technological advances can miss the important role that customers play both in the adoption decision and in subsequent refinements.[38] For instance, marketplace applications of artificial intelligence have been disappointing. Artificial intelligence allows computers to mimic ordinary human intelligence. It includes systems that help machines in factories "see," enable computers to analyze aerial photographs, and permit language recognition for translation or dictation. The most promise is in expert systems, software packages that can imitate the reasoning and decision processes of specialists in various fields by applying the rules the specialists use and the data they have available.

Venture capital funds and talented technical people who were attracted to the field, however, abandoned it. Despite its promise, the developers of artificial intelligence did not show a good understanding of potential markets. For instance, Applied Expert Systems tried to sell a $50,000 software package to professional financial planners. The claim was that the computer could produce a better financial plan than the planners. Understandably, the professional planners felt threatened by this claim, so they refused to buy the package. The artificial intelligence industry may have been hampered by the founders: They were researchers with limited understanding of market forces. Initially very well funded, they spent money freely without concern for the time and budget limits that are needed to make a commercial success.

Another example of failure to pay sufficient attention to the market is Motorola. Its excellence as an engineering company is widely recognized.[39] It won the prestigious Malcolm Baldrige National Quality Award in the United States and the Nikkei Prize in manufacturing in Japan. However, it was unable to keep its customers from defecting to rivals such as Intel, Sun Microsystems, and MIPS Computer Systems. Motorola's obsession with technological excellence—its engineers had to create the best-designed, fastest, and highest-quality product possible—prevented it from meeting market needs in a timely fashion. It delayed in introducing new products. While competitors were already shipping products to customers, Motorola was still making revisions, refusing to put products on the market before all the bugs were worked out.

IBM chose Intel's chip to be the standard in personal computers not because Motorola's was technically inferior but because Intel was more responsive to IBM's needs. Motorola at one time had nearly 80 percent of the market for microprocessors used in workstations, but that market was much smaller than the personal computer market. Transferring technology from the laboratory to the market is not easily accomplished when technically oriented managers dominate.

Government Uncertainty

New products can be hurt by uncertain government support. For instance, high-definition television (HDTV) was once a favorite among politicians and business lobbyists in Washington, D.C.[40] Sharp images, perfect sound, and the convenience of large, thin screens had great appeal. The consumer market was considered to be worth more than $100 billion. Government and business officials met to map out a strategy to compete with Japan and other foreign nations on HDTV. The idea was to collaborate in developing a new technology standard in the United States. However, the federal government was not cooperative, and support for research was not forthcoming. As a consequence, this promising technology was slow to get off the ground.

Technology Push and Market Pull

The **technology-push model** of innovation starts with discoveries in basic science and engineering, and from these discoveries come new goods and services. Schumpeter posited that science and technology drive technological change:[41] Exceptionally creative entrepreneurs and people in the research labs of large corporations harness the ideas of science and technology and find useful applications. However, numerous empirical studies and descriptions of innovation demonstrate the importance of a clear perception of market needs.[42] Schmookler contested Schumpeter's claim, arguing that market factors are more important than technology, that market growth and potential are the main determinants of innovation.[43] Researchers have concluded that it is the linking of both components—technology-push factors and market-pull factors—over the product life cycle that is important.[44] Studies show that the amount of innovation coming from scientific and technical people is roughly equal to that from manufacturers and users. Frequent interactions between these groups are important. Users have to be sophisticated enough to make technically relevant recommendations. They have to be able to purchase and use the products that incorporate their suggestions. Successful innovations need both scientific/technical and market components.

The challenge innovators and entrepreneurs face is to match technological opportunity with market need. For managers, this means bringing together different in-house functions (such as marketing, R&D, and manufacturing) with knowledge of consumer needs and scientific and technical developments. The essence of successful innovation is that it fuses technological possibility with market demand. Technology-push and market-pull models now are viewed as atypical examples of a more general process in which constant interaction occurs between market requirements and scientific achievement.

Difficulties of Successful Innovation

Entrepreneurship and innovation are hard to pull off successfully for a number of reasons.[45]

1. *The entities that make the discoveries are not always the ones that profit from them.* The EMI scanner was an enormous scientific discovery, as important as anything since X-rays, but EMI suffered great losses in developing it and sold the rights to the technology at a cut-rate price. Relatively small engineering companies routinely produce innovations, such as the bar codes on supermarket products, that others use. Suppliers are the originators of many new ideas for their customers. Developers frequently do not profit from the commercial application of their ideas.

2. *Innovation rarely is instantaneous.* Technologies change as they diffuse. They improve in reliability, quality, and flexibility. In a series of small steps and refinements, they develop an evolving range of applications. Innovation usually starts as a solution to a narrow problem, and innovators rarely know all the ramifications. IBM's Thomas Watson, for instance, thought the computer would be of limited use. He believed the single computer his company made in 1947 would solve all the world's scientific problems but had no commercial application.

3. *Diffusion is very uneven.* Diffusion follows the classic S-shape curve. The first adopters are daring. Other people are slow to change, and only much later do they respond. Large firms in rapidly growing industries are sometimes the first to innovate because they have the necessary financial strength and access to information, but this is not always the case. The early market for innovation is hard to establish. Expectations that prices will fall retard adoption. People wait before they buy because they believe that with further progress prices will go down (think of the market for personal computers). Meanwhile, inventors and developers, who endure most of the risk, may not have the staying power, and second and third movers exploit their inventions.

4. *Since imitators face lower costs, the incentive to be innovative and entrepreneurial is not large.* For many important new ideas, patent protection is not available. The cost of taking out a patent, moreover, is great and may not be worth it. Without protection, the incentive to be innovative diminishes.

Understanding the Innovation Process

New ideas rarely are carried out as expected. Product gestation periods often are longer than anticipated, and R&D costs are underestimated while markets are overestimated. After analyzing numerous innovations, Van de Ven and colleagues concluded the innovation process typically goes through many stages, as outlined in Exhibit 7.11.[46] The gestation period of an invention lasts for many years, after which seemingly coincidental events occur that set the stage for innovation to be initiated. Often, internal or external shocks to an organization get things going. Dissatisfaction is needed to move people from the status quo. The plans submitted by the developers of an invention to the resource controllers are in the form of sales pitches, not realistic assessments of the costs and the obstacles as the innovation unfolds.

Once development begins, those involved usually discover there is disagreement and lack of clarity about what the innovation entails. Ideas proliferate, making the challenge of managing the innovation very difficult. Continuity among innovation personnel is broken as people come and go for many reasons, including frustration with the process as well as alternative career opportunities. Emotions run high and frustration levels build as normal setbacks are encountered, mistakes are made, and blame is apportioned.

EXHIBIT 7.11
The Innovation Journey—A Typical Path

- Coincidental events initiate gestation of many years:
  - Without shocks, level of apathy great
  - Need dissatisfaction to move from status quo
- Present plans to resource controllers in form of sales pitches.
- At start, there is disagreement and lack of clarity.
- Ideas proliferate, making managing difficult.
- Lack of continuity is found among personnel.
- Emotions run high, leading to frustration setbacks, mistakes, and blame.
- Problems snowball and patience of resource providers weakens.
- A struggle for power ensues.
- Resources run out before dreams fulfilled.

EXHIBIT 7.12
An Augmented View of Innovation

Source: Adapted from A. H. Van de Ven and R. Garud, "A Framework for Understanding the Emergence of New Industries," *Research on Technological Innovation Management and Policy,* Vol. 4, pp. 295–325.

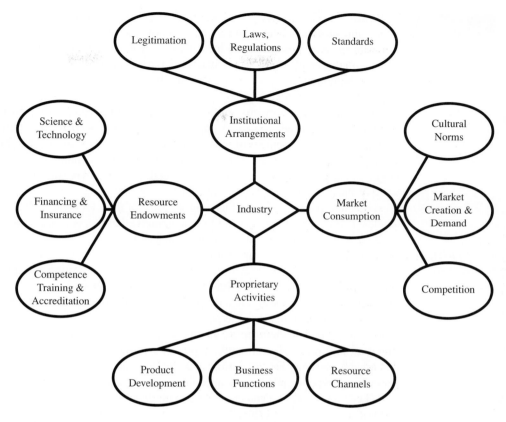

At first, schedules are adjusted and additional resources are provided to compensate for the unanticipated problems, but as the problems snowball, the patience of the resource providers weakens.

The goals of the resource providers and innovation managers may begin to diverge and a struggle for power emerges about project goals and how the project should be evaluated. Resources tend to get tight and can run out before the dreams of the developers are fulfilled. Innovations often are terminated because new resources are not forthcoming. The ideas continue to show promise, but the resource providers lose patience. As mentioned at the start of this chapter, the ability to see a project to the end is critical to the successful completion of an innovation. Seeing a project through to the end is a hard undertaking.

Technological innovations are collective achievements that occur over long periods. Their realization involves an entire industrial infrastructure that consists of institutional arrangements such as laws and regulations as well as resource endowments, proprietary activity, and markets (see Exhibit 7.12). No project evaluation technique has been developed that would make this process smoother or that would resolve the inherent difficulties. Thus, hunches, persistence, and what the economist John Maynard Keynes has called "animal spirits" are needed for innovations to succeed.

Summary

Achieving success in new business ventures is a long process that involves many stages. Innovators and entrepreneurs must have the staying power and commitment needed to see an idea through to realization. Many barriers have to be overcome. For new products and services to be commercialized, entrepreneurs, innovative companies, investors, and government support are needed.

Commercialization means not only finding new opportunities for business innovation but also exploiting them. The new opportunities can be discerned from trends, the opinions of experts, the development of alternative scenarios, and examining an era's leading-edge industries that drive innovation and entrepreneurship. In postindustrial societies, the leading-edge industries are apt to rely on human creativity to uncover ways to use less material to achieve the same or more economic value.

Biotechnology is a potential leading industry of the 21st century, but it faces many obstacles. Perhaps the largest barrier to its commercialization is lack of public acceptance.

In general, environmental challenges can lead businesses to new opportunities for innovations and entrepreneurship. These challenges provide huge promise, but they are risky and businesses must be sure footed about the comparative price and quality of environmentally sound substitutes to already existing technologies.

The obstacles to innovation and entrepreneurship start with uncertainty about the future. Because risk is great, managers, especially in existing firms, tend to be very cautious. They innovate slowly and on the margins. To innovate, they must have an optimistic bias, even if it is not always warranted. Uncertainty can prevent innovation and entrepreneurship. There is considerable uncertainty before, during, and after a product reaches the market; there is general business uncertainty; and there is uncertainty about customer and about government support.

Success at innovation and entrepreneurship requires matching market demand with technological capabilities. Evaluating the promise of a new venture requires careful assessment of both the maturity of the technologies on which it is based and their market potential. Both of these factors work together in the successful launching of new ventures.

Since entities that make discoveries often are not the ones that profit from them, innovation is rarely instantaneous, and because diffusion is uneven, the incentive to innovate is not great. Often, innovation takes years, and resource providers may abandon a project before it comes to successful fruition. Persistence is needed.

Because of the many disappointments that exist in developing new business ideas, creative entrepreneurs need to play their hunches and work against the odds. If they were to just calculate in a dispassionate and even-handed way the odds of success against the risk of failure, they might not proceed. Society would be the loser.

Endnotes

1. Gary Hamel, "Strategy as Revolution," *Harvard Business Review,* July–August 1996, p. 69.

2. Ibid., pp. 69–82.

3. M. Porter, *Competitive Strategy* (New York: Free Press, 1980).

4. H. Aldrich and C. Fiol, "Fools Rush In," *Academy of Management Review* 19 (1994), pp. 645–70.

5. Hamel, "Strategy as Revolution."

6. J. Harrison, *Strategic Management* (New York: Wiley and Sons, 2003).

7. G. Starling, *The Changing Environment of Business,* 3rd ed. (Boston: PWS-Kent Publishing Company, 1988).

8. Ibid.

9. Ibid.

10. Ibid.

11. A. Marcus, *Strategic Forecasting: A New Look at Scenarios* (New York: Palgrave McMillan, 2009).

12. J. Schumpeter, *Business Cycles* (New York: McGraw-Hill, 1939).

13. Ibid.

14. N. Kondratiev, "The Major Economic Cycles," *Voprosy Konjunktury* 1 (1925), pp. 28–79; English translation reprinted in *Lloyd's Bank Review,* no. 129 (1978).

15. I. Kirzner, *Perception, Opportunity, and Profit* (Chicago: University of Chicago Press, 1979); and Schumpeter, *Business Cycles.*

16. R. Rothwell and W. Zegveld, *Reindustrialization and Technology* (Armonk, NY: M. E. Sharpe, Inc., 1985).

17. D. Bell, *The Coming of Post-Industrial Society* (New York: Basic Books, 1973).

18. G. Gilder, "The World's Next Source of Wealth," *Fortune,* August 28, p. 116.

19. Ibid.

20. Ibid.

21. Ibid.

22. R. Shapiro, "Growth through Global Sustainability: An Interview," *Harvard Business Review,* January–February 1997, pp. 79–88.

23. A. Marcus, *Reinventing Environmental Regulation* (Washington, DC: Resources for the Future, 2002).

24. M. Porter and C. van der Linde, "Green and Competitive," *Harvard Business Review* 73 (1995), pp. 120–34.

25. A. Marcus, "Ringer: Overcoming Obstacles," National Pollution Prevention Center for Higher Education, University of Michigan, June 1998, http://css.snre.umich.edu/.

26. A. Marcus, "Osmonics Incorporated: Creating Competitive Advantage," National Pollution Prevention Center for Higher Education, University of Michigan, June 1998, http://css.snre.umich.edu/.

27. A. Marcus, "The Deluxe Corporation's PrintWise System," National Pollution Prevention Center for Higher Education, University of Michigan, June 1998, http://css.snre.umich.edu/.

28. P. Keegan, "Recharging Detroit" *Fortune,* April 15, 2009, pp. 54–62.

29. N. Walley and B. Whitehead, "It's Not Easy Being Green," *Harvard Business Review,* May–June 1994, pp. 46–52.

30. C. Freeman, *The Economics of Industrial Innovation,* 2nd ed. (Cambridge, MA: MIT Press, 1982); and F. Knight, *Risk, Uncertainty, and Profit* (New York: Houghton Mifflin, 1921).

31. Freeman, *Economics of Industrial Innovation.*

32. Ibid., p. 155.

33. M. Chase, "Did Syntex Withhold Data on Side Effects of a Promising Drug?" *The Wall Street Journal,* January 8, 1991, p. A1.

34. A. Swasy, "Diaper's Failure," *The Wall Street Journal,* October 9, 1990, p. B1.

35. T. O'Boyle, "GE Refrigerator Woes," *The Wall Street Journal,* May 7, 1990, p. A1.

36. J. White and M. Guiles, "GM's Plan for Saturn," *The Wall Street Journal,* July 9, 1990, p. A1.

37. Ibid.

38. Rothwell and Zegveld, *Reindustrialization and Technology.*

39. S. Yoder, "Motorola Loses Edge," *The Wall Street Journal,* March 4, 1991, p. A1.

40. B. Davis, "High-Definition TV," *The Wall Street Journal,* June 6, 1990, p. A1.

41. Schumpeter, *Business Cycles.*

42. Rothwell and Zegveld, *Reindustrialization and Technology.*

43. J. Schmookler, *Invention and Economic Growth* (Cambridge, MA: Harvard University Press, 1966).

44. E. Von Hippel, "Appropriability of Innovation Benefit as a Predictor of the Functional Locus of Innovation," Sloan School of Management MIT working paper 1084–79, 1979.

45. "Innovation," *The Economist,* January 11, 1992, pp. 17–19.

46. A. Van de Ven, D. Polley, R. Garud, and S. Venkatraman, *The Innovation Journey* (New York: Oxford University Press, 1999).

Repositioning

CHAPTER EIGHT

Continuous Reinvention

"In the martial arts of judo, a combatant uses the weight and strength of his opponent to his own advantage rather than opposing blow directly to blow. Judo strategy is based on three elements—rapid movement, flexibility, and leverage—each of which translates into a competitive principle. The first principle requires judo players to move rapidly to new markets and uncontested ground, thus avoiding head-to-head combat. . . . What judo strategists try to avoid are sumo matches. In a sumo match, combatants wrestle each other directly. . . . Agility and brains matter, but weight and strength matter far more."[1]

David Yoffie and Michael Cusumano

Chapter Learning Objectives

- Reviewing and summarizing the analytical approach to achieving sustained competitive advantage (SCA) so far presented in the book, which involves external and internal analysis followed by a series of moves related to timing, cost, differentiation, business scope, globalization, innovation, and entrepreneurship.
- Being aware that this approach to SCA must be carried out constantly and that a firm's strategy must be regularly reinvented. Effective implementation, then, must be linked to strategy formulation (see Chapter 9).
- Understanding judo as a strategy, which involves rapid movement to sweet spots followed by defense of those spots against competitors' inevitable encroachments.
- Providing examples of how firms have reinvented their strategies through such means as achieving greater closeness to customers, bridging supplier–customer gaps, and putting in place smart business designs.

Introduction

So far this book has prepared you for creating strategies that can help your business best existing and erstwhile rivals. Interesting rivalries in business are numerous and keep growing, such contests as those between: Medtronic and Boston Scientific; Harley Davidson and Kawasaki; Nokia and Apple; and Toyota and Volkswagen. As these rivalries heat up, the uncertainty that businesses face is high.

Because of downturns in the economic cycle, businesses must contend with irregularities in demand and consumption. Under these circumstances, are prior methods firms have used to formulate their strategies adequate? Can employees afford to just wait it out, or should they be more aggressive and use the present circumstances to try to achieve renewed competitive advantage?

Consider Crocs, an innovative shoe manufacturer, which made a meteoric rise prior to the recession of 2008, only to fall just as rapidly. What should it do now? Its footwear incorporates a proprietary resin material, "Croslite," which enables Crocs to produce a soft, light-weight, comfortable shoe for casual and recreational use. With the addition of color and varying designs, Crocs has been able to market its shoes to a very broad range of consumers. The company grew very fast, expanding its geographical reach and manufacturing capabilities and product lines and selling more than 30 million pairs of shoes in over 80 countries in 2007. It went from a company of 130 employees in 2003 to a company of more than 5,000 employees, but the recession struck Crocs hard and the competition heated up, with branded shoe companies responding to its basic model with their own alternatives and "me-too" and substitutes selling cheap look-alike shoes. Crocs's share price fell dramatically in 2008 and it had to lay off more than 2,000 of its employees. What it should do next was not obvious. The choices were many. It could develop new shoe models, open exclusive Crocs stores, turn to other product lines like accessories, reduce prices, market to new segments, use its remaining cash to make acquisitions or do R&D so as to license its proprietary material to other companies.

As the example shows, companies cannot stand still. They must regularly reinvent their strategies. In Crocs's case, its success was anything but permanent. It moved to a strong position but it could not rest safely in that position. It could not defend the position against aggressive rivals.

The need for firms to reposition themselves is constant. Beat back one competitor, and another is sure to follow. Core businesses are most vulnerable, if like Crocs they are relatively easy to copy.

This example suggests that formulating a good strategy in turbulent times is more challenging than ever. A company that correctly repositions itself can emerge stronger than ever, but a company that fails to adequately adjust risks failure. With consumers buying less, searching for deals, and switching brands, product categories, and stores, businesses the world over are challenged by changes in the economic cycle. Many consumers have changed long-held attitudes toward consumption itself. If this change is permanent, how will it affect markets and industries? Businesses cannot expect that a rising tide of consumption will lift all of them out of this predicament. They must pay even greater attention to the basics of branding, pricing, and segmentation.

A company's strategy must be regularly reset. Thus, this chapter reviews and expands on the approach to formulating a strategy developed so far in this book. The goal of strategy is sustained competitive advantage (SCA), but have no doubts about it: SCA is ephemeral. A firm's employees must be alert to strategic turning points and, when they take place, redeploy a firm's assets. How to manage this transition is not likely to be easy. This book has provided you with the key steps to grapple with this dilemma. Systematically examine external opportunities and threats; analyze internal strengths and weaknesses; and make moves related to product positioning, corporate scope, globalization, and innovation and entrepreneurship. If the circumstances call for a reexamination of a firm's strategy, then everything must be on the table. Start with the external environment (EA) and extend the examination to an organization's resources, capabilities, and competencies (IA), the positioning of its products and services (BS), the scope of its businesses (CS), its global reach (GS), and its approach to innovation (IS). Reexamining a firm's strategy also must be accompanied by a deep and penetrating understanding of how a firm will implement the strategy it formulates (see Chapter 9).

Judo Strategy

Rapid Movement and Agility: An Example

In uncertain times, rapid movement and agility are critical. Judo provides a good analogy for how rapid movement and agility might work in business. A classic judo struggle was the contest between Netscape and Microsoft over Internet browsers. This battle has been compared to the one between David and Goliath: a fast, flexible entrant, Netscape, taking on a dominant and powerful firm, Microsoft.[2] In 1997, at the height of the browser wars, Netscape had 700 employees and $80 million in sales, while Microsoft had 17,000 employees and $6 billion in sales (see Exhibit 8.1). In 1996, Netscape peaked with close to 90 percent of the browser market. One year later, its market share was down to less than 50 percent. Ultimately, it was Microsoft and not Netscape that controlled the Internet.

At first, Microsoft more or less ignored Netscape—it was preoccupied with bringing another Windows version to the market. But in December 1995, Bill Gates proclaimed that Microsoft was going to be "hard core" about the Internet. Netscape achieved its initial dominance of the browser market in a number of ways. By releasing a beta version of Navigator in 1994, Netscape received free assistance in developing the product from early users who acted as a quality-assurance team. It then separated the browser from other Internet options sold by vendors (such as dial-up access and e-mail accounts) and virtually gave the browser away for free. The official price was $39, but academics and nonprofit organizations did not have to pay, and anyone could download the browser for a free 90-day trial. Netscape's aim was to build market share and set the industry standard, and then make money through licensing fees for Navigator code used in browsers, intranet and extranet software, e-commerce solutions, Web servers priced in the thousands of dollars, and a portal that competed with Yahoo!, AOL, and InfoSeek.

Microsoft matched these moves. Not only did it give away its Internet Explorer to all users, including corporate clients, but it also bundled it with Windows 95. Internet Explorer popped up on the desktop of every Windows user. Microsoft also outbid Netscape for contracts with Internet service providers, including giant AOL with its millions of customers. In putting AOL's icon on the Windows desktop, however, Microsoft ceded ground to AOL and undercut its own online network, MSN.

Microsoft was determined to break Netscape, particularly because Netscape's managers claimed their system would make the Windows operating system unnecessary. By threatening

EXHIBIT 8.1
Judo Strategy: David versus Goliath

Netscape Navigator	Microsoft Internet Explorer
700 employees and $80 million sales in 1997	17,000 employees and $6 billion sales in 1997
Strategy: build market share, set standard	*Strategy: bundle with Windows 95 or free by downloading*
Open system	Outbid Netscape for customized AOL version
Published source code	Put AOL icon on Windows desktop
Virtual R&D	Undercut MSN network
Essentially free via server	

the existence of Windows, Netscape's executives spurred Microsoft to retaliate. Netscape's managers were not sufficiently prepared for Microsoft's response. In carrying out a judo strategy, it is necessary to be prepared for the determined retaliation that inevitably comes from stronger and more established companies.

Microsoft also was hurt by this battle. The Department of Justice challenged its tactics as violating the Sherman Antitrust Act: As a company with a dominant position—more than 90 percent of the operating-system market—Microsoft could not use its Windows monopoly to defeat a competitor in another market it wished to enter. Microsoft's exclusive bundling deals and the threat it made to cut off customers from Windows if they used Netscape went too far. Microsoft defeated Netscape, which ultimately was purchased by AOL, but Microsoft's long clash with the Justice Department seriously damaged the software maker.

Defense and Exploitation

From the perspective of a new entrant, the lesson is to try to "stay under the radar"—remain unnoticed—for as long as possible. Such companies as Honda in autos, Nucor in steel, and Walmart in retailing launched successful surreptitious attacks from the fringes by not provoking larger and more powerful competitors to retaliate. Their appearance of weakness slowed the response time of their opponents and reduced the magnitude and scope of the response when it came. By the time competitors woke up, the newcomers had gained substantial strength. They were better able to withstand the blows their opponents inflicted and thus better able to defend the territory they occupied. Judo strategy requires not only moving into uncontested space but also being able to defend and exploit it.

Sweet Spots and SCA: Company Analysis

The firms mentioned in Chapter 1 that consistently outperformed their industry tended to operate under the radar (see Exhibit 8.2). Those that achieved SCA moved quickly to "sweet spots," uninhabited niches that they helped create. In moving rapidly to uncontested space, they also built the capabilities and competencies they needed to defend and exploit this space.

For example, both Amphenol and LSI Logic had been hit hard by the collapse of the computer and telecommunications industry. Amphenol's strategy was to penetrate new niche markets in industries other than computers and telecommunications. Starting in 1996, it purchased several companies that had complementary technologies. Its aim was to offer high-priced, specialized products to an array of companies in industries as diverse as aerospace, automobiles, and defense. By 2002, it had more than 10,000 customers worldwide, with no single customer providing more than 5 percent of its revenues. LSI Logic, in contrast, sold expensive and highly specialized products to a very small group of customers; Sony was the largest, typically contributing 12 to 18 percent of LSI's total revenues. Other customers, such as NEC and Toshiba, had the capacity to move backward in the supply chain and make the products on their own. LSI's customers, therefore, had significant bargaining power with regard to price. The niche the company occupied was hard to defend. Amphenol, with its move to uncontested space, was the more agile of the two companies.

Similarly, both SPX and Snap-on started in the same mature auto-parts and testing industry. In 1996, they were direct competitors. However, SPX quickly moved from this industry in search of better opportunities. SPX became a highly diversified company competing in 25 business segments, while Snap-on stuck to the same industry, where it tried to grow within a mature market. SPX was relentless in its pursuit of new sweet spots

EXHIBIT 8.2
Matched Pairs
of Companies
Showing
Competitive
Advantage and
Disadvantage

Companies	5-Year Average Annual Market Return, 1997–2002	Sector
Amphenol	34.0%	Technology
LSI Logic	3.4	
SPX	28.8	Manufacturing/appliance
Snap-on	1.7	
FiServ	31.2	Software
Parametric	−21.2	
Dreyer's	22.4	Food
Campbell Soup	−2.8	
Forest Labs	58.5	Drugs/chemicals
IMC Global	−18.7	
Ball	23.9	Manufacturing/industrial
Goodyear	−11.5	
Brown & Brown	48.7	Financial
Safeco	−1.0	
Family Dollar	36.1	Retail
Gap	9.8	
Activision	24.1	Entertainment/toys
Hasbro	−0.1	

to occupy. When buying a company, SPX rapidly consolidated, cut costs, and closed unprofitable operations to increase margins. SPX was more agile than Snap-on, and it made sure the new spaces it occupied became more defensible.

FiServ is another example of an agile company. It created a new niche for itself as the "back office" for deregulated firms in the financial services industry. It defended this niche by being close to its customers, continuously developing new products and business lines, and being indispensable to customers. Dreyer's, too, moved into a new niche as manufacturer, transporter, and supplier of premium ice cream. It defended this niche by its ability to manage the freezer space for all brands, including those of its main competitors Ben & Jerry's and Häagen Dazs, which made it less vulnerable to attack. Forest Labs also succeeded in creating a new niche by obtaining regulatory approval for and marketing an antidepressant, Celexa, that had previously been available only in Europe. It defended this niche with a large and focused marketing team of detail persons who regularly met with physicians and health care providers and knew their needs well. Ball moved from glass bottles to aluminum and plastics and defended this niche with superior innovation in packaging and superior efficiency in manufacturing.

Once a sweet spot is created, it can be a powerful magnet attracting other firms to enter. These successful companies built mechanisms to protect the spaces they occupied. They were able to realign and reconfigure resources, capabilities, and competencies to make themselves hard to attack. Firms like these had not only the *agility* to move to a sweet spot but also the discipline to protect it.

Focus is another characteristic of firms with SCA. Ball, for instance, did not have a stake in all sides of the business—raw materials and retailing included—as Goodyear did;

EXHIBIT 8.3
Seeking
Sustained
Competitive
Advantage

Attributes	Advantage	Disadvantage
Position	Sweet spot—being in an uncontested space	Sour spot—being in a contested space
Movement	Agility—getting to an uncontested space	Rigidity—not getting to an uncontested space
Hard-to-imitate capabilities	Discipline—protecting an uncontested space	Ineptness—inability to protect an uncontested space
Concentration	Focus—exploiting an uncontested space	Diffuseness—inability to exploit an uncontested space

rather, it just designed and manufactured aluminum cans and plastic bottles. Brown & Brown did not operate at all points in the supply chain, as Safeco did. Rather than underwriting as well as selling insurance, Brown & Brown became an extremely aggressive seller of insurance and niche insurance products originated by many companies. Safeco's sales force was restricted to selling only the products that it originated. Safeco could not keep up with the small and agile Brown & Brown.

Similarly, Gap and Hasbro were vertically integrated and had products in many niches. They could not compete with the more focused Family Dollar and Activision. Family Dollar concentrated on the often-disregarded low-income shopper in large urban areas, while Gap designed and produced clothes, as well as selling them, at different price points for different classes of customers. Gap had stores for the discount shopper (Old Navy), for the upscale shopper (Banana Republic), and for the middle-of-the-road shopper (The Gap). Carrying out such diverse activities in the same organization was challenging. The skills for designing clothing, for instance, did not match the skills that Gap needed to distribute clothes efficiently.

The companies listed in Exhibit 8.2 that achieved SCA did not deviate from what they did best. They chose an area where they had a comparative advantage and extended it. They had the agility to find a sweet spot, the discipline to protect it, and the focus to fully exploit it, while the underperforming firms had the opposite characteristics—rigidity that left them in a contested or "sour spot," ineptness, and diffuseness. Exhibit 8.3 summarizes these attributes.

Reinvention

Firms cannot stand still, especially during tough economic times. They must continually reinvent themselves. As argued in Chapter 1, they always are between two poles: their *mission,* which reflects where they were, what they were good at in the past, and where they had achieved some type of comparative advantage; and their *vision,* where they would like to go and what they would like to be good at in the future to achieve a comparative advantage. Managing this tension is not easy and thus attaining SCA is rare. Many firms achieve temporary advantage, but few make the advantage last through good times and bad.

To succeed over the long term, businesses must regularly remake themselves. In doing so, they must confront two constants: The competition never lets up, and internal lethargy stands in the way of change.

The Dilemma of Change

As discussed in Chapter 1, inflection points are moments of deep-seated departures from the past—momentous shifts in technologies, markets, laws and regulations, global conditions, and the economy. In the last years of the 21st century's first decade, the entire world was going through such an inflection. When an inflection occurs, the pressure for change increases. Firms have little choice but to try to remake themselves. The ones that can better navigate such conditions are the ones that will be better able to thrive. They must struggle against vested interests that do not want to budge from the status quo. They fight staff, for instance, that does not want to honestly confront the challenges that lie in front of them. It is simpler to stick with what they know best than to move forward. Barriers to change abound, and resistance comes from many quarters. Mobilizing the forces of change to overcome these barriers is not easy. Just determining where the firm wants to be next is a difficult decision.

Many staff members focus on what the firm knows best. They do not want to give up what they are currently doing, and they do not want to move to an unknown destination. Developing new capabilities and competencies is demanding, and they are reluctant to do so.

Chapter 1 identified approaches firms can take when dealing with the prospect of making changes:

- Some firms vigilantly guard the past. These are *defenders*.
- Other firms have no hesitation about taking the next steps and moving into the future. They vigorously search for new opportunities. They are *prospectors*.
- Others try to simultaneously cultivate the past while they journey into the future. These are *analyzers*.
- Still others, overwhelmed by change, become confused and do not know what to do. These firms are *reactors*.

When inflection points bear down on firms, the reactors may well be the poorest performers. They are adrift without direction. They may be just trying to keep their options open. At some point, they will have to decide on a direction.

Defenders, too, might be in a poor position. However, if they can effectively mobilize resources, they may be able to protect their current position. As survivors in unattractive industries, they can defend remaining niches. As other firms leave the industry, they can pick up revenue streams and profits.

Prospectors, those who seize opportunities before others realize their value, face many challenges. Key among them is the risk of being too far out in front of competitors. Pioneers rarely realize the full gains of the quick and early thrusts they make into new territory. Early movers face many problems. For instance, they must convince recalcitrant buyers to switch before a new product has been accepted and standards for its manufacture and use have been established. The experiments in which they take part are costly. The efforts they make are often premature; the mistakes are hard to undo. Aggressive second movers learn from and capitalize on pioneers' miscalculations; they take advantage of the first movers' misfortunes. If the early bird gets the worm, the second mouse after the first loses its life in the mousetrap always gets the cheese.

The managers of most firms tend to understand these risks. Seeing the failures of overexuberance all around them, they do not have to be persuaded to be cautious. Many choose to be conscious and deliberate analyzers. Perched between the past and the future, they try to defend and exploit a successful niche and, at the same time, seek out new opportunities for growth and expansion.

This approach requires maintaining a delicate balance. Pulled in two directions at once, the position the firm tries to straddle may not be tenable. The organizational requirements for exploiting a past niche are not necessarily compatible with those for exploiting a future one. The former calls for the utmost efficiency to fend off encroaching competitors, whereas the latter requires maximum creativity to move into uncharted territory. While efficiency depends on having strict command and control structures that may stifle employees' ability to innovate, creativity depends on loosening constraints that stand in the way of new ways of thinking and behaving.

Thus, the ambidextrous organization that has a hand in the past and a hand in the future and that occupies the middle position may not be viable. A firm may have to decide whether to continue as dominant in what it has been doing well or try to become dominant—as soon as possible—in what it would like to do well next. If it tries to simultaneously prospect and defend, it is likely to be mediocre at both and it will fail because it has no comparative advantage (see Chapter 1).

A Strategic Approach to the Dilemma

SCA is fleeting, and managers must be watchful of major turning points in which the dilemma of where to head is most challenging. This book has developed a sequence of steps that managers can take to deal with such change. This approach to strategy can be summarized as follows: SCA is equal to external analysis (EA) plus internal analysis (IA) plus moves (M) that the strategist can take. That is,

$$SCA = EA + IA + M$$

The moves should be taken with as much knowledge as possible of the responses opponents can make and the consequences of those responses.

External and Internal Analysis

External analysis (Chapter 2) and internal analysis (Chapter 3) both have a number of components.

External analysis (EA) is an assessment of industry attractiveness. The industry is defined as best as possible, although industry definition is often problematic because industry boundaries are shifting. In analyzing the external environment, the analyst:

- Examines the *five forces (5F)* in the industry—suppliers, customers, competitors, new entrants, and substitutes. These determine the industry's attractiveness.
- Assesses the *macroenvironmental forces (MF)*—economics, politics, technology, demography, social conditions, and the natural environment—that influence the five industry forces.
- Conducts a *stakeholder analysis (SA)*—an assessment of such key constituencies as shareholders, government, advocacy groups, and the media. This determines the network of ties between the firm and its constituencies.

Each of these assessments should be conducted to the extent possible. Thus,

$$EA = 5F + MF + SA$$

Internal analysis (IA) is an assessment of the firm's strengths and weaknesses. In analyzing the internal environment, the analyst:

- Analyzes the degrees to which the organization is mechanistic or organic and whether there is a good *fit (F)* with the environment.
- Assesses the firm's *value chain (VC)*—its primary and support activities in areas such as inbound and outbound logistics. What are the linkages between the firm's value chain components and those of other firms?
- Examines the firm's *resources, capabilities, and competencies (RCC)*—its strengths. Are they combined in a way that provides something rare, hard to imitate, difficult to substitute, and valuable?

Thus,

$$IA = F + VC + RCC$$

Each part of external and internal analyses provides a more complete picture, but time constraints may preclude a thorough assessment of each element. Before choosing moves, the analyst should ask:

- Given the firm's unique configuration of resources, capabilities, and competencies, how defensible is its position?
- Are the resources, capabilities, and competencies barriers to change, or can they be the drivers of entrepreneurial activity and new business development?

Moves

External and internal analyses are only the start of the strategy process. They are preliminaries to making actual *moves (M)*. The firm's possible moves depend on the options available and on whether the firm should use or forgo these options. Timing plays a role, and competitors' reactions also must be considered.

The strategist needs to understand the possible moves the organization can make. He or she must consider each move by itself and in combination with other moves in an ordered sequence. The strategist then has to determine to what extent the moves have the potential to achieve the organization's goals, given the fact that competitors also are choosing or forgoing moves.

A rational process would be to list all the options available, consider all the consequences, and choose the best, but this degree of comprehensiveness may not be feasible. Given the risks and uncertainties of each action and the limited time and calculating ability of the analyst, precisely estimating results of following every potential course of action is usually not possible. The analyst can, however, try to approximate this type of estimation.

A shortcut for generating a list of options is to think in terms of the moves discussed in Chapters 4 through 7: positioning; mergers, acquisitions, and divestitures; globalization; and innovation. Each of these chapters considered a type of generic move that the analyst might think of pursuing.

Timing and Positioning   Chapter 4 dealt with the *timing (T)* of the moves a firm might make as well as the *positioning (P)*. Should the moves be early or late as well as what combination of low-cost and high-quality attributes should be incorporated into a product or service to create a best-value proposition? These decisions are included in *business strategy (BS):*

$$BS = T + P$$

Mergers, Acquisitions, and Divestitures   Chapter 5 addressed *mergers, acquisitions, and divestitures (MAD)*. At issue here are the size and scope of the firm itself, the extent of its diversification, the degree to which it should focus on one product or market or on many, and the degree to which it should be integrated up or down the value chain. These decisions typically are included in the category of choices called *corporate strategy (CS):*

$$CS = MAD$$

Global Expansion   Chapter 6 dealt with the rationales for a firm's *global expansion (GE)*. Should such expansion be undertaken primarily for marketing, manufacturing, or other reasons? Should it be carried out in a uniform way that promotes low cost or a customized way that requires expensive adaptation? Another issue is the extent to which the firm should *outsource (OS)* its global operations: Should it partner with local allies or internalize them? These are some of the critical elements of *global strategy (GS)*. Thus,

$$GS = GE + OS$$

Innovation and Entrepreneurship   Chapter 7 discussed innovation and entrepreneurship. The roles of entrepreneurs, established firms, funding sources, and backers of the firm, including government, have to be sorted out. The firm has to discover what *opportunities (O)* are available, and it must analyze the obstacles to *commercialization (C)*. It must achieve a match between a technology's development stage and the market's readiness for that technology. This category of moves, which we refer to as *innovation strategy (IS),* can be expressed as

$$IS = O + C$$

Implementation   Chapter 9 will discuss strategy implementation. Strategy is a continuous process of reinvention and implementation (CI).

The Expanded Model   Together, these moves and the external and internal analyses create an expanded model of SCA, as follows:

$$SCA = [EA + IA] + [BS + CS + GS + IS] + CI$$

If a firm continuously engages in this process, it will be better able to deal with inflection points, to redeploy assets, and to reinvent itself when necessary.

Innovations in Strategy

Innovation and entrepreneurship are fundamental factors in the SCA equation that deserve more attention. They encompass not just new technologies, but also new business models. Strategic innovation itself is important. The following example shows just how important it is.

An Example: Retail Food Industry

The retail food industry has experienced a deep-seated transformation. During the past 15 years, changing consumer demographics and lifestyles, alternative whole-meal replacement chains, specialty stores, hypermarkets, cooperatives, deep discounters, and, most significantly, general merchandisers such as Walmart have eroded market positions among traditional grocery stores and supermarkets.[3] By 1995, Walmart had opened 275 supercenters; since then, it has opened another 100 of these stores per year, each selling an average of $20 million worth of food annually. By 2000, Walmart had become the largest grocer in the United States.

Walmart's strategies have posed basic challenges to the industry. The company's distribution costs are about 3 percent of sales, roughly half the cost of the typical supermarket chain. The industry's response to these changes has been a gargantuan campaign to acquire new competencies in supplier and customer relations. The actions it has taken were meant to improve the efficiency of the supply chain, a complicated undertaking involving both people's skill levels and technology. With competition in the food industry rising and a rapidly changing retail environment, acquiring capabilities in supplier and customer relations was a key to grocers' survival. Firms in the industry had to better link suppliers and customers and eliminate waste. They had to acquire new information systems that linked customers, wholesalers, and manufacturers; achieved enhanced food chain integration; and provided for stronger alliances between retailers and vendors, leaner inventories, lower inventory costs, and better logistics.

Thus, the industry's goal was innovation in all its business practices; it tried to reengineer the supply chain with new alliances and incentives that would do away with waste. Stronger alliances between retailers and suppliers were expected to yield leaner inventories, lower inventory costs, better logistics, and improved exchange of information. The goal was to get higher product turnover and greater sales per square foot. The supermarket industry recognized the importance of supply chain management in achieving this goal. It organized a nationwide campaign in efficient consumer response (ECR) to keep up with the supply chain efficiencies of chains such as Walmart.

Supermarkets are at the end point in a long chain of food distribution that starts with the grower and processor/manufacturer and moves through an assortment of wholesalers, distributors, and warehouses before final purchase and consumption by consumers. The average supermarket deals with many suppliers, and the industry understood that supply chain improvement was vital. The entire industry effort was designed to have the right goods available to consumers at the right times and in the right proportions. The Walmart challenge unleashed these innovations in the retail food industry, but it was similar to the challenges many industries faced in the early 21st century.

Competing via Strategic Innovation

Continuous reinventions of business strategy entail a view of the organization as a feedback loop.[4] They start with a recognition of customer needs and end with an attempt to satisfy these needs at a higher level.

Companies must have aggressive goals with respect to the speed and consistency with which they deliver goods and services to their end customers. It is essential to set up critical business processes, as in the retail food industry, to accomplish these ends.

Meeting Customer Needs

Superior information is the basis for meeting customer needs effectively. Dell meets its customer needs with a low-cost plus customization formula. IBM, a hardware and software vendor and also the world's largest information technology consultant, has a different

EXHIBIT 8.4
From Products to Solutions

Source: Adapted from A. Slywotzky and D. Morrison, *Profit Patterns* (New York: Time Business, 1999).

Customer process before the solution: Inefficiency and Confusion

Customer process after the solution: Efficiency and Harmony

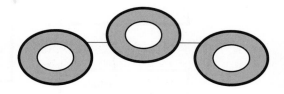

Everything is bought separately; doesn't fit together well.

Supplier simplifies process for customers and provides entire system or complete package of maintenance, service, and financing.

approach. To satisfy customer needs, it relies not just on products but also on customer solutions. Other companies that have gone from products to solutions are Honeywell, which is taking responsibility for Boeing's entire avionics system, and GE, which has been providing customers with a complete package of maintenance, service, and financing (see Exhibit 8.4).

Profits come not from a firm's resource-intensive assets but from knowledge. To capture profitable niches in industries, companies use their know-how. Thus, it is not ownership of hotels, theme parks, and college bookstores that has proved to be extremely profitable but rather the contracts firms such as Marriott, Disney, and Barnes & Noble have for managing them. Such contracts are intangible, knowledge-based assets.

Using Knowledge about Customers

Today, many believe that knowledge provides the competitive edge in industry after industry. Grocers, for instance, have been moving from managing individual stockkeeping units to managing whole categories of foods because of knowledge about customer needs for interrelated categories such as breakfast foods (cereals, yogurts, milk, bagels, coffee, eggs, etc.).

Precision merchandising also is based on the knowledge of a firm's employees. Precision merchandising eliminates mismatches between what is on the shelf and what a firm's customers want. Walmart, for instance, uses the data it collects on customer's purchasing habits to create predictive algorithms for nearly every inch of shelf space in its stores. If it can eliminate discrepancies between what customers want and what is available, it not only reduces shortages but also minimizes closeouts and losses on excess inventory.

EXHIBIT 8.5
Micro-
segmenting
of Customers

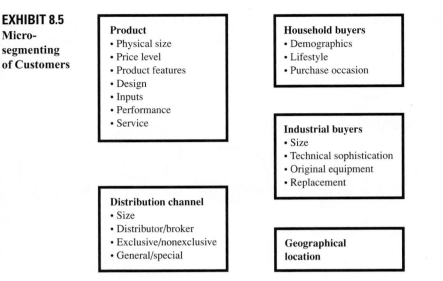

Product
- Physical size
- Price level
- Product features
- Design
- Inputs
- Performance
- Service

Household buyers
- Demographics
- Lifestyle
- Purchase occasion

Industrial buyers
- Size
- Technical sophistication
- Original equipment
- Replacement

Distribution channel
- Size
- Distributor/broker
- Exclusive/nonexclusive
- General/special

Geographical location

Many companies use their knowledge to micro-segment their customers. There are significant differences in customer wants and needs based on age, income, gender, and so on. Because one size does not fit all, managers may divide customers into finer and finer segments, trying to serve a category of one, or nearly one, customer (see Exhibit 8.5).

Micro-segmenting yields a market where customers are willing to pay more for products because the products are better suited to their needs; the products are more personalized and more functional. A firm must use its data to figure out which groups of customers are profitable and which are not. Managers must ask if there is any value to serving some customers at a loss. Do the money-losing customers help to cover fixed costs? Can they be converted to profitable customers? If they have no value, why is the firm serving them?

The firm must analyze and reanalyze its customers to know which are the good ones and how to manage those that are not so good. It has to understand how the brands, styles, designs, functions, performances, and prices that it offers fit together to serve different customer classes.

Closing the Supplier–Customer Gap

The customer analysis discussed above leads managers to think of ways of bringing customers and suppliers closer together. Superstores, for instance, have long understood the value of compressing supply chain channels to more closely link suppliers and customers. With the advent of the superstore, the number of customers has expanded, as has the number of purchases (see Exhibit 8.6).

A company can first compress channels and then multiply them (see Exhibit 8.7). By multiplying channels, it expands the number of customers and increases purchases. The old pattern was to mainly sell in a single channel; now, it is to sell in multiple channels. Coffee, for instance, once was mainly sold in supermarkets and lunch counters but today is sold at bookstores, cafés, kiosks, and convenience stores, among other places. Media

EXHIBIT 8.6
Compressing
the Supply
Chain

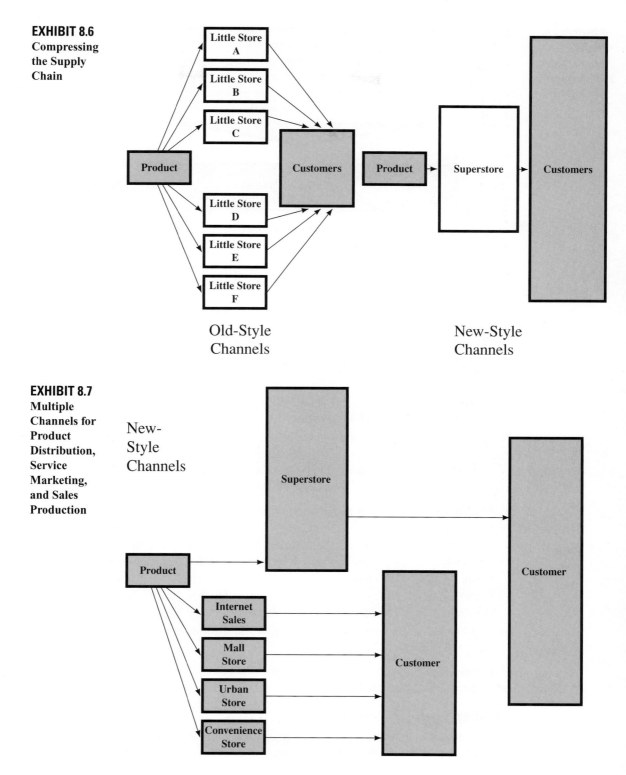

Old-Style
Channels

New-Style
Channels

EXHIBIT 8.7
Multiple
Channels for
Product
Distribution,
Service
Marketing,
and Sales
Production

New-
Style
Channels

EXHIBIT 8.8
Where Can Value Chain Dominance Be Established?

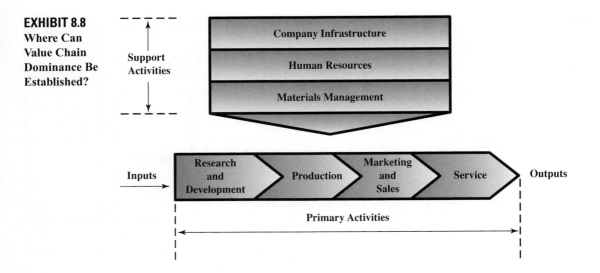

companies such as Viacom, Disney, and AOL/Time Warner have copied this technique to spread creative ideas. They diffuse the ideas in many forms—print, TV, film, video, cable, and so on. They seek to profit again and again from their assets. Thus, Harry Potter is incorporated into toys, clothing, comic books, TV shows, musicals, ice shows, and theme parks. A blockbuster is a powerful platform through which a company profits many times.

Establishing Value Chain Dominance

A company should examine the value chain to see where it can establish dominance. Because it cannot be good at everything, it should divide the value chain into separate elements and determine where it can derive the most value (see Exhibit 8.8). It should concentrate on areas in which it can establish leadership and outsource the rest. Consider these examples:

- Nike has chosen to be a marketing and design company. It outsources most of its manufacturing.
- Merck, a developer of new drugs, acquired Medco, a distributor, but did not hold it for long. Merck divested this company when it realized that distribution was not an area where it could be effective.
- Coca-Cola and PepsiCo, while retaining an interest in their bottling companies, let go of these companies. The bottlers operate as separate companies.
- Gap has run into trouble because it designs and distributes its own clothes, and to do both well is difficult.

A company can dominate in only a few areas of the value chain. It should know what these areas are and specialize in them.

Creating Smart Business Designs

To create smart business designs, strategists must think in terms of customers, suppliers, distribution channels, and competing value chains. These are the main building blocks. **Smart designs** rest on a willingness to regularly reassess them; they cannot be taken for granted.

To achieve this, the firm's goal should be to establish a continuous flow of goods, services, and information from suppliers to customers. The strategist should obtain information about customers from many sources. The firm engages in numerous transactions and communications with customers, so it should try to move from ad hoc, episodic interactions to continuous, accurate interactions. The types of interactions analyzed should reduce guesswork, increase efficiency, and enhance the flexibility and fast response the firm needs.

Forward-Thinking Analysis

The strategist also has to think more than one step into the future. Imagine a 10-year time horizon with three steps of 3 to 4 years each. At step 1, options 2 and 3 might be the most appropriate moves to make; at step 2, options 4 to 6 might be the most appropriate moves; and at step 3, options 8 to 10 might be the most appropriate moves. On careful reflection, it might become clear that options 1 and 11 should never be carried out.

For each stage in the future, the strategist must think not only about the moves he or she is proposing, but also about how competitors will respond. A key lesson in this book is that the analyst must pay attention to competitors' responses. The success of your company is determined not by your moves alone but also by the moves they elicit from your competitors.

Summary

This chapter goes over the basic approach to strategy found in this book. The purpose of strategy is to achieve sustained competitive advantage. Doing so requires a good knowledge of external opportunities and threats and internal strengths and weaknesses. Based on this knowledge the strategist is ready to recommend a series of moves that the firm can make. These moves can involve the cost and quality of the products and services that the firm offers. They can involve expanding or subtracting from the scope of the firm's businesses via mergers, acquisitions, and divestitures. They can consist of globalizing the firm's offerings or engaging in innovation and entrepreneurship with entirely new products, services, or lines of business.

The activity of gaining knowledge about the external and internal environment and considering the moves that the firm can make is not a onetime event. It must be engaged in continuously. A firm must be constantly alert to changes in its external and internal environment and be ready to make moves that reinvent its strategy.

Judo provides yet another analogy for the task of the strategist. A strategy based on this martial art is one in which the strategist searches for uncontested space and recommends that the firm rapidly move to this space. Being in this space is just the start, however, of creating sustained competitive advantage (SCA). The firm must use discipline and focus to protect the space it occupies.

This chapter has shown how in finding a sweet spot, agility, discipline, and focus distinguished firms that enjoy SCA from those that do not. Firms that suffer from sustained competitive disadvantage are likely to be in a contested space, which they are unable to vacate, protect, or exploit.

This chapter has shown how creative business redesigns can bring firms into closer contact with their customers. Enhanced customer intimacy comes from business designs that systematically collect detailed information about customers, break up customers into smaller and smaller segments, and provide them with integrated packages of solutions rather than separate products and services. Smart business designs break down the barriers that stand between firms and their customers and then multiply the points of access or contact points between firms and customers.

Firms move into uncontested spaces that can be protected through smart business designs, which form the basis for long-term advantage. Choosing these designs must be accompanied by effective implementation, the subject of this book's last chapter.

Endnotes

1. D. Yoffie and M. Cusumano, "Judo Strategy," *Harvard Business Review,* January–February 1999, p. 74.
2. Ibid., pp. 71–81.
3. A. Marcus and M. Anderson, "A Dynamic Capability and the Acquisition of Competencies in Supply Chain and Environmental Management," University of Minnesota Carlson School of Management working paper, 2003.
4. A. Slywotzky and D. Morrison, *Profit Patterns* (New York: Time Business, 1999).

CHAPTER NINE

Implementation[*]

"The value of an idea lies in the using of it."

Thomas A. Edison, American inventor

Chapter Learning Objectives

- Being aware that implementation is both a dynamic process and a core competence.
- Understanding that skillful implementation is required to drive results.
- Using past failures to reveal common obstacles to implementation and emphasize the need for a more masterful approach to the process.
- Discerning whether an organization is ready to embark on a strategic change initiative.
- Comprehending the activities required to move from a state of change-readiness to a changed state that continues to stand ready.
- Being conscious of the need to continuously monitor the competitive environment, nurture the organization, and improve the implementation process itself.

Introduction

Implementation is the process of translating a strategy into action—bringing the ideas and decisions covered in previous chapters to life. If an organization cannot effectively manage the process, it will lag behind its rivals in the marketplace.

Unfortunately, the implementation process is often fraught with obstacles: Resources are scarce, resistance to change is great, persistent yet agile leadership is rare, and transparent communications (which show the linkages between executive- and operating-level objectives) are atypical. As a result, numerous organizations have struggled to realize the benefits of even their most well-conceived strategic plans. This book's analytical process for deriving strategic moves—analyzing the external and internal environments and choosing the optimal sequence and combination of moves—will come to naught if implementation is not effective.

[*]This chapter was written by Anne Cohen, Senior Lecturer, Strategic Management and Organization Department, Carlson School of Management.

EXHIBIT 9.1
The Basic
Strategic
Management
Cycle

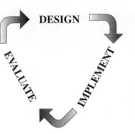

DESIGN

EVALUATE

IMPLEMENT

The purpose of this chapter, therefore, is to examine successes and failures in strategy execution while providing an implementation framework for you to use. Theoretically, implementation is positioned between strategic design and evaluation but, in practice, all these processes must be integrated and synchronized (see Exhibit 9.1).[1] Implementers must be willing to regularly rethink the tactics necessary to achieve their objectives.

The Probability and Anatomy of Failure

Managers have grappled with the gap between organizational strategy and attainment of objectives for quite some time. A 2004 survey conducted by *The Economist* polled both U.S. and Canadian senior operating executives across eight key industries and found that 57 percent of companies did not successfully implement their strategic initiatives.[2] In 2006, the American Management Association and the Human Resources Institute painted an even bleaker picture. Its survey of global executives and HR experts revealed that just 3 percent of respondents rated their companies as very successful at implementing strategies, while 62 percent described their organizations as mediocre or worse.[3] It's obvious that success has not been the norm.

Mistakes in implementation result in an organization losing precious time, money, and momentum versus its rivals. With this in mind, the following section analyzes several high-profile implementation mishaps and warns of obstacles that management might encounter along the way.

Home Depot: Performance-Enhancing Moves versus an Engrained Culture

Home Depot's overall performance had been lackluster when Robert Nardelli, a talented former executive at General Electric, was recruited for the company's top spot. The organization recognized the need for change, but Nardelli brought "the wrong toolbox to the job," mistakenly believing that GE's successful strategies and tactics could be readily transplanted to a big box retail environment. In his efforts to streamline Home Depot's business processes and 2,000 stores, he over-focused on the processes and trampled on Home Depot's highly customer-focused and entrepreneurial culture. He angered the management ranks by firing longtime Home Depot executives to bring in GE alumni, and then he enraged investors by losing out to rival Lowe's when it began to invest heavily in new and more attractive stores. When competition heated up, Nardelli employed manufacturing-appropriate methods to shore up the bottom line, but his tactics, which cut costs by increasing the number of less knowledgeable part-time workers, left full-time employees fuming and crippled customer service. Though cuts allowed Nardelli to reach earnings per share and other growth targets—a "commendable job," according to Barry Henderson, an equities analyst at T. Rowe Price—investors questioned whether the company's top-line growth was sustainable. After years of a declining stock price, Home Depot announced Nardelli's resignation.[4]

Moral of the Story: *Implementation efforts will fail if leadership does not acknowledge that cultural norms can place boundaries on the pace and extent to which new behaviors can be integrated into the existing organizational system—and if executive incentives are not carefully aligned with a comprehensive organizational vision.*

Circuit City: "Me Too" Moves versus Faster, More Savvy Foes

Circuit City's Firedog offering was created to provide customers with an enhanced menu of services delivered at cost levels comparable to the company's low-cost and best-value rivals. Pulling a page from Best Buy's playbook, the Firedog team was to handle technical services for both computer equipment and home theater installations in a way that closely mimicked the Geek Squad. Unfortunately, this move was made well past the company's prime. Complacence and inaction during prior industry inflection points had created a significant long-term disadvantage. Starting in the 1990s, Circuit City failed to secure prime real estate while rivals were snapping up more convenient locales.[5] It reduced the breadth of its product line when it stopped selling appliances, yet did not aggressively pursue the electronics niche with a strong set of gaming offerings. It neglected to improve its Web presence, just as online retailers such as Amazon.com were hitting their stride. Then it lost to Best Buy in a contest to create an Apple presence in its stores.[6] Internally, old inventory levels began to swell and soon Circuit City was unable to buy fresh product or pay off its existing debts. Deep cuts at the front line (which were similar to Nardelli's moves at Home Depot) eliminated over 8,000 of Circuit City's most experienced employees, replacing them with cheaper workers. In the end, the organization only succeeded in mortally wounding its customer service. Its descent was rapid and liquidation was announced by the end of 2008 because it was not able to successfully implement its strategic initiatives.

Moral of the Story: *Poor timing coupled with inadequate management of market dynamics will sink any strategy.*

United Airlines: A Low-Cost Segmentation Move versus Lack of Internal Commitment

United's Ted concept was designed to give United a way to compete with low-cost airlines, such as Frontier, JetBlue, and Southwest. Plans to standardize aircraft with no-frills configurations, and maximize jet use through rapid turnarounds at airport gates, were meant to reduce maintenance and operating costs significantly. These plans were put into play and service was launched on February 12, 2004, in Denver, with 57 Airbus A320 aircraft, in a 156-seat all-economy configuration. However, the airline's overall cost structure lacked alignment with the new initiative, and the low-cost offering was never certified as a separate operating entity. "Ted" was simply a brand name applied in an attempt to differentiate the all-economy service from United's mainline flights. As a result, all Ted flights actually were operated by United Airlines crew flying under the United Airlines operating certificate—and those crews of pilots, flight attendants, and mechanics were not always compensated per Ted's low-cost design. United's own operational needs also interfered with the new brand implementation. Ted aircraft were recruited as needed for mainline United flights, while mainline United aircraft were operated as Ted flights only confusing Ted's customer base and weakening the brand. As a result of this lack of full commitment to the concept, costs at Ted were never as low as those of a genuine discount airline and its operations led to significant losses. The fatal blow to the concept came when fuel prices spiked and parent UAL dumped its gas-guzzling 737 models, reclaimed the A320's from the Ted operations, and reconfigured them to carry higher-margin first-class United passengers. On January 6, 2009, operations were officially folded back into the mainline brand and Ted was dead.[7]

> ***Moral of the Story:*** *Implementation efforts will fail without a lack of full commitment and alignment of structures, procedures, and resources with an organization's strategy.*

Swissair: Empire-Building Moves versus Resource Limitations and EU Law

The conventional wisdom of the airline industry, as in many other mature industries, has been that globalization demands concentration into a small number of operators. Multiple carriers have formed alliances and merged to optimize aircraft utilization levels and build scale economies, but this conventional wisdom is too often oversimplified. Swissair's Hunter strategy was designed to set the airline on a path toward such a global alliance by focusing company resources on markets with the largest growth potential—such as Belgium, Austria, Finland, Hungary, Portugal, and Ireland. With the exception of the Polish carrier LOT, however, all companies acquired were in a desolate financial situation and required significant managerial intervention. EU law, which demanded majority citizen ownership as a condition of retaining an EU operating permit, also complicated Swissair's efforts. Swissair could own only 49.9 percent of each carrier *on paper*, yet it bore the full financial risk of ownership *off balance sheet* to obtain immediate and direct managerial control. Soon, the funds invested were significantly higher than initially approved by the board (which lacked any solid experience in managing an international airline). The culture of excellence, which defined the Swissair brand, was also not as easily transferable to non-Swiss cultures as initially estimated. Massive divestments were undertaken to reduce the steadily growing financing gap. However, these divestments largely represented sale and lease-back transactions involving the group's aircraft fleet—transactions that yielded cash flow and improved the financial picture in the short run but resulted in lease payments in subsequent years. Within two years, off-balance-sheet obligations increased by some CHF 5 billion, and on October 1, 2001, Swissair's liquidity requirements exploded. Regular flight operations could no longer be maintained, so these were suspended October 2, 2001, and, at 3:35 p.m., the airline was grounded.[8]

> ***Moral of the Story:*** *To successfully implement complex moves, an organization must employ skilled foresight—and oversight—of both internal and external dynamics. Inflection points can occur throughout the process.*

The Root Causes of Failure

Although the failures detailed in the previous section involve a variety of strategic moves in different industries on separate continents, the decisions and behaviors of those charged with the implementation of these strategies suggest that the root causes of failure are universal. A strategy-to-performance gap comes about because of "a combination of factors, such as poorly formulated plans, misapplied resources, breakdowns in communication, and limited accountability for results."[9] Exhibit 9.2 features a compilation of the most common obstacles that have challenged successful strategy implementation[10]—a list which includes some of the specific obstacles encountered by the organizations featured above.

EXHIBIT 9.2
Occurrence of Common Obstacles to Successful Strategy Execution

Source: Adapted from Lawrence G. Hrebiniak, *Making Strategy Work* (Upper Saddle River, NJ: Pearson Education, 2005), p. 17.

Common Obstacles to Strategy Execution	Home Depot	Circuit City	United Airlines	Swissair
Inability to manage change effectively or to overcome internal resistance to change	X	X		X
Poor or inadequate information sharing between individuals or business units responsible for strategy execution				X
Trying to execute a strategy that conflicts with the existing power structure	X			
Poor or vague strategy	X	X		
Unclear communication of responsibility and/or accountability for execution decisions or actions			X	
Not having guidelines or a model to guide strategy-execution efforts				X
Lack of feelings of ownership of a strategy or execution plans among key employees	X	X		
Lack of understanding of the role of organizational structure and design in the execution process			X	
Inability to generate buy-in or agreement on critical execution steps or actions	X			
Lack of incentives or inappropriate incentives to support execution objectives	X	X		
Insufficient financial resources to execute the strategy		X	X	X
Lack of upper-management support of strategy execution			X	

It is imperative for any manager to recognize and work to rectify these obstacles as soon as they are encountered. A series of misstarts and hasty implementations attempted without sufficient commitment will eventually destroy the credibility of the strategy your organization is trying to carry out.

A Comprehensive Implementation Framework

At the most basic level, implementation can be viewed as a structured process of (1) creating a portfolio of change programs that will deliver the strategy and (2) attracting, allocating, and managing all of the necessary resources to deliver these change programs.[11] At first glance, the process may appear to be a straightforward task; however, genuine shifts in strategy imply a significant change in emphasis. Implementation is felt throughout the organization. It typically involves changes in customers, suppliers, or markets; new technologies or business processes; and unfamiliar leadership styles or management techniques. Managers must prepare carefully for implementation by assessing an organization's change readiness.

EXHIBIT 9.3 **A Change-Readiness Assessment**

Source: Exhibit created by Anne Cohen and based upon forces identified by IBM's 2008 "Making Change Work" survey.

Forces Against Change versus Forces That Support Change

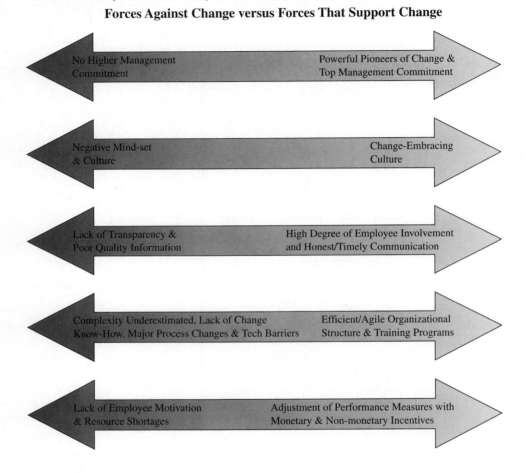

No Higher Management Commitment	Powerful Pioneers of Change & Top Management Commitment
Negative Mind-set & Culture	Change-Embracing Culture
Lack of Transparency & Poor Quality Information	High Degree of Employee Involvement and Honest/Timely Communication
Complexity Underestimated, Lack of Change Know-How, Major Process Changes & Tech Barriers	Efficient/Agile Organizational Structure & Training Programs
Lack of Employee Motivation & Resource Shortages	Adjustment of Performance Measures with Monetary & Non-monetary Incentives

Assess Change Readiness

An organization's **readiness for change** varies greatly based upon the *extent* of the change anticipated and its past *experience* with change. A strategic initiative requiring deep, fundamental transformations of both business model and process may be overwhelming for the current organization; a track record of failed past initiatives erodes trust and increases the probability of subsequent failures. As Mankins and Steele comment:

> Unrealistic plans create the expectation throughout the organization that plans simply will not be fulfilled. Then, as the expectation becomes experience, it becomes the norm that performance (goals) won't be kept. . . . Commitments cease to be binding promises with real consequences. . . . Managers, expecting failure, seek to protect themselves from the eventual fallout. They spend time covering their tracks rather than identifying actions to enhance performance (or stretching to ensure that commitments are kept). . . . The organization becomes less self-critical and intellectually honest about its shortcomings. . . . It loses the capacity to perform.[12]

Before launching any new initiatives, therefore, managers should assess their organization's readiness. Has management shown an unflagging and highly visible commitment to past programs, or is it a fair-weather friend to change? Does information flow freely, or do gate-keepers block and skew the process? The continua shown in Exhibit 9.3 help determine the level of resistance one can expect.

Once this initial assessment is complete, it is essential to develop strategies that leverage the predominant forces for change in an organization and minimize the opposition. The entire organization must be told why everyone must be in a state of change-readiness: The dynamic environment within which today's organizations operate demands nothing less and quickly dispatches those lulled into a false sense of security.

Today, perpetual readiness and expertise in change management is a highly valued organizational competence. The change-ready organization is prepared for the inevitable bumps in the road. It is able to react more quickly and pass more fluidly through all phases needed to implement new strategies.[13]

Install Integrative Leadership

After the organization is readied for change, it must install decisive, yet integrative, leaders to move the implementation process forward. Such **integrative leaders** are effective in maneuvering organizations to resolve the strategy-to-performance gaps that exist in implementation. They are able learn new skills and master new approaches quickly. They have the capacity to examine an initiative from multiple perspectives—from the strategic to the organizational and operational. These leaders create action plans that stretch, but respect, the organization's seemingly invisible process and cultural boundaries. They consider both internal and external forces and, unthreatened by weaknesses, deftly weave new resources into the organizational fold, building competencies and competitive advantage. They are capable of overseeing a program of ever-improving, interdependent activities while building a culture of cooperation, confidence, and performance.

Not every leader, however, is willing to embark upon new initiatives in such an integrative manner. New initiatives often undermine established organizational priorities, resource allocations, and reporting relationships. Implementation can challenge leaders' past decisions, their power, status, scope of responsibility, and business philosophies. Some leaders will simply be incapable of grasping a new set of circumstances or learning new skills. These leaders will erect obstacles to change.

At the other end of the spectrum are leaders who will throw caution to the wind, making radical departures from the norm without considering current organizational realities. For example, when Procter & Gamble launched its Organization 2005 initiative, CEO Durk Jager set out to grow profits and enhance its competitive position with a series of highly aggressive moves: refocusing P&G on developing markets; demanding a high rate of new global brand introductions; standardizing existing brands across all geographic regions; redesigning the company's structure, processes, and culture; and reducing time to market. It soon became obvious, however, that Jager's program was too forceful. His confrontational style and unreasonable demands alienated his management team, the accelerated product pipeline generated products that were only moderately successful, and the organization lost ground in established markets. Jager was soon replaced by A. G. Laffley who took a much more integrative approach, one that balanced existing strengths with competitive realities.[14]

Laffley retained pipeline improvements made under Jager, yet reined new developments back to a more measured pace. He leveraged existing retailer relationships while developing extensions for existing powerhouse brands. He reappropriated underperforming assets, dropping brands that did not fit with P&G's focus. He addressed existing weaknesses in the IT infrastructure, which increased efficiencies across the supply chain. P&G was then able to pursue acquisitions and new-market development from a greater position of strength. Laffley's efforts more than doubled P&G's size. He was the kind of integrative leader needed to successfully implement a strategy.

When an organization is compelled by competitive forces to make a radical shift in strategy, integrative leadership quickly becomes a critical resource. Organizations, therefore, must encourage, develop, reward, and retain leaders that incorporate integrative behaviors into the everyday management of their organizations. These leaders are among the most important factors needed to maintain a change-ready organization.

Create a Consistent Message

Strategic change is typically aborted whenever leadership doesn't act consistently or fails to demonstrate the same commitment to change that they expect from others. The installed leadership team, therefore, must immediately come together to negotiate how each leader will be held accountable for specific elements of the implementation, and to build consensus around a **common message** for all stakeholders—a message that will be shared with both shareholders and operational employees.

Shareholders can exert relentless pressure on an organization to boost profits quarter after quarter. This pressure, often foisted by the board onto senior executives, must be well managed and not allowed to derail the implementation of long-term strategies. A consistent message, a clear plan of action, and open lines of communication from leadership to the board and shareholders is vital to retaining support throughout the process.

Employees must also have a shared understanding of the desired end-state, yet most companies don't communicate strategy broadly or effectively to their employees. A 2005 study by Kaplan and Norton found that up to 95 percent of a company's employees are unaware of, or do not understand, its strategy.[15] If, for example, an organization's strategy is to become "best in class," it must be made very clear to employees whether that means to achieve top-quartile performance, to be the most profitable, to be the most admired, or all of the above. The salesperson on the street, the call-center customer service representative, and the operations manager should be interpreting the organization's desired state in the same way.

To deliver such specific and targeted messages to employees, leaders need to have all hands on deck, intermingling with groups and engaging employees across the organization in discussions about marketplace realities and the organizations desired end-state. Failing to create a common vision up front impedes future progress.

Appoint Cross-Functional Program Teams

Strategic leadership teams alone are not in a position to identify and effectively define the specific changes to successfully implement a strategy. Even if they are, resentment is aroused when management announces a change and mandates the specifics of implementation. The involvement and contributions of knowledgeable middle managers are necessary.

The placement of these middle managers on **cross-functional program teams,** which are both highly visible and accessible, is strongly advised. Such accessible teams give employees from each functional area an opportunity to engage in the implementation process. They send a powerful message that the organization values its employee base. By creating such program teams, leadership is saying, "We now know *what* must happen. How do you think it can *best be done?*"

Ideally, the managers appointed to these program teams have been involved from the earliest stages in the strategic leadership team's diagnosis of the business environment; they have helped build scenarios of change imagining how best the organization can respond to various strategic contingencies.[16] With these middle managers in place and employees on board, the organization can quickly begin work to more clearly identify gaps between the organization's current and desired states. These gaps will be the basis for subsequent decisions and actions.

Solicit Change Program Proposals

When cross-functional program teams effectively engage the employee base in discussions about how to achieve strategic goals, the response is often significant. Employees are able to inform management of additional resources they need, and functional groups can quickly alert leadership if they expect to be significantly affected by the change. Ideas start to flow, specific proposals begin to take shape, and the scope of the original strategic initiative tends to expand. Unfortunately, financial and human resources are never unlimited and are especially stretched during times of transition. Even the process of reviewing proposals can become overwhelming without a solid framework for submissions and selection.

Each proposal that gathers momentum, therefore, should be developed into a formal business case.[17] The case-writing process requires sponsors to consider all facets of implementation and demonstrate how their proposed change programs will contribute to the achievement of the organization's strategic goals. Any acceptable submissions must include the following elements:

- An identification of the necessary changes from the status quo.
- An outline of new resource requirements, timelines, and costs (and how these will compete with ongoing needs for continuity and cash flow).
- A clear definition of the expected benefits.
- A list of the individuals who, with the sponsor, will be responsible and *accountable* for delivering the benefits.

This last element is crucial. Insisting on accountability at this stage eliminates a sponsor's tendencies to underestimate costs and overestimate benefits. Such accountability also leads to more honesty downstream, when certain programs can become irrelevant due to changing business conditions, and their adjustment (or abandonment) becomes necessary.

Select and Prioritize Proposed Change Programs

To select and prioritize change programs, cross-functional teams and senior leadership must utilize a **prioritization plan**—one that relies on objective and transparent criteria to blend current programs, products, and processes with the new strategy. These criteria might include any number of factors, including expected ROI, risks, and so on. Such a prioritization process helps functional areas and the operational front lines balance the realities of a dynamic competitive environment and the need for change with liquidity needs,

EXHIBIT 9.4 **Strategic Program Prioritization Matrix**

Source: An adaptation of the Project Prioritization Matrix created by A. P. Brache and S. Bodley-Scott, "Which Initiatives Should You Implement?" *Harvard Management Update,* April 2009.

Balance		Priority-Setting Criteria	Criteria Weight	Program 1		Program 2		Program 3	
Short-Term	Long-Term			Raw	Weighted	Raw	Weighted	Raw	Weighted
x	x	Criteria 1	10	9	90	5	50	4	40
x	x	Criteria 2	10	7	70	3	30	1	10
	x	Criteria 3	6	8	48	9	54	4	24
x		Criteria 4	3	2	6	6	18	2	6
x		Criteria 5	1	5	5	3	3	8	8
		Combined Weighted Scores =			219		155		88

	Resource Requirements		
Marketing	x		
Operations		x	x
Finance		x	
HR		x	
IT	x	x	
Verdict =	Expedite	Delay	Drop

cost control programs, the sales of existing product lines, and the availability of new capital over the short and long terms. The process also helps the organization estimate how much time it will take to realize specific goals.

While an organization can transform its capabilities over time, there is a limit to how far it can go and how fast. The decisions are never simple and uncertainty always clouds the decision-making process. However, without clearly defined priorities, employees are only left second-guessing the intent of senior management as they attempt to resolve day-to-day conflicts between operational and change resource requirements. Without resolution, most employees will focus on earning revenue from a demanding customer, leaving implementation of the strategic initiative hanging.

In "Which Initiatives Should You Implement?" Alan Brache and Sam Bodley-Scott provide a methodology that management can use to examine the complete portfolio of projects, and to determine which projects must be expedited, which could be combined, and which should be delayed or canceled. An adaptation of the Brache/Bodley-Scott prioritization matrix appears in Exhibit 9.4.[18]

Regardless of the selection criteria utilized, clear communications of which priorities are to be funded, and why, illustrates clear leadership thinking and consistency. A lack of priorities only leads to implementation overload, which wastes resources, distracts the organization from its goals, and dulls its responsiveness to the competitive environment.[19]

Assign Process Owners and Align Resources

Once program-specific priorities are set, the cross-functional teams must then select and assign process owners to oversee the transition from the status quo to the desired state. It is critical that the process owners selected have adequate authority over all programs and areas involved in their processes' implementation as they will also be held accountable for success or failure. Mid- and top-level leaders are recommended.

Working in tandem with cross-functional teams and the sponsors of approved change programs, the new process owners then begin to coordinate activities that span organizational functions. They define new process flows, audit policies, and determine whether current resource levels are adequate to conduct the different phases of the transition. Several questions designed to complete alignment of the new strategy with the existing one must be answered.

Process Issues:

- How should work and process flows change to support new initiatives while improving efficiencies and reducing redundancies across the organization?
- Should specific decisions and activities be centralized or decentralized?
- How should changes to supplier or customer interfaces be managed?
- Which operating systems should be modified, which information systems upgraded, to support new initiatives?

Structural Issues:

- Which employee groups and individuals will be most affected by the new priorities?
- Must resource levels change on a permanent basis to address new workload levels per employee, or will temporary assistance suffice?
- Can projects be combined in any way to share physical assets or human resources?
- Can resources be reappropriated from lower priority/canceled initiatives?
- Do employees need to be relocated and/or retrained, or will new hires be required?
- What other changes should be made to insure that the structure is conducive to rapid, strategy-supportive decision-making and knowledge transfer?

Policy and Culture Issues:

- Which policies create obstacles to the execution of new initiatives?
- Do some incentives encourage the wrong behaviors?
- What is the best way to maintain momentum and continue to nurture a strategy-supportive culture throughout these changes?

Answers to such questions will help guide the organization as it shifts to its desired state. Decision making will be pushed to appropriate levels, and the formation of inefficient functional silos will be prevented. In fact, as more efficient processes are designed, functional boundaries will begin to fade and be replaced with more fluid and productive lateral collaborations. The marketing analyst who needs information from operations to determine capabilities will have a direct link. The operations manager charged with boosting efficiencies at the plant level will have access to finance department expertise. Even field and line employees will benefit from the collaborative environment and will gain a better grasp on the bottom-line impact of their decisions.

It is imperative, therefore, that these coordination activities not be short-circuited, and that management resists the temptation to just strip costs indiscriminately. Modifying structures, eliminating resources, and removing layers of management can reduce costs drastically, but without fundamental changes that reduce process complexity and install strategy-supportive incentives, an organization will eventually return to its original state. Structural change must be the capstone—not the cornerstone—of any organizational transformation.[20]

Secure Funding, Formalize Operational Objectives, and Design Incentives

To proceed with the implementation, each transition initiative requires funding to cover its entire timeline. Assuring adequate funding requires knowing whether internal cash flows will be sufficient to support new initiatives. If they are not, external sources must be tapped and the decision to utilize either stock and/or debt instruments must be made.

Too much debt in an organization's capital structure can reduce the range of actions it will be able to take in response to future threats that jeopardize its survival. On the other hand, issuing an excessive amount of stock will dilute ownership control and affect stock price overall. In the end, managers must determine the best mix of financing options for their organization—stock, debt, or a combination of the two—that will provide maximum earnings per share (which is assumed to be consistent with the maximization of share price and immediate shareholder wealth) and will increase the odds that the organization will continue to thrive. The tool of choice for such a decision is the EPS/EBIT analysis, which compares earnings per share (EPS) and earnings before interest and taxes (EBIT) at various levels of sales—optimistic, pessimistic, and most likely scenarios.

Once funding is assured, all initiatives and their respective timelines must be divided into annual budget cycles. These organizational time constraints force process owners to parse multiyear transition initiatives into several phases. Specific goals must then be defined for each phase, and the goals subdivided so that each phase goal can be linked to each employee's personal objectives and incentives. Employees must be provided with both a clear outline of the decisions and actions for which they will be held responsible, and a set of well-defined success criteria. These updated guidelines and criteria are the new keys to their personal rewards and program success.

It is vital that employees not remain tied to reward schemes based upon objectives that support the status quo. If your organization has just set its sights on being a service leader, managers should rethink any high-volume incentives that are in place to reward customer service reps for keeping their calls short. Replacing such stopwatch systems with customer satisfaction surveys and repeat purchase data will motivate more vision-supportive behaviors. If your organization is hoping to grow profits, it must reward not only volume and market share, but also margin.

Managers must also be sure to incorporate objectives and incentives that reflect the fact that most employees are also responsible for delivering timely and high-quality output to others (so that they can perform their own duties). Take, for instance, a food-packaging manufacturer that hopes to increase profitability by 20 percent over the next two years. At the most basic level, this will place immediate pressure on the organization's sales force, and the sales force will require an increased number of quotations from the home office. Generating these quotations, however, requires the input of both package design staff and plant operations. Any delays in their inputs impacts the timely delivery of quotations, reduces the confidence of the food producer in the capabilities of the packaging manufacturer, and ultimately hurts the likelihood that the producer will enter into a purchase agreement with the manufacturer.

EXHIBIT 9.5   **Horizontal and Vertical Consistencies in Objectives Support Processes**

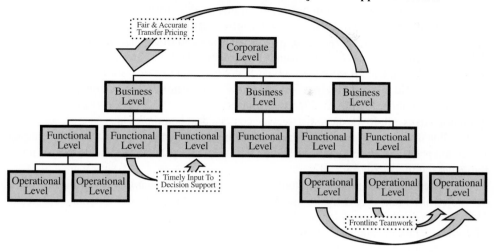

In the end, there must be both vertical and horizontal consistency in the objectives-setting process (see Exhibit 9.5). Vertical consistency yields a strategy-transparent subdivision of duties and responsibilities from the executive to the operating levels, while horizontal consistency encourages collaboration and simultaneous progress across functions. Unfortunately, many organizations fail to persist in this comprehensive approach and, as a result, their employees lack adequate direction and motivation, their budgets swell, their timelines stretch, and they ultimately fail to reach their higher-level goals.

Advance and Continually Monitor Initiatives

Armed with budget monies, clear objectives, and strategy-supportive incentives, programs are now equipped to move forward. New processes are set into motion and monitoring begins. Early wins should be celebrated, and any drift away from stated objectives should be immediately corrected.

However, the monitoring process itself can be very challenging. The gathering of accurate information can be both costly and time-consuming if systems designed to improve processes were not also designed to track the relevant activities of employees, the performance of vendors, the purchases and sentiments of customers, and the countermoves of competitors.

> When performance falls short, executives . . . often have no way of knowing whether critical actions were carried out as expected, resources were deployed on schedule, competitors responded as anticipated, and so on. Unfortunately, without clear information on how and why performance is falling short, it is virtually impossible for top management to take appropriate corrective action.[21]

However, there are many tools that can help managers monitor both their progress and their environment. **Scorecards,** such as Kaplan and Norton's balanced scorecard (mentioned in Chapter 1), are preferred as they measure both leading and lagging factors. Using such a scorecard, your financial results, employee turnover, and inventory changes might be tracked along with the leading indicators from this week's customer focus group or the results of the last month's employee survey. **Dashboards** can also be fully integrated into the operating systems of organizations to provide relevant and timely performance data, aid in decision making, and serve as a constant reminder of the link between employee actions and results. When used properly, dashboards deliver a mix of operational, financial, and program-specific information that is both timely and meaningful to stakeholders. A sales executive's dashboard might track daily revenues, unit sales, and market share against program objectives, while the customer service center's dashboard provides its representatives with call statistics, wait times, and kudos or complaints that reflect customers' changing needs and priorities. An effective dashboard will help an organization synchronize its internal beliefs with its external realities.

The broad appeal of monitoring tools is based on their applicability to almost any organizational situation; they can take the form of either manual or highly automated systems. However, leadership must lead the charge in measuring and adjusting to incoming competitive and operational signals. If they do not participate, the effectiveness of any system will be severely limited. Many complaints about Hewlett-Packard's former CEO, Carly Fiorina, are traced to such a laissez-faire approach to the monitoring and evaluation process, while the amazing turnaround by her successor, David Hurd, is being attributed to his much higher level of engagement. "While Fiorina rarely sat in on divisional reviews, Hurd not only holds them but keeps staffers busy with his follow-ups." Hurd's active monitoring process has been bounded only by his infectious curiosity and self-authored inquiries.[22]

Whether manual or automated, the most effective monitoring systems are used to:

- Alert executives to the development of dangerous economic and competitive trends.
- Help managers identify and limit budget variances, which always spell trouble—use too many resources one year and risk a poor evaluation or program cancellation, use too few and risk future resource shortfalls and virtual program strangulation.
- Help justify the program variances that do occur—protecting program resources and helping the organization maintain positive momentum.
- Provide an objective basis for the distribution of earned incentives across all levels of the organization, while helping an organization to identify and retain its best people and practices, and pinpoint sources of underperformance for review and remediation.
- Continually reinforce the link between an organization's strategy and the benefits realized by both the organization and its loyal employees.

Today, the global recession is forcing organizations around the world to closely monitor events, quickly recognize and adapt to new realities, and make changes on the fly. Businesses must continually revisit priorities to get the most out of their existing resources. Most must prune underutilized or nonperforming assets to survive. Though it's a painful time, the pinch is yielding both valuable lessons in financial discipline, and investment opportunities that will set the stage for a period of growth once business conditions return to normal. Savvy firms are capitalizing on the easy access to good talent and other valuable resources they can use to fight the downturn and expand in a revived economy. Those that have invested during this recession are positioned to leapfrog competitors who have hesitated to make any bold moves.[23]

Fortify Gains and Refine the Implementation Process

Although this last step of our implementation framework seems to imply that this process is coming to a close, in practice, the implementation cycle is never complete. It continually overlaps with the design of new strategies, the evaluation of existing initiatives, and the redirection of current processes.

The organization, its environment, and its processes require constant attention, oversight, and fortification. Managers must recognize that an organization's internal culture is under constant assault as it endures mergers and acquisitions, promotions and retirements, basic turnover and hiring. It is highly susceptible to failure unless leadership takes an active role in continuously fortifying and protecting it.

Accomplishments must be consistently communicated to all employees, supply partners, and key customers. This will help build a sense of pride and loyalty to your brand. Successes must be promptly and generously rewarded. This will cement them into the psyche of the organization. Managers must encourage ongoing strategic thinking and opportunity identification at all levels. This will help the organization preserve its change-ready state and will facilitate modifications as necessitated by both internal and external forces. Leaders must not hesitate to continually test assumptions, revise strategy when necessary, revisit and learn from previous forecast errors, fine-tune the program prioritization process, cut any programs that are not yielding expected benefits, reassign ineffective process owners, adjust policy, develop new incentives, or replace monitoring systems that are no longer relevant to internal changes or able to produce timely market and competitive intelligence.

Employees witnessing such a continuous improvement process will, in turn, become more confident in leadership's ability to deliver positive change and will embrace future initiatives with greater trust and enthusiasm. Yet mastering the implementation process is much like learning to successfully land an aircraft on a carrier: It's not simple and never perfected the first time around. The seas are rough, the skies are turbulent, and the runway target is constantly moving. Only the most skillful and practiced hands will consistently hit the flight deck's sweet spot and emerge from the cockpit ready for the next sortie.

Summary

Failed initiatives leave in their wake suboptimal results—significant cost overruns, demoralized employees and, in the worst of cases, a downward spiral of disgruntled customers and shrinking market shares. Management must learn to identify and rectify the most destructive implementation behaviors, and must begin to consider the process of implementation as a core competence to be continually honed and developed.

This chapter provided a comprehensive framework that:

- Helps managers and executives determine whether their organizations are ready for change.
- Emphasizes the importance of developing and retaining integrative leaders.
- Helps those leaders manage stakeholder pressures.
- Devises special organizational structures and positions to support the change process—from cross-functional program teams to process owners.
- Assists in the diagnosis of misaligned processes, structures, policies, and culture.

- Outlines key funding and budgeting decisions.
- Explains how to create strategy-supportive objectives and incentives.
- Scrutinizes and adjusts both the process and organization as required by internal and external dynamics.

The careful practice of this process will not only deliver fundamental change but will also produce an organization that is much more ready to adapt to the next, inevitable challenge—which is strategy's main point, the capacity to continuously adapt to the challenges your organization confronts.

Endnotes

1. K. Nagendra, "The Recession Dilemma—To Save or To Invest," http://thoughtspotblog. wordpress.com/2009/06/02/the-recession-dilemma-to-save-or-to-invest/.

2. Key industries included manufacturing, oil, like sciences, chemicals, telecoms, health care, consumer goods and retail. "Strategy Execution: Achieving Operational Excellence," Economist Intelligence Unit, http://graphics.eiu.com/files/ad_pdfs/Celeran_EIU_WP.pdf.

3. AMA/HRI survey included those in Europe and Asia. "Most Companies Are Only Moderately Successful—Or Worse—When It Comes to Executing Strategy, Executives Say," http://press. amanet.org/press-releases/97/most-companies-are-only-moderately-successful%E2%80%94or-worse%E2%80%94when-it-comes-to-executing-strategy-executives-say/.

4. "Home Unimprovement: Was Nardelli's Tenure at Home Depot a Blueprint for Failure?" http://knowledge.wharton.upenn.edu/article.cfm?articleid=1636.

5. A. Hamilton, "Why Circuit City Busted, While Best Buy Boomed," http://www.time.com/time/ business/article/0,8599,1858079,00.html.

6. M. Raby, "Apple Expands Best Buy Relationship, Limits Deal with Circuit City," http://www. tgdaily.com/content/view/34543/113/.

7. S. Freeman, "United to Ground Its Ted Carrier," *Washington Post,* June 5, 2008, p. D1; http://www.washingtonpost.com/wp-dyn/content/article/2008/06/04/AR2008060400945.html.

8. Results of Ernst & Young's Investigation Regarding Swissair, January 24, 2003, http://www. liquidator-swissair.ch/uploads/media/untersuchung1_e.PDF.

9. Michael C. Mankins and Richard Steele, "Turning Great Strategy into Great Performance," *Harvard Business Review,* July–August 2005.

10. The Wharton-Gartner Survey (2003) was a joint project between the Gartner Group, Inc., and Lawrence G. Hrebiniak, professor at the Wharton School of the University of Pennsylvania and teacher at the Wharton MBA and Executive Education programs. The short online survey was sent to 1,000 individuals on the Gartner E-Panel database. The targeted respondents were managers who were involved in strategy formulation and execution. The survey yielded responses from 243 individuals. Combined, the Wharton-Gartner Survey and the Wharton Executive Education Survey provided responses on obstacles to strategy execution from more than 400 managers. L. G. Hrebeniak "Making Strategy Work: Overcoming the Obstacles to Effective Execution" *Ivey Business Journal,* March–April 2008.

11. G. Johnson, K. Scholes, and R. Whittington, *Exploring Corporate Strategy,* 7th ed. (Harlow, England: Pearson Education Limited, 2005); W. D. Giles, "Making Strategy Work," *Long Range Planning* 24/5 (1991): 75–91.

12. Mankins and Steele, "Turning Great Strategy into Great Performance," pp. 64–72.

13. From IBM's 2008 study, "Making Change Work." IBM Global Business Services researched change management practices across the globe. The study quizzed over 1,500 project leaders,

sponsors, project managers, and change managers from many of the world's leading organizations, ranging from small to very large.

14. R. Martin, *The Opposable Mind: How Successful Leaders Win Through Integrative Thinking* (Boston: Harvard Business School Press, 2007).

15. R. S. Kaplan and D. P. Norton, "The Office of Strategy Management," *Harvard Business Review,* October 2005, pp. 72–80.

16. A. Marcus, *Strategic Foresight* (New York: Palgrave MacMillan, 2009).

17. A. Franken, C. Edwards, and R. Lambert, "Executing Strategic Change—Understanding the Critical Management Elements That Lead to Success," *California Management Review* 51, no. 3 (Spring 2009), pp. 49–73.

18. A. P. Brache and S. Bodley-Scott, "Which Initiatives Should You Implement?" *Harvard Management Update,* April 2009.

19. See, for example, P. Rothschild, J. Duggal, and R. Balaban, "Strategic Planning Redux," *Mercer Management Journal* 17 (2004), pp. 35–45.

20. G. L. Nielson, K. L. Martin, and E. Powers, "The Secrets to Successful Strategy Execution," *Harvard Business Review,* June 2008.

21. Mankins and Steele "Turning Great Strategy into Great Performance."

22. P. Burrows, "Controlling the Damage at HP," *BusinessWeek,* October 9, 2006, http://www.businessweek.com/magazine/content/06_41/b4004001.htm.

23. Nagendra, "The Recession Dilemma."

A

action-response cycles   Outcomes of competitive battles are determined not by the moves of any single company but by the actions and responses of many firms that interact with each other and alter their strategies in response to their competitors' moves.

agency theory   Holds that the company is obligated to put shareholders first because they are risking the most.

B

balanced scorecard   Multidimensional approach of measuring corporate performance through financial and nonfinancial factors.

barriers to entry   Roadblocks within an attractive industry that deter new companies from entering and secure the place of existing companies.

best-value strategy   Combines the benefits of low cost and differentiation in an attractive value for the money package.

business plan   Consists of a description of the business, an external analysis, an internal analysis, an implementation schedule, an end-game strategy that indicates when the business will be viable, financial projections, and an analysis of risk.

business strategy   How a firm competes in a given business.

C

capabilities   The skills and routines that allow the company to exploit its resources in ways that are valuable and difficult for other firms to imitate; if resources are the company's hardware, capabilities are its software.

classic approach to management theory   Relies on accountability and control starting with the board and top management and extending to employees who are divided into specialties and issued commands with which they are expected to comply.

common message   Organizational communications—whether written, spoken, or implicit—which when delivered to stakeholders illustrate a consistent vision.

community model (of capitalism)   Common in Japan and some European countries; managers are considered senior members in the company and shareholders are one of many stakeholder groups that have to be satisfied; managers are freer from short-term pressures imposed by stock market prices and quarterly profits.

comparative advantage   What a company is able to do best in comparison to all other firms.

competencies   Links key resources and capabilities to satisfy customer needs and provide access to new markets; very hard for competitors to imitate.

co-opetition   Ways in which companies compete and cooperate at the same time to broaden markets and create new value and thereby escape zero-sum games where one company benefits at another's expense.

corporate strategy   Determines what business or businesses the company should be in; a focus on the scope of the firm.

cross-functional program teams   A group of people from different departments (and, preferably, with differing areas of expertise) organized to implement a set of specific strategic activities and moves.

culture   Key values, beliefs, and assumptions about how an organization should conduct its business.

cross-impact matrix   Used in the creation of scenarios to illustrate how one trend may intersect with another.

D

dashboards   Decision support systems that consolidate and display information about the performance of key strategic functions within an organization.

decline   A stage within industry evolution that sees falling prices and margins; companies exit or are squeezed out during this stage.

Delphi method   Developed by Rand Corporation to elicit expert opinion about important trends in society, technology, and government; combines the beliefs of different experts to sharpen the predictions made about developments in these areas.

diamond framework   Porter's reformulation of the five forces to reflect greater globalization; includes factor conditions (production inputs), demand conditions, competitive conditions (firm, strategy, structure, and rivalry), and related and supporting industries.

differentiated position   A way for a firm to distinguish itself through low-volume sales of high-margin items.

distinctive competence   A unique accumulation of capabilities and rigidities that an organization has acquired over time that includes a sense of pride and purpose that can keep the firm from making important strategic adjustments or facilitate these adjustments.

E

eco-efficiency   Reduces the ecological impact that a company has while maintaining the delivery of competitively priced goods and services.

economies of scope   Potential cost savings from combining the production of disparate products provided that they rely on the same management structure, administration systems, marketing departments, R&D, and so on; often used as a justification for the cost savings that are supposed to result from mergers and acquisitions.

economic growth   An increase in the level of production of goods and services by a country.

economic value added (EVA)   Compares what the company is earning for shareholders in relation to the cost of capital; a way to judge over time whether a company is winning competitive battles.

effect uncertainty   Uncertainty about the effects of macroenvironmental factors as they make their impact felt on a particular firm—what do changes in these conditions mean for the individual firm?

embryonic stage   The beginning stage in industry evolution when prices are high, margins low, and profits still not certain; products are of lesser reliability, competition has yet to take hold, and export activity is limited.

entrepreneur   The entity that discovers and starts to exploit new business or other opportunities while assuming the risks.

exporting production   Outsourcing or setting up production and distribution in a foreign company.

external analysis   Assessment of the industry environment; includes the analysis of industry forces, the macroenvironment, and stakeholder groups.

F

five forces   See Porter's five forces.

franchising   Method for a company to disseminate its business methods and models by providing franchisers with a brand identity and a business image; the company gains a percentage of the franchised company's profit.

G

GDP per capita   Total output of goods and services for final use produced by an economy per person; indicates how wealthy the individuals in a country are in comparison to individuals in other countries.

global product-market strategy   A single dominant design or business model; takes advantage of economies of scale and scope and is a highly efficient, low-cost way to expand internationally.

greenfield operations   New manufacturing, production, marketing, or other sets of activities established by a company in a foreign country.

gross domestic product (GDP)   The total value of goods and services produced by a nation, consisting of four components: personal consumption, private investment, government spending, and exports.

growth stage   The stage during industry evolution when prices go down and profits rise; product reliability increases as does the competition, and exports also begin to go up.

H

horizontal integration   Method by which a company increases market share by purchasing companies that share the same business line.

human relations approach to management theory   Emphasizes employee development, motivation, and values, informal coordination, and two-way communication, rather than being hierarchical and based on command and control structures.

hybrid structure   A hybrid sells both high-margin myth products and low-margin commodity products, the high-margin products for profitability and the commodities for growth.

I

industry analysis   An assessment of the attractiveness of an industry based on the five forces—the power of customers, suppliers, competitors, new entrants, and substitutes.

industry environment   The context in which a company operates.

industrial organization (IO) economics   Focuses on the formation of monopolies and near-monopolies.

innovation   Putting an invention or other important discoveries into widespread use.

integrative leaders   Managers and executives with the capacity to synthesize incoming strategic signals with both their past experience and current organizational realities to devise and implement highly insightful and successful new strategies.

internal analysis   Examination of a company's strengths and weaknesses in order to better compete with other companies.

invention   The creation of a new idea and/or its demonstration in prototype form.

J

just-in-time (JIT)   Inventory management approach in which a company produces only what the customer wants, in the quantities the customer actually requires, and when the customer needs it.

L

leading-edge industries   Depend upon newly emerging technologies that provide the impetus for economic growth.

legalistic model (of capitalism)   Emphasizes the obligations that managers as employees of the owners (the shareholders) owe their employers.

licensing   A legal arrangement whereby one company licenses another firm to produce and sell the company's products for a fee.

low-cost position   A way for a firm to distinguish itself through the high-volume sale of low-margin items.

M

M-form   A corporate structure in which top-level executives make strategic choices, interact with shareholders, and allocate resources to separate, independent business units.

macroenvironment   Broad forces that affect the industry environment, including law, politics, technology, demography, society, the economic climate, and the physical environment.

management theory   Various approaches to scrutinizing, investigating, and breaking down an organization's strengths and weaknesses, including the classic approach, the human relations approach, and contingency theory.

material-balance model   Analyzes an organization's production processes based on a study of inputs and outputs in an effort to increase usable products and decrease waste.

maturity   The stage during industry evolution when profits decline as more companies compete for market share; innovation is rare and overcapacity begins; exports blossom because there are few new consumers at home.

matrix structure   An organizational form that establishes multiple reporting arrangements for employees based on the clients they serve, the geography covered, and/or their functional expertise.

micro-segmenting   Dividing customers into finer and finer segments to serve smaller and smaller categories of customers and to provide them with more of precisely what they need.

mission   Typically represents what the company has been good at in the past, what it has accomplished, and where its employees take pride in their achievements.

multidomestic product-market strategy   Adapts and modifies a product or service to each separate country or region; extracts high margins and charges a premium price for delivering customized products and services that meet the needs of individual markets.

N

natural parity   The expected, even competition found in most industries.

O

outliers   Companies that break the natural parity that prevails in their industries and sustain competitive advantage or realize competitive disadvantage for a significant period such as a decade or more.

P

Porter's five forces The forces that need to be examined to determine industry attractiveness: (1) existing rivals, (2) new entrants, (3) substitutes, (4) customers, and (5) suppliers; see industry analysis.

portfolio planning A method that assists large, complex organizations manage their separate business units by focusing on the relative strengths and weaknesses of these units.

positioning A way to gain distinction in an industry by occupying a unique market niche that other companies cannot easily imitate.

postindustrialism An era following industrialism that is categorized by a move from goods to services; the prominence of theoretical knowledge; and the preeminence of technology and technological assessment.

prioritization plan A system used by managers to objectively filter strategic proposals, to select those that have the greatest potential to strengthen the organization, and to determine the most appropriate way to allocate resources between each selected proposal.

prisoner's dilemma A situation in game theory where it is rational for each player—not knowing how the other player will act—to behave in a way that will make both players worse off.

process technologies Enable firms to improve their ability to make goods and services.

product technologies Improvements in the goods and services themselves.

R

readiness for change An organization's ability to transition its processes and structures in a timely and effective manner from the current state to a new state (as required by the demands of the organization's competitive environment).

realized strategies Outcomes are not determined by what any single company intends but by the moves and countermoves of competitors responding to changing conditions over time.

resources An organization's basic financial, physical, and human capital.

resource-based view (RBV) Explains why some firms within industries consistently outperform others; emphasizes the ability of firms to reap higher returns from resources by the way they configure their capabilities and competencies.

response uncertainty Uncertainty about what a firm should do based on its knowledge of conditions in the macroenvironment.

risk Odds of success are known with certainty; to be contrasted with uncertainty, where the odds are not known with certainty.

S

scenario A depiction of a possible future based on the intersection of various trends over time.

scorecards A set of planning and management tools that are used to illustrate the strategic priorities of a business, align the organization's activities to its vision, improve communications between stakeholders, and monitor the organization's performance against its strategic goals.

sensitivity analysis Using different assumptions to estimate different levels of payoffs based on their probabilities.

separate business units (SBUs) Closely related businesses or groups of businesses that have been divided by a larger parent company.

seven S's The seven characteristics that Peters and Waterman used to describe excellent firms: (1) strategy, (2) structure, (3) systems, (4) style, (5) staffing, (6) skill, and (7) shared values.

shared values Unity of purpose—a part of management that Peters and Waterman found was often slighted by U.S. managers in comparison to their Japanese counterparts.

skill The capabilities to compete and generate new business—a part of management that Peters and Waterman found was often slighted by U.S. managers in comparison to their Japanese counterparts.

smart (business) designs Better ways of meeting customer needs through the use of detailed and systematic information about customers; this information allows firms to satisfy customer needs for integrated solutions; better designs often break down barriers between a business and its customers by eliminating redundant supply channels; they take advantage of special niches firms occupy in the value chain and they tend to provide small segments of customers with customized products that meet their unique needs.

staffing Matching jobs with the people available to hold them in an organization—a part of management that

Peters and Waterman found was often slighted by U.S. managers in comparison to their Japanese counterparts.

stakeholder groups   Stakeholders are groups such as shareholders, customers, and communities that affect and are affected by the strategic moves of a company.

stakeholders   Those who affect and are affected by a company's actions and results.

stakeholder theory   Holds that managers are accountable to an array of outside and internal stakeholders to whom managers must provide incentives (wages to workers, taxes to government, products to customers, etc.) to induce their involvement.

state uncertainty   Uncertainty about conditions in the macroenvironment; for instance, where the economy is headed, what the next government will be, how technology will change, and so on.

strategic inflection point   A major point of departure, a point of no return, where a company's competitive environment is radically altered due to new technologies, different regulatory conditions, or changing customer preferences; in response to these changes, the company may be forced to alter its strategies.

strategic groups   Groups of companies with similar positions competing in the same industry space; these companies must find finer and finer points of distinction between them in order to stand out.

strategy   The extent to which an organization has a logical sense of the actions it has to take to gain sustainable competitive advantage over the competition, improve its position in relation to customers, and allocate resources to high-return activities—an aspect of management that Peters and Waterman found was often overemphasized by U.S. managers in comparison to their Japanese counterparts.

structure   A coherent form for dividing labor, allocating responsibilities, coordinating tasks, and ensuring accountability—an aspect of management that Peters and Waterman found was often overemphasized by U.S. managers in comparison to their Japanese counterparts.

style   Extent of actual alignment between management and employees and the organization's real strategic needs as opposed to lip service—an aspect of management that Peters and Waterman found was often slighted by U.S. managers in comparison to their Japanese counterparts.

sustainable society   Based on three principles— protection of the environment, economic equity, and economic growth; in such a society the needs of future generations are not sacrificed for the consumption of the current generation.

sustained competitive advantage (SCA)   The goal of strategic management, which is to consistently outperform relevant competitors for long periods, such as a decade or more; the aim of strategy is to be a dynasty, not a onetime winner. Onetime winners can succeed by luck; being a dynasty requires skill.

SWOT analysis   Strengths, weaknesses, opportunities, and threats analysis; examining the internal strengths and weaknesses of a firm, comparing them with external opportunities and threats, and matching the two in order to choose a strategy based on the analysis.

systems   Description of how critical processes are carried out in an organization—an aspect of management that Peters and Waterman found was often overemphasized by U.S. managers in comparison to their Japanese counterparts.

T

technology   Knowledge of how to convert the factors of production into goods and services.

technology-push model   Innovation starts with discoveries in basic science and engineering, and from these discoveries come new goods and services to the marketplace.

timing dilemma   Difficulty of deciding whether a company should go first and be a pioneer with a new strategy or be a fast follower and allow another firm to take these risks; often the issue is deciding whether to continue with an old product or utilize a new product, business model, or practice.

total quality management (TQM)   Designed to achieve enhanced productivity and greater quality at the same time; breaks with Porter's generic strategies that assume a firm has to choose between low cost or high quality. Under TQM, a firm has a few trusted suppliers rather than having power over many suppliers in accord with Porter's framework.

transnational product-market strategy   Combines global design and local responsiveness; to achieve best value, it both exploits scale economies and adapts to local conditions.

U

uncertainty   Odds of success are unknown; to be contrasted with risk.

V

value chain   The primary and support activities a firm undertakes to deliver products and services to customers; each element in the value chain can be broken down to determine how profitable it is (what are its margins).

value net   Rather than being stuck in a zero-sum game in which one company prevails at another companies' expense, companies can work together with other companies and with their suppliers and customers to create greater value for all of them.

vertical integration   Corporate structure in which a company combines production, distribution, and/or sales within its organization.

vision   Typically based on senior executives' understanding of the company's future possibilities and where it should be moving next. What should the company be aiming for so that it can excel in the future? A vision typically provides employees with a sense of direction. It tells them where the company should be heading. All companies are caught between what they have been good at in the past (their mission) and what they would like to be good at in the future (their vision).

Index